Small Business Made Simple

Limited Liability Company
Small Business Start-Up Kit

Limited Liability Company

Small Business Start-Up Kit

by Daniel Sitarz
Attorney-at-Law

Nova Publishing Company
Small Business and Consumer Legal Books and Software
Carbondale, Illinois

ISBN 10: 1-892949-37-7   ISBN 13: 978-1-8792949-37-0   Book w/CD   ($29.95)
Library of Congress Catalog Card Number 99-28195

Library of Congress Cataloging-in-Publication Data
    Sitarz, Dan, 1948-
        Limited Liability Company : small business start-up kit / Daniel Sitarz
        P. cm-(Small Business Made Simple)
        ISBN 01-892949-04-0
        1. Private companies—United States. 2. Private companies—United States—Forms.
        I. Title. II. Title: Small Business Start-up kit. III. Series
        KF1466.Z9 .S48 2000   346.73'0652-dc21   CIP 99-28195

Nova Publishing Company is dedicated to providing up-to-date and accurate legal information to the public. All Nova publications are periodically revised to contain the latest available legal information.

3rd Edition; 2nd Printing:	February, 2008	1st Edition; 4th Printing:	April, 2004
3rd Edition; 1st Printing	June, 2007	1st Edition; 3rd Printing:	June, 2003
2nd Edition; 2nd Printing:	January, 2006	1st Edition; 2nd Printing:	October, 2001
2nd Edition; 1st Printing:	August, 2004	1st Edition; 1st Printing:	January, 2000

This publication is designed to provide accurate and authoritative information in regard to the subject matter covered. It is sold with the understanding that the publisher and author are not engaged in rendering legal, accounting, or other professional services. If legal advice or other expert assistance is required, the services of a competent professional person should be sought.
—*From a Declaration of Principles jointly adopted by a Committee of the American Bar Association and a Committee of Publishers*

DISCLAIMER

Because of possible unanticipated changes in governing statutes and case law relating to the application of any information contained in this book, the author, publisher, and any and all persons or entities involved in any way in the preparation, publication, sale, or distribution of this book disclaim all responsibility for the legal effects or consequences of any document prepared or action taken in reliance upon information contained in this book. No representations, either express or implied, are made or given regarding the legal consequences of the use of any information contained in this book. Purchasers and persons intending to use this book for the preparation of any legal documents are advised to check specifically on the current applicable laws in any jurisdiction in which they intend the documents to be effective.

Nova Publishing Company   *Distributed by*:
Small Business and Consumer Legal Books and Software   National Book Network
1103 West College St.   4501 Forbes Blvd., Suite 200
Carbondale, IL 62901   Lanham, MD 20706
Editorial: (800) 748-1175   Orders: (800) 462-6420
www.novapublishing.com

Nova Publishing Company Green Business Policies

Nova Publishing Company is committed to preserving ancient forests and natural resources. Our company's policy is to print all of our books on recycled paper, with no less than 30% post-consumer waste de-inked in a chlorine-free process. As a result, for the printing of this book, we have saved:

32.7 trees • 9,450 gallons of water • 5,535 kilowatt hours of electricity • 81 pounds of pollution

Nova Publishing Company is a member of Green Press Initiative, a nonprofit program dedicated to supporting publishers in their efforts to reduce their use of fiber obtained from endangered forests. For more information, go to www.greenpressinitiative.org. In addition, Nova uses all compact fluorescent lighting; recycles all office paper products, aluminum and plastic beverage containers, and printer cartridges; uses 100% post-consumer fiber, process-chlorine-free, acid-free paper for 95% of in-house paper use; and, when possible, uses electronic equipment that is EPA Energy Star-certified. Finally, all carbon emissions from office energy use are offset by the purchase of wind-energy credits that are used to subsidize the building of wind turbines on the Rosebud Sioux Reservation in South Dakota (see www.nativeenergy.com).

Table of Contents

List of Forms-on-CD

Business Start-up Checklist
Business Start-up Checklist (text and PDF form)

Business Plan
Business Plan Worksheet (text and PDF form)
Executive Summary (text and PDF form)

Marketing Plan
Business Marketing Worksheet (text and PDF form)

Financial Plan
Business Financial Worksheet (text and PDF form)
Estimated Profit and Loss Statement (PDF form)
Current Balance Sheet (PDF form)

Limited Liability Company Paperwork
Limited Liability Company Paperwork Checklist (text and PDF form)

Pre-Organization Activities
Pre-Organization Worksheet (text and PDF form)
Pre-Organization Checklist (text and PDF form)
Document Filing Checklist (text and PDF form)
Application for Reservation of Limited Liability Company Name (text and PDF form)

Articles of Organization
Articles of Organization Checklist (text and PDF form)
Articles of Organization (text and PDF form)

Operating Agreement
Operating Agreement Checklist (text and PDF form)
Operating Agreement (text and PDF form)

Members Meetings
First Members Meeting Checklist (text and PDF form)
Minutes of First Members Meeting (text and PDF form)
Annual Members Meeting Checklist (text and PDF form)
Minutes of Annual Members Meeting (text and PDF form)

Amendments to Articles of Organization or Operating Agreement
Amendment to Articles of Organization (text and PDF form)
Amendment to Operating Agreement (text and PDF form)

Termination of Limited Liability Company
Termination Worksheet (text and PDF form)
Termination of Limited Liability Company Agreement (text and PDF form)

Employee Documents
General Employment Contract (text and PDF form)
Independent Contractor Agreement (text and PDF form)
Contractor/Subcontractor Agreement (text and PDF form)

Business Financial Recordkeeping
Financial Recordkeeping Checklist (text and PDF form)

Business Accounts
Income Chart of Accounts (PDF form)
Expense Chart of Accounts (PDF form)
Balance Sheet Chart of Accounts (PDF form)
Sample Chart of Accounts (PDF form)
Current Asset Account (PDF form)
Physical Inventory Report (PDF form)
Periodic Inventory Report (PDF form)
Cost of Goods Sold Report (PDF form)
Fixed Asset Account (PDF form)
Accounts Payable Record (PDF form)
Long-Term Debt Record (PDF form)
Weekly Expense Record (PDF form)
Monthly Expense Summary (PDF form)
Annual Expense Summary (PDF form)
Weekly Cash Report (PDF form)
Monthly Cash Report Summary (PDF form)
Weekly Income Record (PDF form)
Monthly Income Summary (PDF form)
Annual Income Summary (PDF form)
Monthly Credit Sales Record (PDF form)
Credit Sales Aging Report (PDF form)
Invoice (PDF form)
Statement (PDF form)
Past Due Statement (PDF form)
Credit Memo (PDF form)

Business Payroll
Quarterly Payroll Time Sheet (PDF form)
Employee Payroll Record (PDF form)
Payroll Depository Record (PDF form)
Annual Payroll Summary (PDF form)
Payroll Checklist (text and PDF form)

Taxation of Limited Liability Companies
Limited Liability Company Tax Forms Checklist: Taxed As a Partnership (text and PDF form)
Limited Liability Company Tax Forms Checklist: Taxed As a Corporation (text and PDF form)
Limited Liability Company Tax Forms Checklist: Taxed As a Sole Proprietorship (text and PDF form)
Limited Liability Company Tax Schedules Checklist (text and PDF form)

List of Forms Included on CD Only (Not included in book)

The following state-specific forms are provided for 48 states and Washington D. C (On CD only as fillable PDF forms) (Note: Colorado and Georgia provide online registration of Limited Liability Companies)

Application for Reservation of Limited Liability Company Name (or equivalent)
Limited Liability Company Articles of Organization (or equivalent)

The following IRS forms are provided (All IRS forms are PDF forms)

IRS Form SS-4: *Application for Employer Identification Number*
IRS Form 940: *Employer's Annual Federal Unemployment (FUTA) Tax Return*
IRS Form 941: *Employer's Quarterly Federal Tax Return*
IRS Form 1040: *U.S. Individual Income Tax Return*
IRS Schedule E (Form 1040): *Supplemental Income and Loss*
IRS Schedule D (Form 1040): *Capital Gains and Losses*
IRS Schedule C (Form 1040): *Profit or Loss from Business (Sole Proprietorship)*
IRS Schedule C-EZ (Form 1040): *Net Profit from Business (Sole Proprietorship)*
IRS Schedule SE (Form 1040): *Self-Employment Tax*
IRS Form 1040-ES: *Estimated Tax for Individuals*
IRS Form 1065: *U.S. Return of Partnership Income*
IRS Schedule K-1 (Form 1065): *Partner's Share of Income, Credits, Deductions, Etc.*
IRS Form 1096: *Annual Summary and Transmittal of U.S. Information Returns*
IRS Form 1099-Misc: *Miscellaneous Income*
IRS Form 1120: *U.S. Corporation Income Tax Return*
IRS Form 1120-A: *U.S. Corporation Short-Form Income Tax Return*
IRS Form 1120-W: *Estimated Tax for Corporations*

IRS Form 8829: *Expenses for Business Use of Your Home*
IRS Form 8832: *Entity Classification Election*
IRS Form W-2: *Wage and Tax Statement*
IRS Form W-3: *Transmittal of Wage and Tax Statements*
IRS Form W-4: *Employee's Withholding Allowance Certificate*
The following additional forms are provided:
Residential Lease (text and PDF form)
Commercial Lease (text and PDF form)
Assignment of Lease (text and PDF form)
Consent to Assignment of Lease (text and PDF form)
Notice of Assignment of Lease (text and PDF form)
Amendment of Lease (text and PDF form)
Extension of Lease (text and PDF form)
Sublease (text and PDF form)
Consent to Sublease (text and PDF form)
Notice of Breach of Lease (text and PDF form)
Notice of Rent Default (text and PDF form)
Landlord's Notice to Terminate Lease (text and PDF form)
Tenant's Notice to Terminate Lease (text and PDF form)
Mutual Termination of Lease (text and PDF form)
Receipt for Lease Security Deposit (text and PDF form)
Rent Receipt (text and PDF form)
Notice of Lease (text and PDF form)
Notice to Vacate Property (text and PDF form)

Introduction

How to Use This Book

This book and the accompanying Forms-on-CD are designed to be used as a workbook to start your own business as a limited liability company. You will work through various worksheets, complete various checklists, and prepare numerous forms. Before you prepare any of the forms for use, you should carefully read the introductory information and instructions in the section in which the particular form is contained. Try to be as detailed and specific as possible as you fill in these forms. The more precise the description, the less likely that later disputes may develop over what was actually intended by the language chosen. The forms may be carefully adapted to a particular situation that may confront your company. The careful preparation and use of the forms in this book and CD should provide the typical business with most of the documents necessary for day-to-day operations. If in doubt as to whether a particular form will work in a specific application, please consult a competent lawyer. It may also be wise to consult with an experienced accountant as you begin to organize the company. The tax laws regarding limited liability companies are very complex and must be carefully complied with in order to obtain the maximum tax benefits.

Installation Instructions for Installing Forms-on-CD

Installation Instructions for PCs

1   Insert the enclosed CD in your computer.
2.   The installation program will start automatically. Follow the onscreen dialogue and make your appropriate choices.
3   If the CD installation does not start automatically, click on START, then RUN, then BROWSE, and select your CD drive, and then select the file **Install.exe**. Finally, click OK to run the installation program.
4.   During the installation program, you will be prompted as to whether or not you wish to install the Adobe Acrobat Reader® program. This software program is necessary to view and fill in the PDF (potable document format) forms that are included on the Forms-on-CD. If you do not already have the Adobe Acrobat Reader® program installed on your hard drive, you will need to select the full installation that will install this program to your computer.

Installation Instructions for MACs®

1. Insert the enclosed CD in your computer.
2. Copy the folder **Forms for Macs** to your hard drive. All of the PDF and text-only forms are included in this folder.
3. If you do not already have the Adobe Acrobat Reader® program installed on your hard drive, you will need to download the version of this software that is appropriate for you particular MAC® operating system from **www. adobe.com**. Note: The latest versions of the MAC® operating system (OS-X®) has PDF capabilities built into it.

Instructions for Using Forms-on-CD

All of the forms that are included in this book have been provided on the Forms-on-CD for your use if you have access to a computer. If you have completed the Forms-on-CD installation program, all of the forms will have been copied to your computer's hard drive. By default, these files are installed in the **C:\Limited Liability Company** folder which is created by the installation program. (Note for MAC® users: see instructions above). Opening the Forms folder will provide you with access to folders for each of the forms corresponding to forms in the book. Many of the forms are provided in two separate formats:

Text forms which may be opened, prepared, and printed from within your own word processing program (such as Microsoft Word®, or WordPerfect®). The text forms all have the file extension: **.txt**. These forms are located in the TEXT FORMS folders supplied for each chapter's forms. You may wish to use the forms in this format if you will be making changes to any of the text on the forms. To access these forms, please see below.

PDF forms which may be filled in on your computer screen and printed out on any printer. Files in this format may be opened as images on your computer and printed out on any printer. The files in Adobe PDF format all have the file extension: **.pdf**. Although this format provides the easiest method for completing the forms, the forms in this format can not be altered (other than to fill in the information required on the blanks provided) and the completed forms cannot be saved on your computer. To access the PDF forms, please see below. If you wish to alter the language in any of the forms, you will need to access the forms in their text-only versions.

To Access Adobe PDF Forms

1. You must have already installed the Adobe Acrobat Reader® program to your computer's hard drive. This program is installed automatically by the installation program.

2. On your computer's desktop, you will find a shortcut icon labeled **Acrobat Reader®** Using your mouse, left double click on this icon. This will open the Acrobat Reader®

program. When the Acrobat Reader® program is opened for the first time, you will need to accept the Licensing Agreement from Adobe in order to use this program. Click **Accept** when given the option to accept or decline the Agreement.

3. Once the Acrobat Reader® program is open on your computer, click on **FILE** (in the upper left-hand corner of the upper taskbar). Then click on **OPEN** in the drop down menu. Depending on which version of Windows or other operating system you are using, a box will open which will allow you to access files on your computer's hard drive. The files for limited liability company forms are located on your computer's "C" drive, under the folder **Limited Liability Company**. (Note: if you installed the forms folder on a different drive, access the forms on that particular drive).

4. If you desire to work with one of the forms, you should then left double-click your mouse on the sub-folder for the chapter in which the form is located in this book. An additional subfolder is also present: **State-specific Forms** which contains the required forms for each state for Limited Liability Company Articles of Organization (or its equivalent) and the forms for Reservation of a Limited Liability Company Name. A list of forms will appear and you should then left double-click your mouse on the form of your choice. This will open two folders: one for **text forms** and one for **PDF forms**. Left double click your mouse on the **PDF forms** folder and then left double click your mouse on the form of your choice. This will open the appropriate form within the Adobe Acrobat Reader® program.

To Fill in Forms in the Adobe Acrobat Reader® Program

1. A 'hand tool' icon will be your cursor in the Acrobat Reader® program. Move the 'hand tool' cursor to the first blank space that will need to be completed on the form. A vertical line or "I-beam" should appear at the beginning of the first space on a form that you will need to fill in. You may then begin to type the necessary information in the space provided. When you have filled in the first blank space, hit the **TAB** key on your keyboard. This will move the 'hand' cursor to the next space which must be filled in. Please note that some of the spaces in the forms must be completed by hand, specifically the signature and/or notary blanks.

2. Move through the form, completing each required space, and hitting **TAB** to move to the next space to be filled in. When you have completed all of the fill-ins, you may print out the form on your computer's printer. (Please note: hitting **TAB** after the last fill-in will return you to the first page of the form).

3. IMPORTANT NOTE: Unfortunately, the Adobe Acrobat Reader® program does NOT allow you to save the filled-in form to your computer's hard drive. You can only save the form in a printed version. For this reason, you should wait to complete the forms until you have all of the information necessary to complete the chosen form in one

session. You may, of course, leave the Acrobat program open on your computer and leave a partially-completed form open in the program. However, if you close the file or if you close the Acrobat Reader® program, the filled-in information will be lost.

To Access and Complete the Text Forms

For your convenience, all of the forms in this book (other than the state-specific forms) are also provided as text-only forms which may be altered and saved. To open and use any of the text forms:

1. First, open your preferred word processing program. Then click on **FILE** (in the upper left-hand corner of the upper taskbar). Then click on **OPEN** in the drop down menu. Depending on which version of Windows or other operating system you are using, a box will open which will allow you to access files on your computer's hard drive. The files for limited liability company forms are located on your computer's "**C**" drive, under the folder **Limited Liability Company**

2. If you desire to work with one of the forms, you should then left double-click your mouse on the appropriate sub-folder and the form within that subfolder. This will open two folders: one for **text forms** and one for **PDF forms**. Left double-click your mouse on the **text forms** folder and a list of the text forms for that topic should appear. Left double-click your mouse on the form of your choice. This will open the appropriate form within your word processing program.

3. You may now fill in the necessary information while the text-only file is open in your word processing program. You may need to adjust margins and/or line endings of the form to fit your particular word processing program. Note that there is an asterisk (*) in every location in these forms where information will need to be included. Replace each asterisk with the necessary information. When the form is complete, you may print out the completed form and you may save the completed form. If you wish to save the completed form, you should rename the form so that your hard drive will retain an unaltered version of the original form.

Technical Support

Please also note that Nova Publishing Company cannot provide legal advice regarding the effect or use of the forms in this book or on the CD. For questions about installing the Forms-on-CD and software, you may call Nova Technical Support at 1-800-748-1175 or access the Nova Publishing Website for support at **www.novapublishing. com/catalog/faq.php**. For any questions relating to Adobe Acrobat Reader®, please access Adobe Technical Support at **www.adobe.com/support/main.html** or you may search for assistance in the HELP area of Adobe Acrobat Reader® (located in approximately the center of the top line of the program's desktop screen).

CHAPTER 1
Deciding to Start Business as a Limited Liability Company

One of the first decisions that potential business owners must confront is how their business should be structured and operated. This crucial decision must be made even before the business has actually begun operations. The legal documents that will generally accompany the formation of a business can follow many different patterns, depending on the particular situation and the type of business to be undertaken.

Initially, the type of business entity to be used must be selected. There are many basic forms of business operating entities. The five most common forms are:

- Sole proprietorship
- Partnership
- Corporation
- S-corporation
- Limited liability company

The choice of entity for a particular business depends on many factors. Which of these forms of business organization is chosen can have a great impact on the success of the business. The structure chosen will have an effect on how easy it is to obtain financing, how taxes are paid, how accounting records are kept, whether personal assets are at risk in the venture, the amount of control the "owner" has over the business, and many other aspects of the business. Keep in mind that the initial choice of business organization need not be the final choice. It is often wise to begin with the simplest form, the sole proprietorship, until the business progresses to a point where another form is clearly indicated. This allows the business to begin in the least complicated manner and allows the owner to retain total control in the important formative period of the business. As the business grows and the potential for liability and tax burdens increase, circumstances may dictate a re-examination of the business structure. The advantages and disadvantages of the five choices of business operation are detailed below.

Sole Proprietorship

A *sole proprietorship* is both the simplest and the most prevalent form of business organization. An important reason for this is that it is the least regulated of all types of business structures. Technically, the sole proprietorship is the traditional unincorporated one-person business. For legal and tax purposes, the business is the owner. It has no existence outside the owner. The liabilities of the business are personal to the owner and the business ends when the owner dies. On the other hand, all of the profits are also personal to the owner and the sole owner has full control of the business.

Disadvantages

Perhaps the most important factor to consider before choosing this type of business structure is that all of the personal and business assets of the sole owner are at risk in the sole proprietorship. If the demands of the creditors of the business exceed those assets which were formally placed in the name of the business, the creditors may reach the personal assets of the owner of the sole proprietorship. Legal judgments for damages arising from the operation of the business may also be enforced against the owner's personal assets. This unlimited liability is probably the greatest drawback to this type of business form. Of course, insurance coverage of various types can lessen the dangers inherent in having one's personal assets at risk in a business. However, as liability insurance premiums continue to skyrocket, it is unlikely that a fledgling small business can afford to insure against all manner of contingencies and at the maximum coverage levels necessary to guard against all risk to personal assets.

A second major disadvantage to the sole proprietorship as a form of business structure is the potential difficulty in obtaining business loans. Often in starting a small business, there is insufficient collateral to obtain a loan and the sole owner must mortgage his or her own house or other personal assets to obtain the loan. This, of course, puts the sole proprietor's personal assets in a direct position of risk should the business fail. Banks and other lending institutions are often reluctant to loan money for initial small business start-ups due to the high risk of failure for small businesses. Without a proven track record, it is quite difficult for a small business owner to adequately present a loan proposal based on a sufficiently stable cash flow to satisfy most banks.

A further disadvantage to a sole proprietorship is the lack of continuity that is inherent in the business form. If the owner dies, the business ceases to exist. Of course, the assets and liabilities of the business will pass to the heirs of the owner, but the expertise and knowledge of how the business was successfully carried on will often die with the owner. Small sole proprietorships are seldom carried on profitably after the death of the owner.

Advantages

The most appealing advantage of the sole proprietorship as a business structure is the total control the owner has over the business. Subject only to economic considerations and certain legal restrictions, there is total freedom to operate the business however one chooses. Many people feel that this factor alone is enough to overcome the inherent disadvantages in this form of business.

Related to this is the simplicity of organization of the sole proprietorship. Other than maintenance of sufficient records for tax purposes, there are no legal requirements on how the business is operated. Of course, the prudent businessperson will keep adequate records and sufficiently organize the business for its most efficient operation. But there are no outside forces dictating how such internal decisions are made in the sole proprietorship. The sole owner makes all decisions in this type of business.

As was mentioned earlier, the sole proprietorship is the least regulated of all businesses. Normally, the only license necessary is a local business license, usually obtained by simply paying a fee to a local registration authority. In addition, it may be necessary to file an affidavit with local authorities and publish a notice in a local newspaper if the business is operated under an assumed or fictitious name. This is necessary to allow creditors to have access to the actual identity of the true owner of the business, since it is the owner who will be personally liable for the debts and obligations of the business.

Finally, it may be necessary to register with local, state, and federal tax bodies for I.D. numbers and for the purpose of collection of sales and other taxes. Other than these few simple registrations, from a legal standpoint little else is required to start up a business as a sole proprietorship.

A final and important advantage to the sole proprietorship is the various tax benefits available to an individual. The losses or profits of the sole proprietorship are considered personal to the owner. The losses are directly deductible against any other income the owner may have and the profits are taxed only once at the marginal rate of the owner. In many instances, this may have distinct advantages over the method by which partnerships are taxed or the double taxation of corporations, particularly in the early stages of the business.

Partnership

A *partnership* is a relationship existing between two or more persons who join together to carry on a trade or business. Each partner contributes money, property, labor, and/or skill to the partnership and, in return, expects to share in the profits or losses of the business. A partnership is usually based on a partnership agreement of some type, although the agreement need not be a formal document. It may even simply be an oral understanding between the partners, although this is not recommended.

A simple joint undertaking to share expenses is not considered a partnership, nor is a mere co-ownership of property that is maintained and leased or rented. To be considered a partnership for legal and tax purposes, the following factors are usually considered:

- The partners' conduct in carrying out provisions of the partnership agreement
- The relationship of the parties
- The abilities and contributions of each party to the partnership
- The control each partner has over the partnership income and the purposes for which the income is used

Disadvantages

The disadvantages of the partnership form of business begin with the potential for conflict between partners. Of all forms of business organization, the partnership has spawned more disagreements than any other. This is generally traceable to the lack of a decisive initial partnership agreement that clearly outlines the rights and duties of the partners. This disadvantage can be partially overcome with a comprehensive partnership agreement. However, there is still the seemingly inherent difficulty many people have in working within the framework of a partnership, regardless of the initial agreement between the partners.

A further disadvantage to the partnership structure is that each partner is subject to unlimited personal liability for the debts of the partnership. The potential liability in a partnership is even greater than that encountered in a sole proprietorship. This is due to the fact that in a partnership the personal risk for which one may be liable is partially out of one's direct control and may be accrued due to actions on the part of another person. Each partner is liable for all of the debts of the partnership, regardless of which partner may have been responsible for their accumulation.

Related to the business risks of personal financial liability is the potential personal legal liability for the negligence of another partner. In addition, each partner may even be liable for the negligence of an employee of the partnership if such negligence takes place during the usual course of business of the partnership. Again, the attendant risks are broadened by the potential for liability based on the acts of other persons. Of course, general liability insurance can counteract this drawback to some extent to protect the personal and partnership assets of each partner.

Again, as with the sole proprietorship, the partnership lacks the advantage of continuity. A partnership is usually automatically terminated upon the death of any partner. A final accounting and a division of assets and liabilities is generally necessary in such an instance unless specific methods under which the partnership may be continued have been outlined in the partnership agreement.

Finally, certain benefits of corporate organization are not available to a partnership. Since a partnership cannot obtain financing through public stock offerings, large infusions of capital are more difficult for a partnership to raise than for a corporation. In addition, many of the fringe benefit programs that are available to corporations (such as certain pension and profit-sharing arrangements) are not available to partnerships.

Advantages

A partnership, by virtue of combining the credit potential of the various partners, has an inherently greater opportunity for business credit than is generally available to a sole proprietorship. In addition, the assets which are placed in the name of the partnership may often be used directly as collateral for business loans. The pooling of the personal capital of the partners generally provides the partnership with an advantage over the sole proprietorship in the area of cash availability. However, as noted above, the partnership does not have as great a potential for financing as does a corporation.

As with the sole proprietorship, there may be certain tax advantages to operation of a business as a partnership, as opposed to a corporation. The profits generated by a partnership may be distributed directly to the partners without incurring any "double" tax liability, as is the case with the distribution of corporate profits in the form of dividends to the shareholders. Income from a partnership is taxed at personal income tax rates. Note, however, that depending on the individual tax situation of each partner, this aspect could prove to be a disadvantage.

For a business where two or more people want to share in the work and profits, a partnership is often the structure chosen. It is potentially a much simpler form of business organization than the corporate form. Less start-up costs are needed and there is limited regulation of partnerships. However, the simplicity of this form of business can be deceiving. A sole proprietor knows his or her actions will determine how the business will prosper and that he or she is, ultimately, personally responsible for the success or failure of the enterprise. In a partnership, however, the duties, obligations, and commitments of each partner are often ill-defined. This lack of definition of the status of each partner can lead to serious difficulties and disagreements. In order to clarify the rights and responsibilities of each partner and to be certain of the tax status of the partnership, it is good business procedure to have a written partnership agreement. All states have adopted a version of the *Uniform Partnership Act*, which provides an outline of partnership law. Although state law will supply the general boundaries of partnerships and even specific partnership agreement terms if not addressed by a written partnership agreement, it is better for a clear understanding of the business structure if the partner's agreements are put in writing.

Corporation

A corporation is a creation of law. It is governed by the laws of the state where it was incorporated and of the state or states in which it does business. In recent years it has become the business structure of choice for many small businesses. Corporations are, generally, a more complex form of business operation than either a sole proprietorship or partnership. Corporations are also subject to far more state regulations regarding both their formation and operation. The following discussion is provided in order to allow the potential business owner an understanding of this type of business operation.

The corporation is an artificial entity. It is created by filing Articles of Incorporation with the proper state authorities. This gives the corporation its legal existence and the right to carry on business. The Articles of Incorporation act as a public record of certain formalities of corporate existence. Adoption of corporate *bylaws*, or internal rules of operation, is often the first business of the corporation, after it has been given the authority to conduct business by the state. The bylaws of the corporation outline the actual mechanics of the operation and management of the corporation.

There are two basic types of corporations: C-corporations and S-corporations. These prefixes refer to the particular chapter in the U.S. Tax Codes that specify the tax consequences of either type of corporate organization. In general, both of these two types of corporations are organized and operated in similar fashion. There are specific rules that apply to the ability to be recognized by the U.S. Internal Revenue Service as an S-corporation. In addition, there are significant differences in the tax treatment of these two types of corporations. The basic structure and organizational rules below apply to both types of corporations, unless noted.

C-Corporation

In its simplest form, the corporate organizational structure consists of the following levels:

- **Shareholders:** who own shares of the business but do not contribute to the direct management of the corporation, other than by electing the directors of the corporation and voting on major corporate issues

- **Directors:** who may be shareholders, but as directors do not own any of the business. They are responsible, jointly as members of the board of directors of the corporation, for making the major business decisions of the corporation, including appointing the officers of the corporation

- **Officers:** who may be shareholders and/or directors, but, as officers, do not own any of the business. The officers (generally the president, vice president, secretary, and treasurer) are responsible for the day-to-day operation of the corporate business

Disadvantages
Due to the nature of the organizational structure in a corporation, a certain degree of individual control is necessarily lost by incorporation. The officers, as appointees of the board of directors, are answerable to the board for management decisions. The board of directors, on the other hand, is not entirely free from restraint, since it is responsible to the shareholders for the prudent business management of the corporation.

The technical formalities of corporation formation and operation must be strictly observed in order for a business to reap the benefits of corporate existence. For this reason, there is an additional burden and expense to the corporation of detailed recordkeeping that is seldom present in other forms of business organization. Corporate decisions are, in general, more complicated due to the various levels of control and all such decisions must be carefully documented. Corporate meetings, both at the shareholder and director levels, are more formal and more frequent. In addition, the actual formation of the corporation is more expensive than the formation of either a sole proprietorship or partnership. The initial state fees that must be paid for registration of a corporation with a state can run as high as $900.00 for a minimally capitalized corporation. Corporations are also subject to a greater level of governmental regulation than any other type of business entity. These complications have the potential to overburden a small business struggling to survive.

Finally, the profits of a corporation, when distributed to the shareholders in the form of dividends, are subject to being taxed twice. The first tax comes at the corporate level. The distribution of any corporate profits to the investors in the form of dividends is not a deductible business expense for the corporation. Thus, any dividends that are distributed to shareholders have already been subject to corporate income tax. The second level of tax is imposed at the personal level. The receipt of corporate dividends is considered income to the individual shareholder and is taxed as such. This potential for higher taxes due to a corporate business structure can be moderated by many factors, however.

Advantages
One of the most important advantages to the corporate form of business structure is the potential limited liability of the founders of and investors in the corporation. The liability for corporate debts is limited, in general, to the amount of money each owner has contributed to the corporation. Unless the corporation is essentially a shell for a one-person business or unless the corporation is grossly under-capitalized or under-insured, the personal assets of the owners are not at risk if the corporation fails. The shareholders stand to lose only what they invested. This factor is very important in attracting investors as the business grows.

A corporation can have a perpetual existence. Theoretically, a corporation can last forever. This may be a great advantage if there are potential future changes in ownership of the business in the offing. Changes that would cause a partnership to be dissolved or terminated will often not affect the corporation. This continuity can be an important factor in establishing a stable business image and a permanent relationship with others in the industry.

Unlike a partnership, in which no one may become a partner without the consent of the other partners, a shareholder of corporate stock may freely sell, trade, or give away his or her stock unless this right is formally restricted by reasonable corporate decisions. The new owner of such stock is then a new owner of the business in the proportionate share of stock obtained. This freedom offers potential investors a liquidity to shift assets that is not present in the partnership form of business. The sale of shares by the corporation is also an attractive method by which to raise needed capital. The sale of shares of a corporation, however, is subject to many governmental regulations on both the state and federal levels.

Taxation is listed both as an advantage and as a disadvantage for the corporation. Depending on many factors, the use of a corporation can increase or decrease the actual income tax paid in operating a corporate business. In addition, corporations may set aside surplus earnings (up to certain levels) without any negative tax consequences. Finally, corporations are able to offer a much greater variety of fringe benefit programs to employees and officers than any other type of business entity. Various retirement, stock option, and profit-sharing plans are only open to corporate participation.

S-Corporation

The S-corporation is a certain type of corporation that is available for specific tax purposes. It is a creation of the Internal Revenue Service. S-corporation status is not relevant to state corporation laws. Its purpose is to allow small corporations to choose to be taxed, at the Federal level, like a partnership, but to also enjoy many of the benefits of a corporation. It is, in many respects, similar to a limited liability company. The main difference lies in the rules that a company needs to meet in order to qualify as an S-corporation under Federal law. In general, to qualify as an S-corporation under current IRS rules, a corporation must meet certain requirements:

- It must not have more than 100 shareholders
- All of the shareholders must, generally, be individuals and U.S. citizens
- It must only have one class of stock
- Shareholders must consent to S-corporation status
- An election of S-corporation status must be filed with the IRS

The S-corporation retains all of the advantages and disadvantages of the traditional corporation except in the area of taxation. For tax purposes, S-corporation shareholders are treated similarly to partners in a partnership. The income, losses, and deductions generated by an S-corporation are "passed through" the corporate entity to the individual shareholders. Thus, there is no "double" taxation of an S-corporation. In addition, unlike a standard corporation, shareholders of S-corporations can personally deduct any corporate losses.

Limited Liability Company

The limited liability company is the focus of this book. The limited liability company is a hybrid type of business structure. It contains elements of both a traditional partnership and a corporation. The limited liability company form of business structure is relatively new. Only in the last few years has it become available as a form of business in all 50 states and Washington D.C. Its uniqueness is that it offers the limited personal liability of a corporation and the tax benefits of a partnership. A limited liability company consists of one or more members/owners who actively manage the business of the limited liability company. There may also be nonmember managers employed to handle the business.

Disadvantages

In as much as the business form is still similar to a partnership in operation, there is still a potential for conflict among the members/owners of a limited liability company. Limited liability companies are formed according to individual state law, generally by filing formal Articles of Organization of a Limited Liability Company with the proper state authorities in the state of formation. Limited liability companies are, generally, a more complex form of business operation than either the sole proprietorship or the standard partnership. They are subject to more paperwork requirements than a simple partnership but somewhat less than a corporation. Limited liability companies are also subject to far more state regulations regarding both their formation and their operation than either a sole proprietorship or a partnership. In all states, they are also required to pay fees for beginning the company, and in some states, annual franchise fees of often hundreds of dollars are assessed for the right to operate as a limited liability company.

Similar to traditional partnerships, the limited liability company has an inherent lack of continuity. In recent years, however, an increasing number of states have allowed limited liability companies to exist for a perpetual duration, as can corporations. Even if the duration of a limited liability company is perpetual, however, there may be difficulties if the sole member of a one-member limited liability company becomes disabled or dies. These problems can be overcome to some extent by providing, in the Articles of Organization of the limited liability company, for an immediate reorganization of the limited liability company with the deceased member's heirs or estate becoming members of the company. In addition, similar to partnerships, it may be difficult to sell or transfer ownership interests in a limited liability company. Forms for creating Articles of Organization are contained in Chapter 9 and for Operating Agreements in Chapter 10.

Advantages

The members/owners in such a business enjoy a limited liability, similar to that of a shareholder in a corporation. In general, the members' risk is limited to the amount of their investment in the limited liability company. Since none of the members will have personal liability and may not necessarily be required to personally perform any tasks of management, it is easier to attract investors to the limited liability company form of business than to a traditional partnership. The members will share in the potential profits and in the tax deductions of the limited liability company, but will share in fewer of the financial risks involved. Since the limited liability company is generally taxed as a partnership, the profits and losses of the company pass directly to each member and are taxed only at the individual level. Information regarding taxation of limited liability companies is contained in Chapter 18.

A further advantage of this type of business structure is that it offers a relatively flexible management structure. The company can be managed either by members/owners themselves or by managers who may or may not be members. Thus, depending on needs or desires, the limited liability company can be a hands-on, owner-managed company or a relatively hands-off operation for its members/owners with hired managers actually operating the company.

A final advantage is that limited liability companies are allowed more flexibility than corporations in how profits and losses are actually allocated to the members/owners. Thus, one member/owner may be allocated 50 percent of the profits (or losses) even though that member/owner only contributed 10 percent of the capital to start the company.

The decision of which business entity to choose depends upon many factors and should be carefully studied. If the choice is to operate a business as a limited liability company, this book will provide an array of easy-to-use legal forms that will, in most cases, allow the business owner to start and operate the company with minimal difficulty while meeting all of the legal paperwork requirements.

CHAPTER 2
Business Start-up Checklist

Following is the first of many checklists that are provided in this book in order to help you organize your preparation for starting a business. This initial checklist provides an overview of the entire process of starting a business and, in many ways, is your blueprint for your personal business start-up. It incorporates references to many other forms, worksheets, and checklists from throughout this book. Keep this list handy as you proceed through the process of starting your own limited liability company.

Business Start-up Checklist

- ☐ Read through this entire book to understand the process of starting a limited liability company

- ☑ Install the software and forms from the Forms-on-CD if you will be using a computer to complete the forms (Introduction)

- ☐ Complete the Business Plan Worksheet (Chapter 3)

  - ☐ Prepare your written Business Plan

- ☐ Complete the Business Marketing Worksheet (Chapter 4)

  - ☐ Prepare your written Marketing Plan

- ☐ Prepare the Business Financial Worksheet (Chapter 5)

  - ☐ Prepare your written Financial Plan

- ☐ Prepare your written Executive Summary (Chapter 3)

  - ☐ Compile your final Business Plan package

- ☐ Review the Limited Liability Company Paperwork Checklist (Chapter 7)

- ❑ Complete the Pre-Organization Worksheet (Chapter 8)

  - ❑ Review the Pre-Organization and Document Filing Checklists

  - ❑ Prepare and file your Application for Reservation of Limited Liability Company Name (if desired)

- ❑ Prepare and file your Articles of Organization (Chapter 9)

- ❑ Prepare your Operating Agreement (Chapter 10)

- ❑ Hold first members meeting using First Members Meeting Checklist (Chapter 11)

- ❑ Prepare Employment Contracts for managers and employees of the company (Chapter 14)

- ❑ Set up Business Accounting System Chart of Accounts (Chapter 16)

  - ❑ Prepare income, expense, asset, and liability accounts

  - ❑ Open company business bank account

- ❑ Set up business payroll (Chapter 17)

- ❑ Set up company tax payment schedules (Chapter 18)

CHAPTER 3
Developing a Business Plan

One of the most important and often overlooked aspects of starting a business is the process of preparing a Business Plan. It is through preparation of a formal business plan than you begin the process of refining what your business will actually be and, more importantly, how you can make it successful from the start. To develop a useful plan, you will need to research your business idea and determine how it can be developed into a feasible and successful business. You will use your business plan for many purposes: for your own use to continually fine-tune your actual business start-up; for obtaining financing, even it is only from family members; and for presenting your business ideas to potential shareholders, employees, investors, suppliers, and anyone else with whom you may be doing business. Your plan needs to be dynamic and detailed. If you prepare your plan with care and attention, it will help guide you through the process of starting a successful business. If you take shortcuts in researching, thinking about, and preparing your plan, your path to business success will become an everyday struggle.

This book has divided the preparation of your business plan into three separate parts. In this chapter, you will develop your overall plan. However, in the two following chapters, you will also develop plans that will become an integral part of your business plan. Chapter 4 concentrates on the plans to market your business service or product. Chapter 5 provides a worksheet and instructions for preparing and implementing a strategy for financing your business. Together, the three plans that you create will comprise your total Business Plan package. Finally, after completing all three sections, you will prepare an Executive Summary. The instructions for preparing the summary are at the end of this chapter. With the information you will have gathered and set down in your plan, starting a successful business will be simplified and streamlined. Each of these three chapters has a similar format. A worksheet is presented into which you will enter information that you have gathered or researched. Crucial business decisions will need to be made, even at this early stage, in order for you to honestly assess your chances for success. After completing the worksheet, you will use the compiled information to complete a written (typed or printed) plan. This process will take some time to do correctly, but time spent at this stage of your business start-up will save you many times the effort and headaches later in your business' evolution. If you are using a computer, all three of the Business Plan Worksheets are included on the Forms-on-CD. You may enter your answers to the questions directly on the forms which you can open in your own word-processing program. This will allow you to quickly and easily compile the answers that you have written out into the final Business Plan. Following this first worksheet are more detailed instructions for preparing your Business Plan.

Business Plan Worksheet

Preliminary Business Concept Analysis

In one sentence, describe your business concept: _____
_____

What is your business service or product? _____
_____
_____

How long do you estimate that it will take to develop this service or product to the point of being ready for the public? _____
_____

What are the estimated costs of development of this product or service? _____
_____

Why do you think that this business concept will succeed? _____
_____
_____

Who is your target market? _____
_____

Is this market readily identifiable? _____
_____

What are the buying patterns of this market? _____
_____

Is there sufficient advance interest in this type of product or service? _____
_____

What are your expected annual sales/revenue volumes?
Year one: $ _____
Year two: $ _____
Year three: $ _____
Year four: $ _____
Year five: $ _____

Company Description

What is your company's mission? _____
_____

What is the type of business entity of your company?   *Limited Liability Company*

Who will be the directors of the company? _____
_____

Who will serve as the officers of the company?
    President: _____
    Vice President: _____
    Treasurer: _____
    Secretary: _____

What will the physical location of your company be? _____
_____

Where will be the company's main place of doing business? _____

Will there be any additional locations for the company? _____
_____

What geographic areas will your company serve? _____

What are the long-term plans for the business? (Expand, go public, sell to competitor, etc.)
_____
_____

Industry Analysis

In what industry will your company operate? _____

What is the overall size of the industry? _____

What is the growth rate of the industry? _____

What are any seasonal or business cycles in the industry? _____
_____

What have been the main technological advances in the past five years? _____
_____

What are projected technological advances in the industry for the next five years? _____

_____

Do any industry standards apply to your business? _____

_____

Are there any government regulatory approvals or requirements? _____

_____

Are there any local or state licenses necessary for the service or product? _____

_____

What are the main trade or business associations in your industry? _____

_____

To which associations do you currently belong? _____

_____

Product or Service Analysis

Description of product or service: _____

_____

What is the main purpose of the product or service? _____

_____

Is it a luxury item or a necessity? _____

What are the unique features of your product or service? (Cost, design, quality, capabilities, etc.) _____

_____

_____

What is the life of the product or service? _____

How does this product/service compare with the state-of-the-art for the industry? _____

_____

In what stage is the development of the product? (Idea, model, prototype, full production, etc.) _____

Describe the company's facilities: _____

_____

How will the product be produced or the service provided? _____

_____

Is it labor- or material-intensive to produce or supply? _____

What components or supplies are necessary to produce or supply this product? _____

_____

Has the service or product been the subject of any engineering or design tests? _____

_____

What types of quality control will be in place in the business? _____

_____

Are there any special technical considerations? _____

_____

What are the maintenance or updating requirements for the product/service? _____

_____

Can the product be copyrighted, patented, or trade- or service-marked? _____

_____

Are there other products, services, or spin-offs that will be developed and marketed in future years? _____

_____

Are there any known dangers associated with the manufacture, supply, or use of the product/service? _____

What types of liabilities are posed by the product, service, or any other business operations?
    To employees: _____
    To customers: _____
    To suppliers: _____
    To distributors: _____
    To the public: _____

Are there any litigation threats posed by this business? _____

Are there any other problems or risks inherent in this type of business? _____

_____

What types of insurance coverage will be necessary for the business? _____

_____

What are the costs of the needed insurance coverage? _____

What steps will be taken to minimize any potential liabilities, dangers, or risks? _____
_____
_____

Business Operations

Describe the type of facilities that your business will need to operate: _____
_____

Estimate the cost of acquiring and maintaining the facilities for two years: _____
_____

Describe your production plan or service plan: _____
_____
_____

How will orders be filled and your product or service delivered? _____
_____

Will you work through any wholesalers or distributors? _____
_____

Who will be the main wholesalers/distributors? _____
_____

Describe the equipment or machinery that you will need for your business: _____
_____
_____

Who will be the main suppliers of this equipment? _____
_____

What are the estimated costs of obtaining this equipment? _____

What type of inventory will you need? _____

Who will be the main suppliers of the inventory? _____
_____

Estimate the costs of obtaining sufficient inventory for the first two years of operation:
_____

Management Analysis

What will be the organizational structure of the company? (Include an organizational chart)

_____

Who will manage the day-to-day affairs of the company? _____

Describe the management style of the central manager: _____

_____

What are the qualifications of the main management? _____

What type of workforce will be necessary for your business? _____

_____

How many employees will be needed?
Initially: _____
First year: _____
Second year: _____
Third year: _____
Fourth year: _____
Fifth year: _____

What are the job descriptions of the employees? _____

What job skills will the employees need? _____

Are employment and hiring/firing procedures and guidelines in place? _____

What will be the hourly wages or salaries of the employees?
Salaried: _____
Full-time: _____
Part-time: _____

Will any fringe benefits be provided to employees?
Sick pay: _____
Vacation pay: _____
Bonuses: _____
Health insurance or benefits: _____
Profit-sharing or stock options: _____
Other benefits: _____

Estimate the annual cost for employee compensation for the first two years of operations:

_____

Will you need to contract with lawyers, accountants, consultants, designers, or specialists?
_____

Who will be the outside contractors you will use? _____
_____

Estimate the annual cost of outside contractors for the first two years of operations:
_____

Is the business bookkeeping system set up and working? _____

Are business bank accounts set up? _____

Are there administrative policies set up for billings, payments, accounts, etc.? _____

Supporting Documentation

Do you have any professional photos of the product, equipment, or facilities? _____
_____

What contracts have already been signed? _____

Does the company hold any patents, trademarks, or copyrights? _____
_____

Have the company's organizational papers been filed with the state and received? _____
_____

Do you have any samples of advertising or marketing materials? _____

Do you have references and resumés from each of the principals in the business? _____
_____

Do you have personal financial statements from each of the principals in the business?
_____

Have you prepared a time line chart for the company's development for the first five years?
_____

Have you prepared a list of the necessary equipment, with a description, supplier, and cost
of each item noted? _____

Have you prepared current and projected balance sheets and profit/loss statements? _____

Preparing Your Business Plan

Once you have completed the previous worksheet and the worksheets in the next two chapters (relating to marketing and financial plans), you will need to prepare your final Business Plan and complete the Executive Summary. The Executive Summary is, perhaps, the most important document in the entire Business Plan, for it is in this short document that you will distill your entire vision of your company. Do not attempt to prepare the Executive Summary until you have completed all of the other worksheets and plans, for they will provide you with the insight that you will need to craft an honest and enthusiastic Executive Summary for your company.

To prepare your Business Plan, carefully read through the answers you have prepared for the Business Plan Worksheet to obtain a complete overview of your proposed business. Your task will be to carefully put the answers to the questions on the worksheet into a narrative format. If you have taken the time to fully answer the questions, this will not be a difficult task. If you have supplied the answers to the worksheet questions on the computer file version of the worksheet, you should be able to easily cut and paste your Business Plan sections together, adding only sentence and paragraph structure and connecting information. Keep the plan to the point but try to convey both a broad outline of the industry that you will be operating in and a clear picture of how your particular company will fit into that industry and succeed. Emphasize the uniqueness of your company, product, or service, but don't intentionally avoid the potential problems that your business will face. An honest appraisal of your company's risks and potential problems at this stage of the development of your company will convey to investors and bankers that you have thoroughly and carefully investigated the potential for your company to succeed.

For each subsection of the Business Plan Worksheet, use the answers to the questions to prepare your written plan. You may rearrange the answers within each section if you feel that it will present a clearer picture to those who will be reading your Business Plan. Try, however, to keep the information for each section in its own discreet portion of the Business Plan. You will use this same technique to prepare the written Marketing and Financial Plans in the following two chapters. Once you have prepared your written Business, Marketing, and Financial Plans, you are ready to prepare your Executive Summary.

Preparing Your Executive Summary

It is in the Executive Summary that you will need to convey your vision of the company and its potential for success. It is with this document that you will convince investors, suppliers, bankers, and others to take the risks necessary to back your dreams and help you to make them a reality. The Executive Summary portion of your Business Plan should be about one to three pages long. It should be concise, straightforward, and clearly written. Don't use any terms or technical jargon that the average person cannot understand. You may go into more detail in the body of the Business Plan itself, but keep the Executive Summary short and to the point. This document will be a distillation of the key points in your entire Business Plan. It is in the Executive Summary that you will need to infuse your potential backers with your enthusiasm and commitment to success. However, you will need to remain honest and forthright in the picture that you paint of your business and its competition. Use the following outline as a guide to assist you in preparing your Executive Summary. You will, of course, be using the information that you have included in your written Business, Marketing, and Financial Plans to prepare the Executive Summary. After completing your Executive Summary, there are some brief instructions to assist you in compiling your entire Business Plan package.

Executive Summary

Business Plan of _____

Executive Summary

In the year _____ , _____ was organized as a limited liability company in the State of _____ .

The purpose of the company is to: _____
_____
_____ .

Our mission statement is as follows: This company is dedicated to providing the highest quality _____ to a target market of _____ . Our long-term goals are to: _____
_____ .

Industry Analysis

The industry in which this company will operate is: _____
_____ .

The annual gross sales of the _____ industry are approximately $ _____ .

Continue with a brief explanation of how your company will fit into this industry: _____
_____

Product or Service Analysis

The product/service that this company will provide is: _____ .

It is unique in its field because: _____ .

Continue with a brief explanation of product/service: _____
_____
_____ .

Business Operations

Prepare a brief explanation of how the business will operate to obtain and deliver the product/service to the market. Include short explanations of strategies you will use to beat the competition: _____

_____

_____ .

Management of the Company

The company will be managed by: _____

_____ .

Include a brief summary of the management structure and the qualifications of the key management personnel and how their expertise will be the key to the success of the company:

_____

_____

_____ .

Market Strategy

The target market for this product/service is: _____

_____ .

Prepare a brief analysis of your market research and marketing plans and why your product/service is better than any competitors: _____

_____

_____ .

Financial Plans

In this section, briefly review the data on your Current Balance Sheet and Estimated Profit and Loss Statements and describe both the annual revenue projections and the company's immediate and long-term needs for financing: _____

_____

_____

_____ .

Compiling Your Business Plan

1. Prepare a Title Page filling in the necessary information:

    > Business Plan of (*name of limited liability company*),
    > Organized in the State of (*name of state*)
    > Address:
    > Phone:
    > Fax:
    > Internet:
    > E-mail:
    > Date:
    > Prepared by (*name of preparer*)

2. Include a Table of Contents listing the following items that you have:

    - Executive Summary
    - Business Plan
        Business Concept and Objectives
        Industry Analysis
        Product/Service Analysis
        Business Operations
        Management Analysis
    - Marketing Plan
        Target Market Analysis
        Competitive Analysis
        Sales and Pricing Analysis
        Marketing Strategy
            Advertising and Promotion
            Publicity and Public Relations
    - Financial Plan
        Financial Analysis
        Estimated Profit/Loss Statement
        Current Balance Sheet
    - Appendix
        Photos of Product/Service/Facilities
        Contracts
        Organization Documents
        Bank Account Statements
        Personal Financial Statements of Principals
        Proposed List of Equipment/Supplies/Inventory
        Proposed Time Line for Company Growth

3. Neatly print or type the necessary Business/Marketing/Financial Plans.

4. Compile all of the parts of your Plan and have multiple photocopies made.

5. Assemble all of the parts into a neat and professional folder or notebook.

Congratulations! Your completed Business Plan will serve as an essential guide to understanding your business and will allow potential backers, investors, bankers, and others to quickly see the reality behind your business goals.

CHAPTER 4
Developing a Marketing Plan

An integral part of the process of starting a business is preparing a Marketing Plan. Whether the business will provide a service or sell a product, it will need customers in some form. Who those customers are, how they will be identified and located, and how they will be attracted to the business are crucial to the success of any small business. Unfortunately, it is also one part of a business start-up that is given less than its due in terms of time and effort spent to fully investigate the possibilities. In this chapter, a Business Marketing Worksheet is provided to assist you in thinking about your business in terms of who the customers may be and how to reach them. In many ways, looking honestly at who your customers may be and how to attract them may be the most crucial part of starting your business, for if your understanding of this issue is ill-defined or unclear, your business will have a difficult time succeeding.

In order to create your written Marketing Plan, simply follow the same process that you used in creating your Business Plan in Chapter 3. Take the answers that you have supplied on the following worksheet and edit them into a narrative for each of the four sections of the worksheet:

- Target Market Analysis
- Competitive Analysis
- Sales and Pricing Analysis
- Marketing Strategy

By following this process, you should be able to create a clear and straightforward description of your own business's marketing objectives and methods.

Business Marketing Worksheet

Target Market Analysis

What is the target market for your product/service? _____
_____

What types of market research have you conducted to understand your market? _____
_____

What is the geographic market area you will serve? _____

Describe a typical customer:
    Sex: _____
    Marital status: _____
    Age: _____
    Income: _____
    Geographic location: _____
    Education: _____
    Employment: _____

Estimate the number of potential people in the market in your area of service: _____
_____

What is the growth potential for this market? _____

How will you satisfy the customers' needs with your product/service? _____
_____

Will your product/service make your customers' life more comfortable? _____

Will your product/service save your customers' time or money or stress? _____

Competitive Analysis

Who are your main competitors? _____

Are there competitors in the same geographic area as your proposed business? _____
_____

Are the competitors successful and what is their market share? _____

How long have they been in business? _____

Describe your research into your competitors' business operations: _____
_____

Are there any foreseeable new competitors? _____

What are the strengths and/or weaknesses of your competitor's product/service? _____
_____

Why is your product/service different or better than that of your competitors? _____
_____
_____

What is the main way that you will compete with your competitors (price, quality, technology, advertising, etc.)? _____
_____

How will your customers know that your product/service is available? _____
_____

What is the main message that you want your potential customers to receive? _____
_____

Why is your product/service unique? _____
_____

How will you be able to expand your customer base over time? _____
_____

Sales and Pricing Analysis

What are your competitors' prices for similar products/services? _____

Are your prices higher or lower, and why? _____

Will you offer any discounts for quantity or other factors? _____

Will you accept checks for payment? _____

Will you accept credit cards for payment? _____

Will you have a sales force? Describe: _____

What skills or education will the sales force need? _____

Will there be sales quotas? _____

Will the sales force be paid by salary, wages, or commission? _____

Are there any geographic areas or limitations on your sales or distribution? _____
_____

Will you sell through distributors or wholesalers? Describe: _____

Will there be dealer margins or wholesale discounts? _____

Do you have any plans to monitor customer feedback? Describe: _____
_____

Do you have warranty, guarantee, and customer return policies? Describe: _____
_____

Will any customer service be provided? Describe: _____
_____

What is your expected sales volume for the first five years?
　　Year one: _____
　　Year two: _____
　　Year three: _____
　　Year four: _____
　　Year five: _____

Marketing Strategy

What is your annual projected marketing budget? _____

Have your company's logo, letterhead, and business cards already been designed?
_____

Do you have a company slogan or descriptive phrase? _____

Has packaging for your product/service been designed? _____

Has signage for your facility been designed? _____

Describe your advertising plans:

Signs: _____

Brochures: _____

Catalogs: _____

Yellow Pages: _____

Magazines: _____

Trade journals: _____

Radio: _____

Television: _____

Newspapers: _____

Internet: _____

Trade shows: _____

Videos: _____

Billboards: _____

Newsletters: _____

Have advertisements already been designed? _____

Have you prepared a media kit for publicity? _____

Describe your plans to receive free publicity in the media via news releases or new product/ service releases:

Radio: _____

Television: _____

Newspapers: _____

Magazines: _____

Internet: _____

Have you requested inclusion in any directories, catalogs, or other marketing vehicles for your industry? _____

Describe any planned direct mail campaigns: _____

Describe any planned telemarketing campaigns: _____

Describe any internet-based marketing plans:

E-mail account: _____

Website: _____

Will there be any special or seasonal promotions of your product/service? _____
_____

How will your customers actually receive the product/service? _____
_____

CHAPTER 5
Developing a Financial Plan

The third crucial part of your initial Business Plan entails how your business will obtain enough money to actually survive until it is successful. The failure of many small businesses relates directly to underestimating the amount of money needed to start *and* continue the business. Most business owners can, with relative ease, estimate the amount of money needed to start a business. The problem comes with arriving at a clear estimate of how much money will be necessary to keep the business operating until it is able to realistically support itself. If you can honestly determine how much is actually necessary to allow the business time to thrive before you can take out profits or pay, the next challenge is to figure out where to get that amount of money. To help you arrive at a clear picture of your business's finances, a Business Financial Worksheet follows. This worksheet will lead you through a number of questions to help you determine the amount of money needed and where it might be obtained. Following the worksheet are instructions on preparing both a Estimated Profit and Loss Statement and a Current Balance Sheet. Both of these financial forms will help you actually put some real numbers into your plans.

When you have completed the Business Financial Worksheet and your two financial forms, you will again need to prepare a written Financial Plan from your worksheet answers and the data that you have compiled on your Profit and Loss Statement and Balance Sheet. Use the same technique that you used in Chapters 3 and 4 to convert your answers to a narrative. After your written Financial Plan is completed, you will need to return to the instructions at the end of Chapter 3, complete your Executive Summary, and compile your completed parts into your entire final Business Plan package. You may then use your formal plan for presentations to prospective investors, bankers, family, or friends as you go in search of the assistance you will need to make your business a success. You will also need to develop a financial recordkeeping system. This and other accounting-related details are explained in Chapters 15 through 17.

Business Financial Worksheet

Describe the current financial status of your company: _____
_____
_____

Income and Expenses

Estimate the annual expenses for the first year in the following categories:

Advertising expenses: _____

Auto expenses: _____

Cleaning and maintenance expenses: _____

Charitable contributions: _____

Dues and publications: _____

Office equipment expenses: _____

Freight and shipping expenses: _____

Business insurance expenses: _____

Business interest expenses: _____

Legal and accounting expenses: _____

Business meals and lodging: _____

Miscellaneous expenses: _____

Postage expenses: _____

Office rent/mortgage expenses: _____

Repair expenses: _____

Office supplies: _____

Sales taxes: _____

Federal unemployment taxes: _____

State unemployment taxes: _____

Telephone/internet expenses: _____

Utility expenses: _____

Wages and commissions: _____

Estimate the first year's annual income from the following sources:

Sales income: _____

Service income: _____

Miscellaneous income: _____

Estimate the amount of inventory necessary for the first year: _____
_____

Estimate the amount of inventory that will be sold during the first year: _____

_____

Estimate the Cost of Goods Sold for the first year: _____

Using the above information, complete the Estimated Profit and Loss Statement as explained later.

Assets and Liabilities

What forms of credit have already been used by the business? _____

_____

How much cash is available to the business? _____

What are the sources of the cash? _____

What types of bank accounts are in place for the business and what are the balances?

_____

_____

What types of assets are currently owned by the business?
    Current assets: _____
    Inventory: _____
        Cash in bank: _____
        Cash on hand: _____
    Accounts receivable: _____
    Fixed and depreciable: _____
    Autos/trucks: _____
        Buildings: _____
        Equipment: _____
        Amount of depreciation taken on any of above:_____
    Fixed non-depreciable: _____
        Land: _____
    Miscellaneous: _____
        Stocks/bonds: _____

What types of debts does the business currently have?
    Current liabilities: _____
        Taxes due: _____
        Accounts payable: _____
        Short-term loans/notes payable: _____
        Payroll accrued: _____
        Miscellaneous: _____

Long-term liabilities: _____
    Mortgage: _____
    Other loans/notes payable: _____

Financial Needs

Based on the estimated profits and losses of the business, how much credit will be necessary for the business?

    Initially: _____
    First year: _____
    Second year: _____
    Third year: _____
    Fourth year: _____
    Fifth year: _____

Estimate the cash flow for the business for the first five years:

    First year: _____
    Second year: _____
    Third year: _____
    Fourth year: _____
    Fifth year: _____

From what sources are the necessary funds expected to be raised?

    Cash on hand: _____
    Personal funds: _____
    Family: _____
    Friends: _____
    Conventional bank financing: _____
    Finance companies: _____
    Equipment manufacturers: _____
    Leasing companies: _____
    Venture capital: _____
    U.S. Small Business Administration: _____
    Equity financing (*check with current Securities and Exchange rules on sales of shares*): _____

Preparing a Profit and Loss Statement

A Profit and Loss Statement is the key financial statement for presenting how your business is performing over a period of time. The Profit and Loss Statement illuminates both the amounts of money that your business has spent on expenses and the amounts of money that your business has taken in over a specific period of time. Along with the Balance Sheet, which is discussed later in this chapter, the Profit and Loss Statement should become an integral part of both your short- and long-range business planning.

This section will explain how to prepare an Estimated Profit and Loss Statement for use in your Business Plan. The Estimated Profit and Loss Statement can serve a valuable business planning service by allowing you to project estimated changes in your business over various time periods and examine what the results may be. Projections of various business plans can be examined in detail and decisions can then be made on the basis of clear pictures of future scenarios. Your estimates of your business profits and losses can take into account industry changes, economic factors, and personal business decisions. Your estimates are primarily for internal business planning purposes, although it may be useful to use an Estimated Profit and Loss Statement to convey your future Business Plans to others. As a trial exercise, you should prepare an Estimated Profit and Loss Statement using your best estimates before you even begin business. You may wish to prepare such pre-business statements for monthly, quarterly, and annual time periods. You may also desire to prepare Estimated Profit and Loss Statements for the first several years of your business's existence.

The Estimated Profit and Loss Statement differs from the other type of Profit and Loss Statements in that the figures that you will use are projections based on expected business income and expenses for a time period in the future. The value of this type of financial planning tool is to allow you to see how various scenarios will affect your business. You may prepare this form as either a monthly, quarterly, or annual projection. To prepare this form, use the data that you have collected for the above Business Financial Worksheet. For more information on Profit and Loss Statements, please see Chapter 15.

1. The first figure that you will need will be your Estimated Gross Sales Income. If your business is a pure service business, put your estimated income on the "Estimated Service Income Total" line. If your business income comes from part sales and part service, place the appropriate figures on the correct lines.

2. If your business will sell items from inventory, you will need to calculate your Estimated Cost of Goods Sold. In order to have the necessary figures to make this computation, you will need to prepare a projection of your inventory costs and how many items you expect to sell. Fill in the Estimated Cost of Goods Sold figure on the Estimated Profit and Loss Statement. If your business is a pure service business,

skip this line. Determine your Estimated Net Sales Income Total by subtracting your Estimated Cost of Goods Sold from your Estimated Gross Sales Income.

3. Calculate your Estimated Total Income for the period by adding your Estimated Net Sales Income Total and your Estimated Service Income Total and any Estimated Miscellaneous Income (for example: interest earned on a checking account).

4. Fill in the appropriate Estimated Expense account categories on the Estimated Profit and Loss Statement. If you have a large number of categories, you may need to prepare a second sheet. Based on your future projections, fill in the totals for each of your separate expense accounts. Add in any Estimated Miscellaneous Expenses.

5. Total all of your expenses and subtract your Estimated Total Expenses figure from your Estimated Total Income figure to determine your Estimated Pre-Tax Profit for the time period.

Estimated Profit and Loss Statement

For the period of:

ESTIMATED INCOME			
Income	Estimated Gross Sales Income		
	Less Estimated Cost of Goods Sold		
	Estimated Net Sales Income Total		
	Estimated Service Income Total		
	Estimated Miscellaneous Income Total		
	Estimated Total Income		

ESTIMATED EXPENSES		
Expenses	Advertising expenses	
	Auto expenses	
	Cleaning and maintenance expenses	
	Charitable contributions	
	Dues and publications	
	Office equipment expenses	
	Freight and shipping expenses	
	Business insurance expenses	
	Business interest expenses	
	Legal and accounting expenses	
	Business meals and lodging	
	Miscellaneous expenses	
	Postage expenses	
	Office rent/mortgage expenses	
	Repair expenses	
	Office supplies	
	Sales taxes	

Federal unemployment taxes	
State unemployment taxes	
Telephone/Internet expenses	
Utility expenses	
Wages and commissions	
Estimated General Expenses Total	
Estimated Miscellaneous Expenses	
Estimated Total Expenses	

Estimated Pre-Tax Profit (Income less Expenses)	

Preparing a Balance Sheet

A Profit and Loss Statement provides a view of business operations over a particular period of time. It allows a look at the income and expenses and profits or losses of the business during the time period. In contrast, a Balance Sheet is designed to be a look at the financial position of a company on a specific date. It shows what the business owns and owes on a fixed date. Its purpose is to depict the financial strength of a company as shown by its assets and liabilities. It is merely a visual representation of the basic business financial equation: assets – liabilities = equity (or *net worth*). Essentially, the Balance Sheet shows what the company would be worth if all of the assets were sold and all the liabilities were paid off. A value is placed on each asset and on each liability. These figures are then balanced by adjusting the value of the owner's equity figure in the equation. Your Balance Sheet will total your current and fixed assets and your current and long-term liabilities. Even if your business is very new, you will need to prepare a Balance Sheet of where the business currently stands financially. Use the figures that you have gathered for the previous Business Financial Worksheet to complete your Current Balance Sheet. For further information on Balance Sheets, please refer to Chapter 15. Please follow the instructions below to prepare your Current Balance Sheet for your Business Financial Plan:

1. Your Current Assets consist of the following items:

   - Cash in Bank (from your business bank account balance)
   - Cash on Hand
   - Accounts Receivable (if you have any yet)
   - Inventory (if you have any yet)
   - Prepaid Expenses (these may be rent, insurance, prepaid supplies, or similar items that have been paid for prior to their actual use)

2. Total all of your Current Assets on your Current Balance Sheet.

3. Your Fixed Assets consist of the following items, which should be valued at your actual cost:

   - Equipment
   - Autos and Trucks
   - Buildings

4. Total your Fixed Assets (except land) on your Current Balance Sheet. Total all of the depreciation that you have previously deducted for all of your fixed assets (except land). Include in this figure any business deductions that you have taken for Section 179 write-offs on business equipment. *Note*: If you are just starting a business, you will not have any depreciation or Section 179 deductions as yet. En-

ter this total depreciation figure under "Less Depreciation" and subtract this figure from the figure for Total Fixed Assets (except land).

5. Enter the value for any land that your business owns. Land may not be depreciated. Add Total Fixed Assets (except land) amount, minus the (less depreciation) figure, and the value of the land. This is your Total Fixed Assets value.

6. Add any Miscellaneous Assets not yet included. These may consist of stocks, bonds, or other business investments. Total your Current, Fixed, and Miscellaneous Assets to arrive at your Total Assets figure.

7. Your Current Liabilities consist of the following items:

   • Accounts Payable (if you have any yet)
   • Miscellaneous Payable (include here the principal due on any short-term notes payable. Also include any interest on credit purchases, notes, or loans that has accrued but not been paid. Also list the current amounts due on any long-term liabilities. Finally, list any payroll or taxes that have accrued but not yet been paid)

8. Your Fixed Liabilities consist of Loans Payable (the principal of any long-term note, loan, or mortgage due). Any current amounts due should be listed as "Current Liabilities."

9. Total your Current and Fixed Liabilities to arrive at Total Liabilities.

10. Subtract your Total Liabilities from your Total Assets to arrive at your Owner's Equity. For a corporation, this figure represents the total of contributions by the owners or stockholders plus earnings after paying any dividends. Total Liabilities and Owner's Equity will always equal Total Assets.

Current Balance Sheet

As of:

ASSETS			
Current Assets	Cash in Bank		
	Cash on Hand		
	Accounts Receivable		
	Inventory		
	Prepaid Expenses		
	Total Current Assets		
Fixed Assets	Equipment (actual cost)		
	Autos and Trucks (actual cost)		
	Buildings (actual cost)		
	Total Fixed Assets (except land)		
	(less depreciation)		
	Net Total		
	Add Land (actual cost)		
	Total Fixed Assets		
	Total Miscellaneous Assets		
	Total Assets		
LIABILITIES			
Current Liabilities	Accounts Payable		
	Miscellaneous Payable		
	Total Current Liabilities		
Fixed Liabilities	Loans Payable (long-term)		
	Total Fixed Liabilities		
	Total Liabilities		
Owner's Equity	Net Worth or Capital Surplus + Stock Value		

CHAPTER 6
Operating a Limited Liability Company

Limited liability companies are a relatively new form of business organization, first recognized in the United States by the state of Wyoming in 1977. Since then, legislation has been enacted in all 50 states and the District of Columbia (Washington D.C.) to allow businesses to organize as limited liability companies. A limited liability company is a separate legal entity, as is a corporation. The business structure is actually a hybrid type of business entity—between a corporation and a partnership. It is organized in a fashion similar, but not identical, to that of corporations. It also offers owners the limits on personal liability that were previously available only to shareholders in corporations. Like the shareholders of a corporation, the *members* (or owners) are not liable for the debts and obligations of the company beyond their actual contributions to the company. In addition, in most cases, if the company is organized properly, it is taxed at the Federal level as a partnership, or even possibly as a sole proprietorship. This means that there will only be one level of taxation. The profits and losses of the company are passed through to the individual owners, in the same manner as in the taxation of partnerships. Corporations, on the other hand, are subject to a double taxation—first at the corporate level and then at the individual level—after corporate profits in the form of dividends are passed on to shareholders.

Another flexibility that limited liability companies are afforded is the ability to distribute profits and losses to its members in any proportion that they choose. For common corporations, this flexibility is not present. Shareholders in corporations do not share directly in the profits or losses of the corporation. They only receive dividends if so decided by the directors of the corporation. S-type corporations pass their profits and losses through to the shareholders, but are generally restricted to dividing the profits and losses on the basis of percentage of ownership of each individual shareholder. Limited liability companies have the greater flexibility to choose to distribute their profits and losses in any manner that they wish, regardless of the percentage of ownership of the members. There are a few restrictions on such distributions, however, if a limited liability company is to be treated as a partnership for Federal tax purposes. They must abide by two particular partnership distribution rules: that the distribution allocations must have some "substantial economic" relation to the actual economic risks or rewards of the members and that the members may be subject to income tax on their contribution of future services to the limited liability company. If you wish for the manner in which your limited liability company distributes its profits and losses to its members to deviate far from the actual proportionate contributions of its members, a competent tax professional should be consulted to avoid any problems.

The limited liability company also offers management possibilities that are more flexible than those of either corporations or limited partnerships. These unique characteristics make this form of business operation one of the fastest growing forms of organization. Many of the actual operational characteristics of limited liability companies are set by what are termed *default rules*, which are rules that are set by statute in each state. A default rule is essentially a rule that governs the affairs of the company, *unless* the rule has officially been changed by the company in its official documents. Thus, in all states, there are certain rules that will govern the limited liability company but there is also, in all states, a manner by which a limited liability company can change these rules. Thus, by creatively using the formation and operating documents of the limited liability company, members can choose to operate the limited liability company in a wide variety of manners. How these default rules come into play as you plan your limited liability company will be examined below.

Organization of a Limited Liability Company

Limited liability companies are, in some ways, organized in a manner similar to corporations. The shareholders of a corporation have their counterpart in limited liability companies as its *members*. These members are the owners of the company, in much the same way that shareholders are the actual owners of a corporation. Most states now allow a limited liability company to be formed by one member, and that member need not always be a natural person. *Note*: One-member limited liability companies are generally taxed as sole proprietorships, not partnerships. One of the management capabilities of a limited liability company is that the members may choose to manage the company themselves or they can select managers to manage the company. Most states have a default rule that the members are the managers of the company. This is unlike corporations, in which the shareholders elect the directors, who, in turn select the officers of the corporation, who then manage the company. In limited liability companies, the members may either remain as the managers or they can select managers to run the company. If management is desired by managers, these managers may either be members of the limited liability company or they can be nonmembers. In addition, the managers of a limited liability company need not necessarily be *natural* (actual) persons, unlike the requirement that corporate directors must be natural persons. This affords the limited liability company a flexibility of management styles that is not available in other forms of business.

Articles of Organization

Similar to a corporation, there are two initial forms that outline the actual operation of the limited liability company. The first form is known in most states as the Articles of Organization. A few states refer to this central organizing document by another name: for instance, the state of Washington calls it a Certificate of Formation. For ease of understanding, the title "Articles of Organization" will be used throughout this book. Please check the appendix to verify the particular usage in your own state. This form parallels, in many ways, the function of the Articles of Incorporation of the business corporation. Its function is to provide the state with information regarding the framework of the business. All states require that it be filed, generally, with the Secretary of State or a similar state agency. There will be a filing fee for such filing, which may range from $40.00 to upwards of $500.00, depending on your particular state. In addition, some states base this fee on the capitalization of the company, generally charging more for companies with capitalization of over $50,000. Finally, there may be an additional initial fee charged for an annual or biennial report for the company. These are generally in the $100.00 range. For details of the fee requirements for your state, check the appendix.

Each state also has requirements that certain information be provided in the Articles of Organization. This is to enable the state to keep tabs on specific information regarding the company. Most states also require that such information be updated on a regular basis, either annually or biennially. In general, the basic requirements for information are similar to those required of corporations. Most states do not require all of the information listed below to be provided. Some states require a bare minimum of information. Most states will also provide a pre-printed fill-in-the-blanks Articles of Organization form, although, in general, the use of these forms is not mandatory. A very few states, notably Arizona and New York, also require that notice of filing the Articles of Organization be published in a newspaper. Please note that you should check your state's listing in the appendix for the specific requirements. How to prepare your Articles of Organization is outlined in Chapter 9. Following is a list of most of the basic information requirements for Articles of Organization:

- Name of the company
- Duration of the company, if less than perpetual
- Purpose of the company
- Registered agent's name and address
- Initial members' names and addresses
- Any reservation of the right to admit new members
- The right of the company to continue business following an act of dissolution
- Whether the company will be managed by members or managers
- Managers' names and addresses, if managed by managers
- Contributions by members to the company
- Future contributions to the company required of members

Operating Agreement

The second important document for a limited liability company is the Operating Agreement. This document is the limited liability company equivalent of a set of corporate bylaws. Within this document, the basic rights and responsibilities of the members or managers are defined. If matters relating to these areas are not covered by an adequate Operating Agreement, the state's default rules will, generally, take effect. It is within the Operating Agreement that the limited liability company management structure will be decided, the division of profits and losses will be laid out, the members' contributions of money, services, or property will be defined, and members' voting and other rights will be laid out. This document is the key to the success of the limited liability company and must be prepared with care and foresight. Instructions for preparing your limited liability company Operating Agreement are contained in Chapter 10.

Management

Basically, there are three methods by which a limited liability company can be managed: by members only, by members and nonmembers, or by nonmember managers only. The reasons for selecting each of these methods is set out below.

Management by Members Only

This is, by far, the most common approach taken to managing a limited liability company. Most small business owners prefer to take the hands-on approach and manage their own companies. However, if there is a large number of members of the limited liability company, this approach can become unwieldy. It is possible under this approach that not all members will manage the company and that some of the investing members will choose that the company be run by other members. However, even nonvoting nonmanaging members of a member-managed limited liability company will be considered to have earned the profits of the company and, thus, will be required to pay personal income tax on any limited liability company income that passes to them. However, there is a special tax situation that may arise regarding those members who do not participate in the management of the company. They may avoid paying self-employment taxes on their share of the company's profits if they work for 500 hours or less at the company's business. If one or more of your members fall into this category, a competent tax professional should be consulted. In addition, in limited liability companies that are managed entirely by members and in which all members participate, the ownership interests are generally not considered to be securities under state and Federal law. This eliminates an enormous amount of paperwork and regulation from the operation of the member-managed limited liability company. In most situations, this will be the management style with the most flexibility.

Management by Members and Nonmember Managers

It is possible to run a limited liability company by a combination of members and non-members. This choice may be appropriate for limited liability companies that desire to have an outsider (nonmember) with particular expertise participate in the management decisions. For any number of reasons, the nonmember manager may be desired: so that all profits are passed only to members, so that all losses are sustained only by members, or for any other reasons specific to your particular business situation. Again, there is a special tax situation that may arise regarding those members who do not participate in the management of the company. They may also avoid paying any self-employment taxes on their share of the company profits if they work at the company's business for 500 hours or less. If one or more of your members fall into this category, a competent tax professional should be consulted. Finally, the ownership and transfer of membership interests in a limited liability company that is managed, even in part, by managers may possibly subject the limited liability company to regulation under state and Federal securities laws. If you choose this type of management structure, a competent tax professional should be consulted.

Management by Nonmember Managers Only

Although this type of management style is possible, it is chosen in relatively few companies. This style may be chosen if the members have little or no expertise in the particular business and desire a skilled manager or management team to handle all the affairs of the business. Again, for this form of management, there is a special tax situation that may arise regarding members who do not participate in the management of the company. They may avoid paying self-employment taxes on their share of the company's profits if they work for 500 hours or less at the company's business. Finally, the ownership and transfer of membership interests in a limited liability company that is managed solely by nonmember managers may possibly subject the limited liability company to regulation under state and Federal securities laws. If you choose this type of management structure, a competent tax professional should be consulted.

Limited Liability Company Existence

As noted already, a limited liability company is a separate legal entity that offers its members a manner by which to assure that the personal assets of the owners are not at risk in the business. In a sole proprietorship or partnership, an owner's personal property and real estate can be accessed by creditors and courts to fulfill the legal obligations of the business. For corporations and limited liability companies, this is generally not true. Special care must be taken at the time of formation of the business to be certain as to when this limit on liability takes effect. States have several different general times when the limited liability company is considered to be officially formed for the purposes of determining liability. In general, a limited liability company is formed when either:

- Its Articles of Organization are filed with the state
- Its Articles of Organization have been approved by the state
- The Articles of Organization have been approved by the state, but the official formation date may be made retroactive to the date of original submission
- The company has chosen to delay the date of effectiveness to a date later than the filing or approval of the company's submission of the Articles of Organization

If your company will be involved in an enterprise that will have potential liability immediately upon formation, it will be wise to understand the particulars of your state's rules in this area. Please check the appendix for information on your state.

Division of Profits and Losses

As noted earlier, one of the principal flexibilities of the limited liability company is the ability to structure the division of profits and losses to members in any reasonable manner. Members may be provided their distribution of profits and losses in direct proportion to their contributions of money, services, or property to the company. This, in fact, is most often the clearest method by which to structure distribution. However, this form of business entity allows endless possibilities to tailor such distributions to the circumstances of your business. If a member is contributing a particular expertise, they may be compensated by a greater percentage of share in the profits of the business. If members choose not to participate in the management of the company, those members who do manage may earn a greater percentage share in the profits and losses. Look closely at your particular business organization and contributions to decide the fairest manner in which to distribute the proceeds or losses of your limited liability company.

Voting Rights of Members

The default rules that are in effect in most states provide that a member's right to vote is allocated in proportion to the member's contributions to the limited liability company. A few states provide that member's voting rights are *per-capita*, in other words, each member gets only one vote. In some states, managers are also given one vote in the affairs of the company. State default rules also typically provide that limited liability company matters be decided by either a majority or unanimous vote of the members. In all states, the Operating Agreement of the company may override most of these provisions and provide for voting divisions in any proportions desired, including denying voting rights to certain members. However, in many states, the default rules may not be overridden with regard to decisions on major company matters, such as the sale of all company assets, the dissolution of the company, or amendments to the Operating Agreement or Articles of Organization. Also note that in order to place any such restrictions in the Operating Agreement or Articles of Organization, it will be necessary to abide by the state default rules in order to adopt the original version of each document. Please consult the appendix for the situation in your particular state.

Membership and Management Meetings

Most states do not require regular membership or management meetings. However, it is often prudent for the members and/or managers to meet at least on an annual basis to review the conduct of the company and plan for the future. In addition, meetings may be necessary more often in order to handle major affairs of the business that are beyond the scope of the managers alone, such as dissolving the company.

Member and Manager Liability to Others

One of the most important benefits of forming a limited liability company is that the owners are not personally liable for any debts or obligations of the company. Every state statute has this provision included in it. In addition, many states also extend such limited liability to others in the company, such as employees, nonmember managers, and agents of the company. However, please note that anyone who is shielded from personal liability for the normal debts and obligations of a company, whether he or she is director of a corporation or member of a limited liability company, is *not* shielded from personal liability for his or her own negligence, recklessness, or criminal activity. If this issue is critical, please check your state limited liability statute directly for information on the rules regarding the limits of the liability shield in your state.

Additional Default Rules

Each state's statute regarding limited liability companies contains additional default rules that will apply to your limited liability company unless it is officially altered in either the Articles of Organization or the Operating Agreement. Each state may have a different version of each of these rules. Please check the statutes in your state if these issues are critical. These rules generally cover the following items:

- **Continuity of the company:** This default rule states whether or not the company will be automatically dissolved if a member withdraws from the company
- **Transferability of interests:** This default rule governs the ability of a member to transfer his or her ownership interest in the limited liability company to another person by gift, sale, or otherwise. Most states require either a majority or

unanimous vote of the members in order to obtain consent to transfer a limited liability company ownership interest

- **Operating distributions:** The method by which operating distributions are to be distributed to the members of an limited liability company are noted under this default rule in most states. The variations on this particular rule are distribution on a per-capita basis, a proportionate basis based on each member's contribution, or a per-profit share basis

Taxation of Limited Liability Companies

In general, the owners of limited liability companies have a choice regarding how they are to be taxed. If the company has only one member, it will be treated as a sole-proprietorship for Federal tax purposes, unless the member/owner elects otherwise. Being taxed as a sole proprietorship means that all of the profits and losses of the company will be reported on the member/owner's personal income tax return, using Internal Revenue Service Schedule C (Form 1040): *Profit or Loss from Business (Sole Proprietorship)*. The single-member limited liability company may, however, choose to be taxed as a corporation by filing IRS Form 8832: *Entity Classification Election*, and selecting "A domestic eligible entity electing to be classified as an association taxable as a corporation." If the company makes this election, the company must file a normal corporate tax form, IRS Form 1120: *U.S. Corporation Income Tax Return*, and pay corporate income tax on any profits.

If the limited liability company has two or more members, it will be taxed as a partnership under IRS rules, unless it elects to be taxed otherwise. Being taxed as a partnership means that all of the profits and losses of the company will be passed through to the members in the proportion determined by the Articles of Organization or the Operating Agreement of the company. This pass-through will be reported on IRS Schedule K-1 (Form 1065): *Partner's Share of Income, Credits, Deductions, etc*. A multiple-member limited liability company may also, however, choose to be taxed as a corporation by filing IRS Form 8832: *Entity Classification Election*, and selecting "A domestic eligible entity electing to be classified as an association taxable as a corporation." If the company makes this election, the company must file a normal corporate tax form, IRS Form 1120: *U.S. Corporation Income Tax Return*, and pay corporate income tax on any profits.

Additional information and schedules on taxation of limited liability companies are contained in Chapter 18.

CHAPTER 7
Limited Liability Company Paperwork

The business arena in America operates on a daily assortment of legal forms. There are more legal forms in use in American business than are used in the operations and governments of many foreign countries. The limited liability company is not immune to this flood of legal forms. Indeed, the operation of a limited liability company, in general, requires more legal documents than many other forms of business. While large corporations are able to obtain and pay expensive lawyers to deal with their legal problems and paperwork, most small businesses cannot afford such a course of action. The small business limited liability company must deal with a variety of legal documents, usually without the aid of an attorney.

Unfortunately, many businesspeople who are confronted with such forms do not understand the legal ramifications of the use of these forms. They simply sign them with the expectation that they are fairly standard documents, without any unusual legal provisions. They trust that the details of the particular document will fall within what is generally accepted within the industry or trade. In most cases, this may be true. In many situations, however, it is not. Our court system is clogged with cases in which two businesses are battling over what was really intended by the incomprehensible legal language in a certain legal document.

Much of the confusion over company paperwork comes from two areas: First, there is a general lack of understanding among many in business regarding the framework of law. Second, many business documents are written in antiquated legal jargon that is difficult for even most lawyers to understand and nearly impossible for a layperson to comprehend.

The various legal documents that are used in this book are, however, written in plain English. Standard legal jargon, as used in most lawyer-prepared documents, is, for most people, totally incomprehensible. Despite the lofty arguments by attorneys regarding the need for such strained and difficult language, the vast majority of legalese is absolutely unnecessary. As with any form of communication, clarity, simplicity, and readability should be the goal in legal documents.

Unfortunately, in some specific instances, certain obscure legal terms are the only words that accurately and precisely describe some things in certain legal contexts. In those few cases, the unfamiliar legal term will be defined when first used. Generally, however, simple terms are used throughout this book. In most cases, masculine and feminine terms have been eliminated and the generic "it," "they," or "them" have been used instead. In the few situations in which this leads to awkward sentence construction, her/his or she/he may be used instead.

All of the legal documents contained in this book have been prepared in essentially the same manner by which attorneys create legal forms. Many people believe that lawyers prepare each legal document that they compose entirely from scratch. Nothing could be further from the truth. Invariably, lawyers begin their preparation of a legal document with a standardized legal form book. Every law library has multi-volume sets of these encyclopedic texts that contain blank forms for virtually every conceivable legal situation. Armed with these pre-prepared legal forms, lawyers, in many cases, simply fill in the blanks and have their secretaries retype the form for the client. Of course, the client is generally unaware of this process. As lawyers begin to specialize in a certain area of legal expertise, they compile their own files containing such blank forms.

This book provides those businesspersons who wish to form a limited liability company with a set of legal forms that have been prepared with the problems and normal legal requirements of the small business limited liability company in mind. These forms are intended to be used in those situations that are clearly described by their terms. Of course, while most document use will fall within the bounds of standard business practices, some legal circumstances will present nonstandard situations. The forms in this book are designed to be readily adaptable to most usual business situations. They may be carefully altered to conform to the particular transaction that confronts your business. However, if you are faced with a complex or tangled business situation, the advice of a competent lawyer is highly recommended. If you wish, you may also create forms for certain standard situations for your limited liability company and have your lawyer check them for compliance with any local legal circumstances.

The proper and cautious use of the forms provided in this book will allow the typical limited liability company to save considerable money on legal costs over the course of the life of the business, while enabling the business to comply with legal and governmental regulations. Perhaps more importantly, these forms will provide a method by which the businessperson can avoid costly misunderstandings about what exactly was intended in a particular situation. By using the forms provided to clearly document the proceedings of everyday company operations, disputes over what was really meant can be avoided. This protection will allow the business to avoid many potential lawsuits and operate more efficiently in compliance with the law.

The Importance of Recordkeeping

The amount of paperwork and recordkeeping required by the use of the limited liability company form of business may often seem overwhelming. Sometimes, it may even seem senseless. However, there are some very important reasons why detailed records of company operations are necessary. A limited liability company is a fiction. It is a creation of the government to enable businesses to have flexibility to function in a complex national and even international marketplace. This form of enterprise provides one of the most adaptable type of business entity in today's world. Through the use of a limited liability entity, a business may respond quickly to the changing nature of modern business. Of course, the limited liability of investors is also a great advantage over other forms of business organization.

A limited liability company is, in many cases, afforded the legal status of a person. It may sue or be sued in its own name. A limited liability company may own property in its own name. In most situations, a limited liability company is treated as if it has a life of its own. In a legal sense, it does have a life of its own. It was born by filing the limited liability company Articles of Organization with a state and it may die upon filing Articles of Dissolution with the state. While a limited liability company is alive, it is said to exist. During its existence, it can operate as a separate legal entity and enjoy the benefits of its status, as long as certain formalities are observed. The importance of following these basic formalities cannot be overemphasized. All of the advantages of operating under the limited liability form of business are directly dependent upon careful observance of a few basic paperwork and management requirements.

Each major action that a limited liability company undertakes must be carefully documented. Even if there are only a few members, or even a single member, complete records of company activities must be recorded. There must be *minutes*, records of meetings that outline the election of managers of the limited liability company. This is true regardless of the size of the limited liability company. In fact, as the size of the limited liability company decreases, the importance of careful recordkeeping actually increases.

The legal existence of a limited liability company can be challenged in court. This will most likely happen in circumstances where a creditor of the limited liability company or victim of some company disaster is left without compensation, due to the limited liability of the limited liability company. Despite the fact that the limited liability company has been accepted by the state as a legal entity, if the formalities of its existence have not been carefully followed, the owners of a limited liability company are at risk. The court may decide that a single-member limited liability company merely used the limited liability company as a shell to avoid liability. The court is then empowered to declare that the limited liability company was actually merely the alter ego of the owner and to disregard the existence of the limited liability company, and creditors or victims can then reach the personal assets of the owner. This will occur most often when a limited liability company is formed without sufficient capitalization to reasonably cover normal business affairs, the limited liability company has not maintained sufficient insurance to cover standard contingencies, the owner has mingled company funds with his or her own, and there are no records to indicate that the limited liability company was actually operated as a separate entity. The results of such a lawsuit can be devastating. The loss of personal assets and the loss of legal status for tax purposes can often lead to impoverishment and bankruptcy.

The best defense against an attack on the use of the limited liability company business form is to always have treated the limited liability company as a separate entity. This requires documenting each and every major business activity in minutes, records, and agreements. When it is desired that the limited liability company undertake a particular activity, the members should meet and adopt an agreement that clearly identifies the action and the reasons for the action. This is true even if there is only one member. With such records, it is an easy task to establish that the actions taken were done for the benefit of the limited liability company and not for the personal betterment of the individual member/owner or members/owners. As long as it can be clearly shown that the owners respected the company's separateness, the company's existence cannot be disregarded by the courts. It is not the size of the limited liability company, but rather the existence of complete records that provides the protection from liability for the owners of the limited liability company. It is crucial to recognize this vital element in operating a limited liability company. Careful, detailed recordkeeping is the key to enjoying the tax benefits and limited liability of the limited liability company business structure.

Limited Liability Company Paperwork Checklist

The following checklist outlines the various company documents that should be prepared and maintained during the life of a limited liability company:

- ☐ Pre-Organization Checklist (see Chapter 8)

- ☐ Application for Reservation of Limited Liability Company Name (filed with state)

- ☐ Articles of Organization (filed with state)

- ☐ Amendment to Articles of Organization (filed with state)

- ☐ Operating Agreement of the limited liability company (in company record book)

- ☐ Amendment to the Operating Agreement of the limited liability company (in company record book)

- ☐ Minutes of the first meeting of the members (in company record book)

- ☐ Minutes of the annual meetings of the members (in company record book)

- ☐ Member proxies (in company record book)

- ☐ Limited liability company loans to members (in company record book)

- ☐ Limited liability company pension or profit-sharing plans (in the company record book)

- ☐ Limited liability company insurance or health benefit plans (in company record book)

- ☐ Limited liability company accounting books

- Annual financial reports (in company record book)

- Termination of Limited Liability Company Agreement (in company record book)

- Articles of Dissolution (filed with the state)

- Limited liability company tax records (filed with state and Federal tax authorities)

- Application to qualify as foreign limited liability company (filed with other states in which the limited liability company desires to conduct active business)

CHAPTER 8
Pre-Organization Activities

The planning stage is vital to the success of any limited liability company. The structure of a new limited liability company, including the number of members, distribution of profits and losses, and other matters, must be carefully tailored to the specific needs of the business. Attorneys typically use a Pre-Organization Worksheet to assemble all of the necessary information from which to plan the organization process.

By filling out a Pre-Organization Worksheet, potential business owners will be able to have before them all of the basic data to use in preparing the necessary organization paperwork. The process of preparing this worksheet will also help uncover any potential differences of opinion among the persons who are desiring to form the limited liability company. Often conflicts and demands are not known until the actual process of determining the company's structure begins. Frank discussions regarding the questions of voting rights, distribution of profits, amounts of contributions, and other management decisions often will enable potential associates to resolve many of the difficult problems of company management in advance. The use of a written worksheet will also provide all persons involved with a clear and permanent record of the information. This may provide the principals of the limited liability company with vital support for later decisions that may be required.

All persons involved in the planned limited liability company should participate in the preparation of the following worksheet. Please take the time to carefully and completely fill in all of the spaces. Following the worksheet, there is a Pre-Organization Checklist that provides a clear listing of all of the actions necessary to organize a limited liability company business. Follow this checklist carefully as the organization process proceeds. After this Pre-Organization Checklist, there is a Document Filing Checklist that provides a listing of the documents that are normally required to be filed with the state agency or office that handles limited liability companies. Finally, there is a discussion and form for reserving the company name with the state limited liability company department. If desired or required, this will be the first form filed with the state.

Unfamiliar terms relating to limited liability companies are explained in the glossary of this book. As the Pre-Organization Worksheet is filled in, please refer to the following explanations:

Address of state limited liability company department: The appendix of this book provides this address. You should write to this department immediately, requesting all available information on organization of a business limited liability company in your state. Although the forms in this book are designed for use in all states and the appendix provides up-to-date information on state requirements, state laws, and fees charged for organization are subject to change. Having the latest available information will save you time and trouble. Many states provide fill-in the-blank forms that make filing the Articles of Organization a simple task. However, you will still need to prepare this worksheet to determine how best to complete any state-supplied forms.

Company name: The selection of a name is often crucial to the success of a limited liability company. The name must not conflict with any existing company names, nor must it be deceptively similar to other names. It is often wise to clearly explain the business of the limited liability company through the choice of name. All states allow for a reservation of the company name in advance of actual organization. Check the appendix listing for your state.

Parties involved: This listing should provide the names, addresses, and phone numbers of all of the people who are involved in the planning stages of the limited liability company.

Principal place of business: This must be the address of the actual physical location of the main business. It may not be a post office box. If the limited liability company is home-based, this address should be the home address.

Purpose of limited liability company: All states provide for the use of an "all-purpose" business purpose clause in describing the main activity of the business; for example, to conduct any lawful business. The Articles of Organization that are used in this book provide this type of clause.

State/local licenses required: Here you should note any specific requirements for licenses to operate your type of business. Most states require obtaining a tax ID number and a retail, wholesale, or sales tax license. A Federal tax ID number (FEIN) must be obtained by all limited liability companies. Additionally, certain types of businesses will require health department approvals, state board licensing, or other forms of licenses. If necessary, check with a competent local attorney for details regarding the types of licenses required for your locality and business type.

Patents/copyrights/trademarks: If patents, copyrights, or trademarks will need to be transferred into the limited liability company, they should be noted here.

State of organization: In general, the limited liability company should be organized in the state in which it will conduct business.

Company existence: The choices here are *perpetual* (forever) or limited to a certain length. In virtually all cases, you should choose perpetual.

Proposed date to begin company business: This should be the date on which you expect the limited liability company to begin its legal existence. Until this date (actually, until the state formally accepts the Articles of Organization), the organizers of your limited liability company will continue to be legally liable for any business conducted on behalf of the proposed limited liability company.

Organizers: This should be the person (or persons) who will prepare and file the Articles of Organization.

Number of members: Most states allow a limited liability company to have a single member. Please check the appendix for the requirements in your particular state.

Proposed members: Here you should list the names and addresses of the proposed members of the company. Although not a requirement in every state, the Articles of Organization used in this book provide that these persons be listed.

Limited liability company's registered agent and address: Here you should list the name and actual street address of the person who will act as the registered agent of the limited liability company. All states require that a specific person be available as the agent of the limited liability company for the *service of process* (accepting subpoenas or summons on behalf of the limited liability company). The person need not be a member of the limited liability company. The registered agent need not be a lawyer. Normally, the main owner or the attorney of the limited liability company is selected as the registered agent.

Initial investment: This figure is the total amount of money or property that will be transferred to the limited liability company upon its beginning business. This transfer will be in exchange for ownership interests in the limited liability company. This is also referred to as "paid-in-capital." List also the dates on which the contributions are to be made.

Additional contributions by members: If there are to be planned additional member contributions of money, services, or property, list them here.

Initial indebtedness: If there is to be any initial indebtedness for the limited liability company, please list it here.

Share of profits and losses: Under this heading is noted how the members decide in what proportions the profits and losses of the business will be distributed to the members. This may, but need not, be based on the amount of the contributions of the members to the company.

Distribution of profits and losses: Here decide how the limited liability company will distribute its profits and losses to each partner. If the company will retain a portion of the profits for reinvestment, note that here.

Management of the limited liability company: If the business is to be managed by members only, members and managers, or managers only, note the decision here. Also note who will actually comprise the management of the company.

Date of first members meeting: This will be the date proposed for holding the first meeting of the members, at which the company Operating Agreement will be officially adopted.

Proposed bank for company bank account: In advance of organization, you should determine the bank that will handle the company accounts. Obtain from the bank the necessary bank resolution form, which will be signed by the members at the first members meeting.

Cost of organization: The state fees for organization are listed in the appendix. This cost should also reflect the cost of obtaining professional assistance (legal or accounting), the cost of procuring the necessary supplies, and any other direct costs of the organization process.

Out-of-state qualification: If the limited liability company desires to actively conduct business in a state other than the main state of organization, it is necessary to "qualify" the limited liability company in that state. This generally requires obtaining a Certificate of Authority to Transact Business from the other state. In this context, a limited liability company from another state is referred to as a "foreign" limited liability company. If you desire that your limited liability company qualify for activities in another state, you are advised to consult a competent business attorney.

Required quorum for members: This is the percentage of ownership shares in the limited liability company that must be represented at a members meeting in order to officially transact any company business. This is normally set at a majority (more than 50 percent), although this figure can be set higher.

Annual members meeting: The date, time, and place of the annual members meeting should be specified.

Required vote for member action: Once it is determined that a quorum of members is present at a meeting, this is the percentage of ownership shares of the limited liability company that must vote in the affirmative in order to officially pass any member business. This is normally set at a majority (more than 50 percent), although this figure can be set higher and can be made to be unanimous.

Fiscal year and accounting type: For accounting purposes, the fiscal year and accounting type (cash or accrual) of the limited liability company should be chosen in advance. Please consult with a competent accounting professional.

Financial authority: Here list the authority of each proposed member to sign checks, borrow money in the company name, or sign documents in the name of the limited liability company.

Loans to members: In this item, decide if you wish the company to have the ability to make loans directly to its members.

Salaries to members: Here you should decide if the members will earn a salary for their work on behalf of the company.

Transfer of membership interests: Under this listing, a decision should be noted as to whether and how members are to be allowed to transfer their ownership interests in the limited liability company to third parties. This may range from "not at all" to "freely" or may be by unanimous or majority consent of the other members.

Expulsion of members: Here you should consider the terms and conditions for the removal of members.

Insurance: Under this heading, consider the types of insurance that you will need, ranging from general casualty to various business liability policies. Also consider the need for the members or the company to provide the members with life and/or disability insurance.

New members: Will new members be allowed in the company? Here note the terms and conditions for their entry.

Termination of limited liability company: How will the company end? Here list any considerations relating to the dissolution of the limited liability company that you may wish to be considered.

Amendments to Articles of Organization: Here should be the determination of how the limited liability company will amend the Articles of Organization. The forms in this book are designed to allow the Articles of Organization to be amended by unanimous or majority approval of the members of the company.

Amendments to Operating Agreement: Here should be the determination of how the limited liability company will amend its Operating Agreement. The forms in this book are designed to allow the Operating Agreement to be amended by unanimous or majority approval of the members of the company.

Following the Pre-Organization Worksheet are a Pre-Organization Checklist and a Document Filing Checklist. Please use these checklists to be certain that you have completed all of the necessary steps for organization. Once all of the persons involved have completed the Pre-Organization Worksheet, agreed on all of the details, and reviewed the Pre-Organization and Document Filing Checklists, the actual process of organization may begin. If the choice for a company name may be similar to that of another business or if the incorporators wish to insure that the name will be available, an Application for Reservation of Limited Liability Company Name may be filed. This is a simple form that requests that the state limited liability company department hold a chosen company name until the actual Articles of Organization are filed, at which time the name will become the official registered name of the limited liability company. At the end of this chapter, there is a sample of this form. There will be a fee required for the filing of this form, and some states prefer that preprinted state forms be used. Please check in the appendix and with the specific state limited liability company department for information. In any event, the information required will be the same as is necessary for this sample form.

Pre-Organization Worksheet

Name/Address of State Limited Liability Company Department
(from Appendix)

_____
_____
_____

Proposed Name of the Limited Liability Company

First choice:_____

Alternate choices: _____

_____

Parties Involved in Forming the Limited Liability Company

Name	*Address*	*Phone*
_____	_____	_____
_____	_____	_____
_____	_____	_____
_____	_____	_____
_____	_____	_____
_____	_____	_____

Location of Business

Address of principal place of business: _____

_____

Description of principal place of business: _____

_____
_____

Ownership of principal place of business (own or lease?): _____

_____

Other places of business: _____
_____
_____
_____

Type of Business

Purpose of limited liability company: _____
_____
_____
_____

State/local licenses required: _____
_____

Patents/copyrights/trademarks: _____
_____
_____
_____

Organization Matters

State of organization: _____

Company existence (limited or perpetual?): _____

Proposed date to begin company business: _____

Names and addresses of those who will act as organizers:

Name	*Address*
_____	_____
_____	_____
_____	_____
_____	_____
_____	_____

Number of proposed members: _____

Proposed members of the company:

Name	Address	Phone
_____	_____	_____
_____	_____	_____
_____	_____	_____
_____	_____	_____
_____	_____	_____
_____	_____	_____

Limited liability company's registered agent and office address: _____

_____

_____

Initial investment total: $ _____

Date when due: _____

Name	Cash/Property/Services	Value
_____	_____	_____
_____	_____	_____
_____	_____	_____
_____	_____	_____
_____	_____	_____
_____	_____	_____

Additional contributions: $ _____

Date when due: _____

Name	Cash/Property/Services	Value
_____	_____	_____
_____	_____	_____
_____	_____	_____
_____	_____	_____
_____	_____	_____

Members' share of profits and losses:

Name	Proportionate Share of Profits and Losses
_____	_____
_____	_____
_____	_____
_____	_____
_____	_____

Distribution and retention of profits and losses: _____
_____

    Initial indebtedness: $ _____

Management of the company:

Name	*Proportionate Share of Management*
_____	_____
_____	_____
_____	_____
_____	_____
_____	_____

Proposed date of first members meeting: _____

Proposed bank for company bank account: _____
_____

Cost of organization: _____

Is qualification in other states necessary? _____

Company Operating Agreement

Required quorum for members meetings: _____

Annual members meeting

Place	*Date*	*Time*
_____	_____	_____

Required vote for members actions: (majority/%/unanimous?): _____

Fiscal year: _____

Accounting type (cash or accrual?): _____

Financial authority:

Name	*Type of Authority*
_____	_____
_____	_____
_____	_____

Loans to members: _____
_____

Salaries of members:

Name	Salary
_____	_____
_____	_____
_____	_____
_____	_____
_____	_____

Transfer of membership interests: _____
_____

Expulsion of members: _____
_____

Insurance needs: _____
_____

New members: _____
_____
_____

Termination of limited liability company: _____
_____

Amendments to Articles of Organization (majority/%/unanimous?): _____
_____

Amendments to Operating Agreement (majority/%/unanimous?): _____
_____

Pre-Organization Checklist

- ☐ Contact state limited liability company office for information (see appendix)

- ☐ Complete Pre-Organization Worksheet

- ☐ Check annual fees and filing requirements

- ☐ Reserve company name, if desired, by filing with the state

- ☐ Prepare Articles of Organization (use state-specific forms on CD)

- ☐ Prepare Operating Agreement

- ☐ If desired, have attorney review Articles of Organization prior to filing

- ☐ Review tax impact of organization with an accountant

- ☐ Check state tax, employment, licensing, unemployment, and workers' compensation requirements

- ☐ Check insurance requirements

- ☐ Prepare company accounting ledgers

- ☐ Prepare company record book (looseleaf binder)

Document Filing Checklist

- ☐ Application for Reservation of Limited Liability Company Name (if desired)

- ☐ Articles of Organization (mandatory)

- ☐ Amendments to Articles of Organization (mandatory, if applicable)

- ☐ Annual or biennial company reports (generally, mandatory)

- ☐ Change of Address of Registered Agent (mandatory)

- ☐ Articles of Dissolution (mandatory, if applicable)

- ☐ Any other required state forms (see appendix)

Application for Reservation of Limited Liability Company Name

TO:

I, _____ , with an office located at:

acting as an organizer, apply for reservation of the following company name:
_____ .

This company name is intended to be used for a limited liability company in the State of _____ , County of _____ .

I request that this company name be reserved for a period of _____ days. Please issue a certificate of reservation of this company name.

Enclosed please find our check in the amount of $ _____ to cover the registration fee.

Dated: _____ , 20 _____

_____
Signature of Organizer

_____
Printed Name of Organizer

CHAPTER 9
Articles of Organization

The central legal document for any limited liability company is the Articles of Organization. In some states, this document may be called a Certificate of Formation or a Certificate of Organization. Please check the appendix for the requirements in your particular state. For clarity, however, this book will refer to the organizer-prepared document as the Articles of Organization. This form outlines the basic structure of the limited liability company and details those matters that are relevant to the public registration of the limited liability company. The name, purpose, owners, registered agent, address, and other vital facts relating to the existence of the limited liability company are filed with the state by using this form. Upon filing of the Articles of Organization, payment of the proper fee, and acceptance by the state limited liability company department, the limited liability company officially begins its legal existence. Until the state has accepted the Articles, the organizers are not shielded from personal liability by the limited liability company form.

There are a number of items that are required to be noted in all Articles of Organization. The Articles may also include many other details of the limited liability company's existence. Please check the appendix and with your state department for specific details. Following is a checklist of items that are generally included in the Articles of Organization.

Articles of Organization Checklist

The details for Articles of Organization under most state laws are:

- [ ] The name of the limited liability company

- [ ] The principal place of business of the company (optional in some states)

- [ ] The purpose of the limited liability company

- [ ] The duration of the limited liability company

- [ ] The name and address of each member

- [ ] The name of the registered agent of the limited liability company

- [ ] The office of the registered agent of the limited liability company

- [ ] Amount of initial and future contributions to capital of the limited liability company (optional in most states)

- [ ] Provisions outlining the management of the company (optional in some states)

- [ ] Reservation of the right to admit new members (optional in some states)

- [ ] Right of the company to continue business following an act of dissolution or dissociation (optional in some states)

- [ ] Standard Industrial Code [SIC] for the company (optional in most states)

- [ ] Federal Employer Identification Number [FEIN] for the company (optional in most states)

- [ ] The signature(s) of the organizer(s)

- [ ] The signature of the registered agent

The Articles of Organization for your limited liability company should include all of the required information. Since Articles are a public record, all of the information in them will be available for inspection. Much of the information that is not required in the Articles may instead be put into the Operating Agreement of the limited liability company. In this manner, the actual management structure and details will remain unavailable for public inspection.

Note: All states (except Colorado and Georgia, which provide online LLC forms) provide official forms for Articles of Organization that are required to be used for filing. The information required, however, will be the same as noted in the sample Articles of Organization in this chapter and it will be helpful to read through this chapter and fill in the information as noted on the sample forms. Transferring it to the state form will then be a simple task. In addition, some states supply forms listing the requirements for filing the particular documents. Please check the appendix and the state-specific forms included on the Forms-on-CD.

Articles of Organization may be amended at any time. However, this generally requires a formal filing with the state and the issuance of a Certificate of Amendment of Articles of Organization. It also normally requires the payment of a fee. For these reasons, it is often a good idea to put only those items in the original Articles that are unlikely to require changes in the near future.

This chapter contains sample clauses for preparing Articles of Organization. An explanation is provided for each clause. You should check the appendix and any information noted on your state-specific form to be certain that you have included all of the necessary information for your state. A few states may require additional Articles. Most of the information required for preparing the clauses for this form will be on your Pre-Organization Worksheet, which you prepared in Chapter 8. Once you have chosen which of the clauses you will use, fill in the Articles. If state-specific documents are used, fill them in with the information you have prepared in this book. Optional clauses may be added to state-supplied forms where necessary. If you have access to a computer, you can use your own word-processing program or Adobe Acrobat Reader to enter the correct information on the forms that are supplied on the attached Forms-on-CD.

The Articles must then be properly signed. Although not required by all states, the form in this book is designed to be notarized. In addition, a few states require that the Articles be published as legal notices in newspapers. Please check the appendix for the requirements in your particular state. The signed Articles of Organization and the proper fee should be sent to the proper state office. Upon receipt, the state department will check for duplication or confusing conflicts with the names of any other registered companies. They will also check to be certain that all of the statutory requirements have been fulfilled and that the proper fee has been paid. If there is a problem, the Articles will be returned with an explanation of the difficulty. Correct the problem and refile the Articles. If everything is in order, the business will officially be organized and able to begin to conduct business as a limited liability company entity. Some states have different procedures for indicating the beginning of existence of a limited liability company. A completed sample Articles of Organization is included at the end of this chapter.

Title and Introduction

Check the appendix and also with your state limited liability company department for any changes to this clause. If your state has a different title for this document, please insert the proper title (for example: "Certificate of Formation of _____ "). The name of the limited liability company should include the company designation (see below under "Name of Limited Liability Company").

Articles of Organization of _____

The undersigned person(s), acting as organizer(s) for the purpose of forming a business limited liability company under the laws of the State of _____ , adopt(s) the following Articles of Organization:

Name of Limited Liability Company

The name of the limited liability company should be unique. It should not be confusingly similar to any other business name in use within your state. In addition, it should not contain any terms that might lead people to believe that it is a government or financial institution. Finally, it must generally contain an indication that the business is a limited liability company, such as "LLC," "Llc," "limited liability company," or "Limited." Some states allow the use of the word "Company" in the names of limited liability companies. Others do not. If you wish to use a term of designation other than "limited liability company" or "limited" (or abbreviations of these), please check the appendix and with your state limited liability company department.

Article ☐. The name of the limited liability company is

_____ .

Principal Place of Business

This should be the street address of the planned principal place of business of the limited liability company. Post office box addresses are not sufficient. It must be an actual street address.

> Article ☐. The principal place of business of the company is:
>
> _____

Purpose and Powers of the Limited Liability Company

Many states allow a general statement of purpose: "to transact any and all lawful business for which limited liability companies may be organized under the Business Limited Liability Company Act of the State of _____ ." Others may require that you specifically state the purpose of your limited liability company. If you are required to state a specific purpose, try to be broad enough to allow your business flexibility without the necessity of later amending the Articles of Organization to reflect a change in direction of your business. Choose the clause appropriate for your state and circumstances (please note that Kentucky and Massachusetts are referred to as "Commonwealths," rather than "States").

> Article ☐. The purpose for which this limited liability company is organized is to transact any and all lawful business for which limited liability companies may be organized under the laws of the State of _____ , and to have all powers that are afforded limited liability companies under the laws of the State of _____ .

Or:

> Article ☐. The purpose for which this limited liability company is organized is: _____ . This limited liability company shall have all powers that are afforded limited liability companies under the laws of the State of _____ .

Duration of Limited Liability Company

Most states allow for a perpetual duration for limited liability companies, meaning that the limited liability company can continue in existence forever. Unless there is a specific business reason to indicate otherwise, this is generally the safest choice.

> Article ☐. The duration of this limited liability company shall be perpetual.

Number of Members

The minimum number of members allowed is generally one. However, a few states require two. Please check the appendix.

> Article ☐. The number of members of this limited liability company is
> _____ .

Name and Addresses of Initial Members

This clause provides for listing the initial members of the limited liability company.

> Article ☐. The names and addresses of the initial members of this limited liability company are as follows:
>
> | Name | Address |
> |------|---------|
> | _____ | _____ |
> | _____ | _____ |
> | _____ | _____ |

Name of Registered Agent

The registered agent for a limited liability company is the person upon whom service of process (summons, subpoena, etc.) can be served. This person must be an adult who is a resident of the state of organization. The usual choice is the main owner or manager of the limited liability company. Please see the appendix and check with your state limited liability company department. There is a place at the end of the Articles of Organization for the registered agent to sign.

> Article ☐. The initial registered agent of this limited liability company is _____ . By his or her signature at the end of this document, this person acknowledges acceptance of the responsibilities as registered agent of this limited liability company.

Address of Registered Agent

This address must be an actual place, generally the offices of the limited liability company. It may not be a post office box or other unmanned location.

> Article ☐. The initial address of the office of the registered agent of this limited liability company is _____ ,
> City of _____ , in the County of _____ ,
> State of _____ .

Capitalization

This clause refers to the amount of capital that will form the initial basis for operating the limited liability company. Several states require that specific dollar amounts of capital to be contributed to a limited liability company be noted for the purpose of collecting additional fees for organization. All other states have no such requirement and you may delete this clause. Please check the appendix and with your state limited liability company department.

> Article ☐. The total amount of initial capitalization of this limited liability company is $ _____ .

Management of the Company

Under this clause, which is mandatory in several states, you will outline whether the management of the company will be by members only, by members and non-member managers, or by nonmember managers only. Check your state's listing in the appendix and choose the appropriate clause.

Article ☐. The company will be managed by the following (*members only, members and nonmember managers,* or *nonmember managers only*):

       Name   *Address*

_____   _____

_____   _____

_____   _____

Reservation of Right to Admit New Members

In this clause, which is optional in most states, the company can reserve the right to admit new members. In most states, this information may instead be listed in the Operating Agreement of the limited liability company, if preferred.

Article ☐. The company reserves the right to admit new members at any time.

Right of Company to Continue

This clause allows the company to reserve the right to continue, without dissolution, upon an act of dissolution or dissociation under the laws of the particular state. This clause is optional in most states. Please check the appendix.

Article ☐. The company reserves the right to continue without dissolution, under the terms as set forth in the company Operating Agreement, upon any act that might otherwise cause the dissolution of the company or the dissociation of a member under the laws of the State of _____ .

Standard Industrial Code

In this clause, list the Standard Industrial Code, or SIC, for the company. Please contact your appropriate state office for the listing of SIC codes.

> Article ☐. The Standard Industrial Code for the company is _____ .

Federal Employer Identification Number

This clause, which is not required in most states, provides the state with your Federal Employer Identification Number, or FEIN.

> Article ☐. The Federal Employer Identification Number of the company is _____ .

Additional Articles

This clause may be used to adopt any additional articles that may be desired.

> Article ☐. This limited liability company adopts the following additional articles:
>
> _____
> _____
> _____
> _____

Closing and Signatures

This clause provides a statement certifying that the facts as stated are true and correct. It also provides for the registered agent to sign, acknowledging his or her acceptance of the responsibilities of this job. This should be signed in front of a Notary Public.

I certify that all of the facts stated in these Articles of Organization are true and correct and are made for the purpose of forming a business limited liability company under the laws of the State of _____ .

Dated: _____ , 20 _____

_____   _____
Signature of Organizer   Printed Name of Organizer

_____   _____
Signature of Organizer   Printed Name of Organizer

_____   _____
Signature of Organizer   Printed Name of Organizer

State of _____
County of _____

Before me, on _____ , 20 _____ , personally appeared
_____ , _____ , and
_____ , named as the organizer(s), who is/are known to me to be the person(s) who subscribed his or her name(s) to this document, and acknowledged that he or she did so for the purposes stated.

_____
Signature of Notary Public

Notary Public, In and for the County of _____
State of _____

My commission expires: _____   Notary Seal

I acknowledge my appointment as registered agent of this limited liability company and accept the appointment.

Dated: _____ , 20 _____

_____   _____
Signature of Registered Agent   Printed Name of Registered Agent

Sample Articles of Organization

Articles of Organization of ABCXYZ Limited Liability Company

The undersigned person, acting as organizer for the purpose of forming a business limited liability company under the laws of the State of Superior adopts the following Articles of Organization:

Article 1. The name of the limited liability company is ABCXYZ Limited Liability Company.

Article 2. The purpose for which this limited liability company is organized is to transact any and all lawful business for which limited liability companies may be organized under the laws of the State of Superior, and to have all powers that are afforded to limited liability companies under the laws of the State of Superior.

Article 3. The duration of this limited liability company shall be perpetual.

Article 4. The total number of initial members of this company is two (2), and their names and addresses are as follows:

Name	Address
Mary Celeste	1234 Main Street, Capitol City, Superior
John Celeste	1234 Main Street, Capitol City, Superior

Article 5. The initial registered agent of this limited liability company is Mary Celeste.

Article 6. The initial address of the office of the registered agent of this limited liability company is 1234 Main Street, in the County of Inferior, State of Superior.

Article 7. The total amount of initial capitalization of this limited liability company is $1,000.00.

Article 8. This company will be managed by the following persons whose names and addresses are as follows:

Name	Address
Mary Celeste	1234 Main Street, Capitol City, Superior
John Celeste	1234 Main Street, Capitol City, Superior

Article 9. The company reserves the right to admit new members at any time.

Article 10. The company reserves the right to continue, without dissolution, under the terms as set forth in the company Operating Agreement, upon any act that might otherwise cause the dissolution of the company or the dissociation of a member under the laws of the State of Superior.

Article 11. The Standard Industrial Code for the company is 6123 .

Article 12. The Federal Employer Identification Number of the company is 44-1111111.

Article 13. This limited liability company adopts the following additional articles: none.

I certify that all of the facts stated in these Articles of Organization are true and correct and are made for the purpose of forming a business limited liability company under the laws of the State of Superior.

Dated: June 4, 2008

Mary Celeste
Signature of Organizer

Mary Celeste
Printed Name of Organizer

State of Superior
County of Inferior

Before me, on June 4, 2008, personally appeared Mary Celeste, named as the organizer, who is known to me to be the person who subscribed her name to this document, and acknowledged that she did so for the purposes stated.

Andrea Doria
Signature of Notary Public

Notary Public, In and for the County of Inferior
State of Superior

My commission expires: June 5, 2009   Notary Seal

I acknowledge my appointment as registered agent of this limited liability company and accept the appointment.

Dated: June 5, 2008

Mary Celeste
Signature of Registered Agent

Mary Celeste
Printed Name of Registered Agent

CHAPTER 10
Operating Agreement

The Operating Agreement of a limited liability company is the third part of the triangle that provides the framework for the management of company business. Along with state law and the Articles of Organization, the Operating Agreement provides a clear outline of the rights and responsibilities of all parties to a limited liability company. In particular, the Operating Agreement provides the actual details of the operational framework for the business. The Agreement is the internal document that will contain the basic rules for how the limited liability company is to be run. Every limited liability company must have an Operating Agreement. Many of the provisions cover relatively standard procedural questions relating, for example, to quorums or voting. Other provisions may need to be specifically tailored to the type of business for which the Operating Agreement is intended. The provisions are able to be amended by vote of the members.

The Operating Agreement can contain very specific or very general provisions for the internal management of the company. Typically, the Agreement covers five general areas:

- Rights and responsibilities of the members
- Rights and responsibilities of the managers
- Financial matters
- Methods for amending the Operating Agreement
- Member withdrawal and dissolution of the company

This chapter contains sample clauses for preparing your limited liability company Operating Agreement. Once you have filled in any required information, retype or print the Operating Agreement double-spaced in black ink on one side of 8½" x 11" white paper. If you are using a computer and word processing program, simply select those clauses from the Forms-on-CD that you wish to use in your Operating Agreement. Your completed Operating Agreement should be formally adopted at the first members meeting. Following is a checklist for use in preparing your Operating Agreement:

Operating Agreement Checklist

☐ The name of the limited liability company

☐ Power to designate the location of the principal office of the limited liability company

☐ Power to designate the registered agent and agent's office of the limited liability company

☐ The name and address of each member of the limited liability company

☐ Liability of members and managers of the company

☐ Tax treatment of the company

☐ Amount of contributions and initial capital to the limited liability company

☐ Any additional planned contributions to the limited liability company

☐ Penalties on failure to make contributions

☐ Interest on capital contributions

☐ Loans to the limited liability company

☐ Each member's share in the profits or losses of the company

☐ Distribution of profits and losses of the limited liability company

☐ Management of the limited liability company

☐ Authority of manager(s) of the limited liability company

☐ Signature for checking

- ❑ Authorization to borrow money
- ❑ Authorization to sign documents
- ❑ Date and time of annual members meetings
- ❑ Place of annual members meeting
- ❑ Members quorum
- ❑ Members proxies
- ❑ Members voting
- ❑ Members consent agreements
- ❑ Powers of the members
- ❑ Fiduciary duties of members and managers
- ❑ Accounting matters
  - ❑ Cash or accrual accounting
  - ❑ Calendar- or other fiscal-year periods
- ❑ Financial matters
- ❑ Bank account
- ❑ Loans to managers or members
- ❑ Draws and salaries to members
- ❑ Expense accounts

- [ ] Transfer of limited liability company interests

- [ ] Expulsion of member

- [ ] Automatic expulsion of member

- [ ] Limit on remedies of expelled member

- [ ] Insurance

  - [ ] Life insurance

  - [ ] Disability insurance

- [ ] Mediation or binding arbitration for dispute resolution

- [ ] Admission of new member

- [ ] Responsibility of new member

- [ ] Withdrawal from limited liability company

- [ ] Agreement not to compete

- [ ] Termination of limited liability company

- [ ] Amendments to Operating Agreement

- [ ] Amendments to Articles of Organization

- [ ] Additional provisions

- [ ] General provisions

- [ ] Signature(s) of member(s)

Title and Introductory Matter

This Limited Liability Company Operating Agreement is for the
_____ , organized
under the laws of the State of _____ , by the filing of its
organizational documents on _____ , 20 _____ .

Agreement

The parties to this agreement agree to operate a limited liability
company under the following terms and conditions:

Company Office and Registered Agent

☐. **Company Office and Registered Agent.** The members have the
power to determine the location of the limited liability company's
principal place of business. The members also have the power to
designate the limited liability company's registered agent, who may
be a member.

The company's principal place of business shall be: _____
_____

The name and address of the company's registered agent shall be:
_____

Initial Membership

☐. **Initial Membership.** The initial members of the company are
as follows:

Name	Address
_____	_____
_____	_____
_____	_____

Liability of Members and Managers

☐. **Liability of Members and Managers.** No members or managers of the limited liability company shall be personally liable for any debts, obligations, expenses, liabilities, or any claims made against the company.

Tax Treatment of Company

Use this clause to select tax treatment as a partnership, corporation, or sole proprietorship:

☐. **Tax Treatment of Company.** The members of the limited liability company elect to have the company treated as a
_____ for state and federal income tax purposes. The members agree to execute and file any documents necessary to secure this tax treatment.

Contributions and Start-up Capital

Use this first clause to delineate how the company will assemble its start-up capital:

☐. **Contributions and Start-up Capital.** The start-up capital will be a total of $ _____ . Each member of the limited liability company agrees to contribute the following property, services, or cash to this total amount on or before the date indicated:

Name	Cash/Services/Property	Value	Date Due
_____	_____	_____	_____
_____	_____	_____	_____
_____	_____	_____	_____

Additional Contributions

Select "majority" or "unanimous" vote.

☐. **Additional Contributions.** If additional capital is required by the limited liability company and is determined by a _____ vote of the members, then each member shall be required to contribute to such additional capital in such proportions and by a certain date as determined by such vote.

Failure to Make Contributions

☐. **Failure to Make Contributions.** If any member shall fail to make his or her initial or additional contributions as indicated by this agreement, any amendment to this agreement, or any additional agreement between the members, then this company shall continue as a limited liability company of only those members who have satisfied their contribution requirements. Any member who has failed to satisfy his or her contribution requirements will not be a member of this limited liability company. Each member who has made a contribution shall then be entitled to a share of limited liability company profits and losses in proportion to the amount of his or her contribution to the total contributions. If any additional limited liability company contributions are necessary, such additional contributions shall be determined by the remaining members as specified under the terms of this agreement regarding "Additional Contributions."

Interest on Capital Contributions

☐. **Interest on Capital Contributions.** Interest at the rate of _____ percent per annum shall be paid on each member's capital contributions that were paid in cash. The interest shall be an expense of the limited liability company and paid on an annual basis to the member who is entitled to it.

Loans to Limited Liability Company

☐. **Loans to Limited Liability Company.** In addition to capital contributions, the following cash or property will be loaned to the limited liability company under the terms specified:

Name of Member	Cash/Property Loaned	Terms of Loan
_____	_____	_____
_____	_____	_____
_____	_____	_____

Share of the Limited Liability Company

☐. **Share of the Limited Liability Company.** Each member's proportionate share of the profits and losses of the limited liability company shall be as follows:

Name	Percent of Ownership of Limited Liability Company
_____	_____
_____	_____
_____	_____

Distribution of Profits and Losses

Select the time period for distribution of profits and losses ("monthly," "quarterly," or "annual"). Also indicate a percentage of profits for each period that will be retained by the company for reinvestment (this can be zero percent [0%]).

☐. **Distribution of Profits and Losses.** Any profits or losses of the limited liability company shall be determined and distributed to the members on a _____ basis according to their proportionate share of the profits and losses of the limited liability company. However, the first _____ of the profits for each such period shall be retained by the limited liability company for reinvestment in the limited liability company.

Management

Choose the type of management for the company ("members only," "members and non-member managers," or "non-member managers only") and the voting amount needed to select (and remove) the persons who will manage the company ("majority" or "unanimous"):

> ☐. **Management.** The management of the company shall be exclusively by _____. The actual person(s) to manage the company and the salary of an such person(s) shall be set by a _____ vote of the members of the limited liability company, and may be removed, with or without cause, by a like vote.

Manager(s)' Authority

The manager(s)' authority is set in this clause as well as the limit to a manager(s)' ability to borrow money on behalf of the company. Additionally, indicate the voting amount needed ("majority" or "unanimous") for management decisions, other than major decisions. Finally, list major decisions for which unanimous vote will be required such as purchase of real estate, business loans, etc.:

> ☐. **Manager(s)' Authority.** One or more managers may be selected under the terms of this agreement. If a single individual is selected to manage the company, such person shall have exclusive authority to make all management decisions. Otherwise, all limited liability company decisions will be made by _____ vote among the persons selected to manage the company, except the major company decisions noted below, which must be decided by unanimous vote of the persons selected to manage the company: The manager(s) shall have the authority to conduct the day-to-day business of the limited liability company, without consultation with the other members. This shall include hiring and firing employees, signing limited liability company checks, withdrawing funds from limited liability company accounts, borrowing money up to the amount of $ _____ , and maintaining the books and records of the limited liability company. Major decisions are defined as follows:

Date and Time of Annual Members Meeting

☐. **Date and Time of Annual Members Meeting.** The annual limited liability company members meeting will be held on the _____ of every year at the corporate offices at _____ o'clock ___ . m. This meeting is for the purpose of assessing the current status of the limited liability company and transacting any necessary business. If this day is a legal holiday, the meeting will be held on the next day.

Place of Annual Members Meeting

☐. **Place of Annual Members Meeting.** The place for the annual members meeting will be the principal office of the limited liability company, located at _____ .

Members Quorum

☐. **Members Quorum.** A quorum for a members meeting will be a majority of the members. Once a quorum is present, business may be conducted at the meeting, even if members leave prior to adjournment.

Members Proxies

☐. **Members Proxies.** At all meetings of members, a member may vote by signed proxy or by power of attorney. To be valid, a proxy must be filed with the limited liability company prior to the stated time of the meeting. No proxy may be valid for more than 11 months, unless the proxy specifically states otherwise. A proxy may always be revoked prior to the meeting for which it is intended. Attendance at the meeting for which a proxy has been authorized always revokes the proxy.

Members Voting

Choose "majority" or "unanimous:"

☐. **Members Voting.** A _____ vote of the members entitled to vote will be sufficient to decide any matter, unless a greater number is required by this agreement or by state law. Adjournment shall be by majority vote of those shares entitled to vote.

Members Consent Agreements

☐. **Members Consent Agreements.** Any action that may be taken at a company meeting may be taken instead without a meeting if an agreement is consented to, in writing, by all members who would be entitled to vote.

Powers of the Members

☐. **Powers of the Members.** The members will, jointly, have all powers available under state law, including the power to: appoint and remove managers and employees; change the offices; borrow money on behalf of the limited liability company, including the power to execute any evidence of indebtedness on behalf of the limited liability company; and enter into contracts on behalf of the limited liability company. Such powers may be exercised by a single member only upon unanimous approval of all of the members.

Fiduciary Duty of Members and Managers

☐. **Fiduciary Duty of Members and Managers.** Each member and manager owes a fiduciary duty of good faith and reasonable care with regard to all actions taken on behalf of the limited liability company. Each member and manager must perform his or her duties in good faith in a manner that he or she reasonably believes to be in the best interests of the limited liability company, using ordinary care and prudence.

Accounting Matters

Select an accounting method ("cash" or "accrual") and an accounting time-period ("calendar" or some other fiscal year):

☐. **Accounting Matters.** The limited liability company will maintain accounting records that will be open to any member for inspection at any reasonable time. These records will include separate income and capital accounts for each member. The accounting will be on the _____ basis and on a _____ -year basis. The capital account of each member will consist of no less than the value of the property, cash, or services that the member shall have contributed with his or her initial or additional contributions to the limited liability company.

Financial Matters

☐. **Financial Matters.** All notes, mortgages, or other evidence of indebtedness shall be signed by all of the members of the limited liability company, unless otherwise allowed under the terms of this agreement.

Bank Account

☐. **Bank Account.** The limited liability company will maintain a business checking bank account at: _____.

Loans to Managers or Members

Indicate the vote needed for loans ("majority" or "unanimous"):

☐. **Loans to Managers or Members.** The limited liability company may not lend any money to a manager or member of the limited liability company unless the loan has been approved by a _____ vote of all members of the limited liability company.

Draws to Members

Select the time period for member draws (such as "monthly," "quarterly," "annual," or some other period). Also determine the vote amount needed for draws ("majority" or "unanimous"):

☐. **Draws to Members.** All members are entitled to _____ draws from the expected profits of the limited liability company. The draws will be debited against the income account of the member. The dollar amount of the draws shall be determined by a _____ vote of the members.

Salaries to Members

☐. **Salaries to Members.** All members are eligible to be paid reasonable salaries for work or services they perform in the limited liability company business, unless such work is in the capacity of a manager or is to be considered as a contribution to the company.

Expense Accounts

☐. **Expense Accounts.** Each member shall receive an expense account for up to $ _____ per month for the payment of reasonable and necessary business expenses in the regular course of limited liability company business. Each member shall provide the limited liability company with a written record of such expenses in order to obtain reimbursement.

Transfer of Limited Liability Company Interests

☐. **Transfer of Limited Liability Company Interests.** A member may transfer all or part of his or her interest in the limited liability company to any other party only with the unanimous consent of the other members. In addition, the limited liability company has the right of first refusal to purchase the member's interest on the same terms and conditions as the member's offer from the third party. This option to buy must be exercised by the limited liability company within 30 days from notice of the offer to buy by a third party.

Expulsion of Member

☐. **Expulsion of Member.** A member may be expelled from the limited liability company at any time by the unanimous consent of the other members. Upon expulsion, the expelled member shall cease to be a member and shall have no interest, rights, authority, power, or owner-ship in the limited liability company or any limited liability company property. The expelled member shall be entitled to receive value for his or her interest in the limited liability company as determined by the terms of this agreement. The limited liability company shall continue in business without interruption without the expelled member.

Automatic Expulsion of Member

☐. **Automatic Expulsion of Member.** A member is automatically expelled from the limited liability company at any time upon the occurrence of any of the following:

(a) A member files a petition for or becomes subject to an order for relief under the Federal Bankruptcy Code
(b) A member files for or becomes subject to any order for insolvency under any state law
(c) A member makes an assignment for the benefit of creditors
(d) A member consents to or becomes subject to the appointment of a receiver over a substantial portion of his or her assets
(e) A member consents to or becomes subject to an attachment or execution of a substantial portion of his or her assets

On the date of any of the above events, the expelled member shall cease to be a member and shall have no interest, rights, authority, power, or ownership in the limited liability company or any limited liability company property. The expelled member shall be entitled to receive value for his or her interest in the limited liability company as determined by the terms of this agreement. The limited liability company shall continue in business without interruption without the expelled member.

Limit on Remedies of Expelled Member

☐. **Limit on Remedies of Expelled Member.** The expulsion of a member shall be final and shall not be subject to mediation, arbitration, or review by any court of any jurisdiction.

Insurance

☐. **Insurance.** The limited liability company shall buy and maintain life insurance on the life of each member in the amount of $ _____ . The limited liability company shall also buy and maintain disability insurance on each member in the amount of $ _____ . Such life and disability insurance shall be considered assets of the company. On the withdrawal, termination, or expulsion of any member for any reason other than his or her death or disability, any insurance policies on the member's life or health on which the limited liability company paid premiums shall become the personal property of the departing member and the cash value (if any) of such policy shall be considered as a draw against the departing member's income account.

Dispute Resolution

Select a form of dispute resolution ("mediation" or "binding arbitration"). Also select a vote amount ("majority" or "unanimous"):

☐. **Dispute Resolution.** Except as otherwise provided by this agreement, the members agree that any dispute arising related to this agreement will be settled by _____ .
The person hired for such dispute resolution shall be chosen by a _____ vote of the members. All costs of such dispute resolution will be shared equally by all members involved in the dispute.

Admission of New Member

Select a vote amount ("majority" or "unanimous"):

☐. **Admission of New Member.** A new member may be admitted to the limited liability company by _____ consent of the members. Admission of a new member shall not cause the termination of the original limited liability company entity, but rather, it shall continue with the additional member.

Responsibility of New Member

☐. **Responsibility of New Member.** Any new member to the limited liability company shall be responsible for and assume full personal liability equal to all other members for all limited liability company debts, liabilities, and obligations whenever incurred for which the other members of the company have assumed personal liability.

Withdrawal from Limited Liability Company

☐. **Withdrawal from Limited Liability Company.** If any member withdraws from the limited liability company for any reason (including the death or disability of the member), the limited liability company shall continue and be operated by the remaining members. The withdrawing member or his or her personal representative will be obligated to sell that member's interest to the remaining members and those remaining members will be obligated to buy that interest. The value of the withdrawing member's interest will be his or her proportionate share of the total value of the limited liability company. If necessary, the total value of the limited liability company will be assessed by an independent appraisal made within 90 days of the member's withdrawal. The costs of the appraisal will be shared equally by all members, including the withdrawing member.

Agreement Not to Compete

Choose a time limit and geographical limit for member competition:

☐. **Agreement Not to Compete.** No member, during or after the operation of the limited liability company, shall engage in any business that is in competition in any manner with the limited liability company. The prohibition against competition shall continue for a period of _____ years after the member leaves the limited liability company and for any business within _____ miles of the limited liability company's principal place of business. This noncompetition agreement shall end with the termination of the limited liability company.

Termination of the Limited Liability Company

☐. **Termination of the Limited Liability Company.** The limited liability company may be terminated at any time by unanimous consent of the members. Upon termination, the members agree to apply the assets and money of the limited liability company in the following order:

(a) To pay all the debts and obligations of the limited liability company
(b) To distribute the members' income accounts to them in their proportionate share
(c) To distribute the members' capital accounts to them in their proportionate share
(d) To distribute any remaining assets to them in their proportionate share

Amendments to the Operating Agreement

Select a vote amount ("majority" or "unanimous"):

☐. **Amendments to the Operating Agreement.** This Operating Agreement may be amended in any manner by _____ vote of the members.

Amendments to the Articles of Organization

Select a vote amount ("majority" or "unanimous"):

☐. **Amendments to the Articles of Organization.** This Articles of Organization may be amended in any manner by _____ vote of the members.

Additional Provisions

☐. **Additional Provisions.** The following additional provisions are part of this agreement:

General Provisions

Note which state's laws will apply to this agreement.

☐. **General Provisions.** No modification of this agreement shall be effective unless it is in writing and approved by the required number of members set forth in this agreement. This agreement binds and benefits all members and any successors, inheritors, assigns, or representatives of the members. Time is of the essence of this agreement. This document is the entire agreement between the members. Any attached papers that are referred to in this agreement are part of this agreement. Any alleged oral agreements shall have no force or effect. This agreement is governed by the laws of the State of _____ . If any portion of this agreement is held to be invalid, void, or unenforceable by any court of law of competent jurisdiction, the rest of the agreement shall remain in full force and effect.

Signatures Clause

Dated: _____ , 20 _____

_____   _____
Signature of Member   Printed Name of Member

_____   _____
Signature of Member   Printed Name of Member

_____   _____
Signature of Member   Printed Name of Member

Sample Operating Agreement

Operating Agreement of ABCXYZ Limited Liability Company

This Limited Liability Company Operating Agreement is for the ABCXYZ Limited Liability Company organized under the laws of the State of Superior, by the filing of its organizational documents on June 4, 2008.

The parties to this agreement agree to operate a limited liability company under the following terms and conditions:

1. The members have the power to determine the location of the limited liability company's principal place of business. The members also have the power to designate the limited liability company's registered agent, who may be a member.

   The company's principal place of business shall be 1234 Main Street, Capitol City, Superior.

   The name and address of the company's registered agent shall be Mary Celeste, 1234 Main Street, Capitol City, Superior.

2. The initial members of the company are as follows:

Name	Address
Mary Celeste	1234 Main Street, Capitol City, Superior
John Celeste	1234 Main Street, Capitol City, Superior
Tom Celeste	4321 Superior Road, Capitol City, Superior
Cathy Celeste	4321 Superior Road, Capitol City, Superior
Pat Celeste	1009 Main Street, Capitol City, Superior
Debbie Andrews-Celeste	1009 Main Street, Capitol City, Superior
Michael Celeste	1009 Main Street, Capitol City, Superior

3. No members or managers of the limited liability company shall be personally liable for any debts, obligations, expenses, liabilities, or any claims made against the company.

4. The members of the limited liability company elect to have the company treated as a corporation for state and federal income tax purposes. The members agree to execute and file any documents necessary to secure this tax treatment.

5. The start-up capital will be a total of $30,000.00. Each member of the limited liability company agrees to contribute the following property, services, or cash to this total amount on or before the date indicated:

Name	Cash/Services Property	Value	Date Due
Mary Celeste	cash	$ 4,000.00	6/10/08
John Celeste	cash	$ 6,000.00	6/12/08
Tom Celeste	cash	$ 1,000.00	6/12/08
Cathy Celeste	cash	$ 1,000.00	6/12/08
Pat Celeste	services	$ 2,000.00	6/10/08
Debbie Andrews-Celeste	property	$10,000.00	6/7/08
Michael Celeste	property	$ 6,000.00	6/7/08

6. If additional capital is required by the limited liability company and is determined by a unanimous vote of the members, then each member shall be required to contribute to such additional capital in such proportions and by a certain date as determined by such vote.

7. If any member shall fail to make his or her initial or additional contributions as indicated by this agreement, any amendment to this agreement, or any additional agreement between the members, then this company shall continue as a limited liability company of only those members who have satisfied their contribution requirements. Any member who has failed to satisfy his or her contribution requirements will not be a member of this limited liability company. Each member who has made a contribution shall then be entitled to a share of limited liability company profits and losses in proportion to the amount of their contribution to the total contributions. If any additional limited liability company contributions are necessary, such additional contributions shall be determined by the remaining members as specified under the terms of this agreement regarding "Additional Contributions" above.

8. Interest at the rate of eight percent (8%) per annum shall be paid on each member's capital contributions that were paid in cash. The interest shall be an expense of the limited liability company and paid on an annual basis to the member who is entitled to it.

9. In addition to capital contributions, the following cash or property will be loaned to the limited liability company under the terms specified:

Name of Member	Cash/Property Loaned	Terms of Loan
Mary Celeste	computer	1 year
John Celeste	$2,000.00	8% interest
Tom Celeste	office furniture	3 years
Cathy Celeste	$1,500.00	8% interest
Pat Celeste	computer	2 years
Michael Celeste	truck	1 year

10. Each member's proportionate share of the profits and losses of the limited liability company shall be as follows:

Name	Percent of Ownership of Limited Liability Company
Mary Celeste	13.333%
John Celeste	20.000%
Tom Celeste	3.333%
Cathy Celeste	3.333%
Pat Celeste	6.667%
Debbie Andrews-Celeste	33.333%
Michael Celeste	20.000%

11. Any profits or losses of the limited liability company shall be determined and distributed to the members on a quarterly basis according to their proportionate share of the profits and losses of the limited liability company. However, the first twenty-five percent (25%) of the profits for each such period shall be retained by the limited liability company for reinvestment in the limited liability company.

12. The management of the company shall be exclusively by members only. The actual person(s) to manage the company and the salary of an such person(s) shall be determined by a unanimous vote of the members of the limited liability company, and the management may be removed at any time, with or without cause, by a like vote.

13. One or more managers may be selected under the terms of this agreement. If a single individual is selected to manage the company, such person shall have exclusive authority to make all management decisions. Otherwise, all limited liability company decisions will be made by unanimous vote among the persons selected to manage the company, except the major company decisions noted below, which must be decided by unanimous vote of the persons selected to manage the company. The manager(s) shall have the authority to conduct the day-to-day business of the limited liability company, without consultation with the other members. This shall include hiring and firing employees, signing limited liability company checks, withdrawing funds from limited liability company accounts, borrowing money up to the amount of $250.00, and maintaining the books and records of the limited liability company. Major decisions are defined as follows: Purchasing real estate, company vehicles, purchases over $250.00, and borrowing money.

14. The annual limited liability company members meeting will be held on the 12th of June of every year at 10 o'clock a.m.. This meeting is for the purpose of assessing the current status of the limited liability company and transacting any necessary business. If this day is a legal holiday, the meeting will be held on the next day.

15. The place for the annual members meeting will be the principal office of the limited liability company, located at: 1234 Main Street, Capitol City, Superior.

16. A quorum for a members meeting will be a majority of the members. Once a quorum is present, business may be conducted at the meeting, even if members leave prior to adjournment.

17. At all meetings of members, a member may vote by signed proxy or by power of attorney. To be valid, a proxy must be filed with the limited liability company prior to the stated time of the meeting. No proxy may be valid for more than 11 months, unless the proxy specifically states otherwise. A proxy may always be revoked prior to the meeting for which it is intended. Attendance at the meeting for which a proxy has been authorized always revokes the proxy.

18. A unanimous vote of the members entitled to vote will be sufficient to decide any matter, unless a greater number is required by this agreement or by state law. Adjournment shall be by majority vote of those shares entitled to vote.

19. Any action that may be taken at a company meeting may be taken instead without a meeting if an agreement is consented to, in writing, by all members who would be entitled to vote.

20. The members will, jointly, have all powers available under state law, including the power to: appoint and remove managers and employees; change the offices; borrow money on behalf of the limited liability company, including the power to execute any evidence of indebtedness on behalf of the limited liability company; and enter into contracts on behalf of the limited liability company. Such powers may be exercised by a single member only upon unanimous approval of all of the members.

21. Each member and manager owes a fiduciary duty of good faith and reasonable care with regard to all actions taken on behalf of the limited liability company. Each member and manager must perform his or her duties in good faith in a manner that he or she reasonably believes to be in the best interests of the limited liability company, using ordinary care and prudence.

22. The limited liability company will maintain accounting records that will be open to any member for inspection at any reasonable time. These records will include separate income and capital accounts for each member. The accounting will be on the cash basis and on a calendar-year basis. The capital account of each member will consist of no less than the value of the property, cash, or services that the member shall have contributed with his or her initial or additional contributions to the limited liability company.

23. All notes, mortgages, or other evidence of indebtedness shall be signed by all of the members of the limited liability company, unless otherwise allowed under the terms of this agreement.

24. The limited liability company will maintain a business checking bank account at First Bank of Capitol City, 565 Grand Ave., Capitol City, Superior.

25. The limited liability company may not lend any money to a manager or member of the limited liability company unless the loan has been approved by a unanimous vote of all members of the limited liability company.

26. All members are entitled to quarterly draws from the expected profits of the limited liability company. The draws will be debited against the income account of the member. The dollar amount of the draws shall be determined by a majority vote of the members.

27. All members are eligible to be paid reasonable salaries for work or services they perform in the limited liability company business, unless such work is in the capacity of a manager or is to be considered as a contribution to the company.

28. Each member shall receive an expense account for up to $500.00 per month for the payment of reasonable and necessary business expenses in the regular course of limited liability company business. Each member shall provide the limited liability company with a written record of such expenses in order to obtain reimbursement.

29. A member may transfer all or part of his or her interest in the limited liability company to any other party only with the unanimous consent of the other members. In addition, the limited liability company has the right of first refusal to purchase the member's interest on the same terms and conditions as the member's offer from the third party. This option to buy must be exercised by the limited liability company within 30 days from notice of the offer to buy by a third party.

30. A member may be expelled from the limited liability company at any time by the unanimous consent of the other members. Upon expulsion, the expelled member shall cease to be a member and shall have no interest, rights, authority, power, or ownership in the limited liability company or any limited liability company property. The expelled member shall be entitled to receive value for his or her interest in the limited liability company as determined by the terms of this agreement. The limited liability company shall continue in business without interruption without the expelled member.

31. A member is automatically expelled from the limited liability company at any time upon the occurrence of any of the following:

    (a) A member files a petition for or becomes subject to an order for relief under the Federal Bankruptcy Code
    (b) A member files for or becomes subject to any order for insolvency under any state law
    (c) A member makes an assignment for the benefit of creditors

(d) A member consents to or becomes subject to the appointment of a receiver over a substantial portion of his or her assets

(e) A member consents to or becomes subject to an attachment or execution of a substantial portion of his or her assets

On the date of any of the above events, the expelled member shall cease to be a member and shall have no interest, rights, authority, power, or ownership in the limited liability company or any limited liability company property. The expelled member shall be entitled to receive value for his or her interest in the limited liability company as determined by the terms of this agreement. The limited liability company shall continue in business without interruption without the expelled member.

32. The expulsion of a member shall be final and shall not be subject to mediation, arbitration, or review by any court of any jurisdiction.

33. The limited liability company shall buy and maintain life insurance on the life of each member in the amount of $50,000.00. The limited liability company shall also buy and maintain disability insurance on each other member in the amount of $25,000.00. Such life and disability insurance shall be considered assets of the company. On the withdrawal, termination, or expulsion of any member for any reason other than his or her death or disability, any insurance policies on the member's life or health on which the limited liability company paid premiums shall become the personal property of the departing member and the cash value (if any) of such policy shall be considered as a draw against the departing member's income account.

34. Except as otherwise provided by this agreement, the members agree that any dispute arising related to this agreement will be settled by binding arbitration. The person hired for such dispute resolution shall be chosen by a majority vote of the members. All costs of such dispute resolution will be shared equally by all members involved in the dispute.

35. A new member may be admitted to the limited liability company by majority consent of the members. Admission of a new member shall not cause the termination of the original limited liability company entity, but rather, it shall continue with the additional member.

36. Any new member to the limited liability company shall be responsible for and assume full personal liability equal to all other members for all limited liability company debts, liabilities, and obligations whenever incurred for which the other members of the company have assumed personal liability.

37. If any member withdraws from the limited liability company for any reason (including the death or disability of the member), the limited liability company shall continue and be operated by the remaining members. The withdrawing member or his or her personal representative will be obligated to sell that member's interest to the remaining members

and those remaining members will be obligated to buy that interest. The value of the withdrawing member's interest will be his or her proportionate share of the total value of the limited liability company. If necessary, the total value of the limited liability company will be assessed by an independent appraisal made within 90 days of the member's withdrawal. The costs of the appraisal will be shared equally by all members, including the withdrawing member.

38. No member, during or after the operation of the limited liability company, shall engage in any business that is in competition in any manner with the limited liability company. The prohibition against competition shall continue for a period of five (5) years after the member leaves the limited liability company and for any business within 300 miles of the limited liability company's principal place of business. This noncompetition agreement shall end with the termination of the limited liability company.

39. The limited liability company may be terminated at any time by unanimous consent of the members. Upon termination, the members agree to apply the assets and money of the limited liability company in the following order:

    (a) To pay all the debts and obligations of the limited liability company
    (b) To distribute the members' income accounts to them in their proportionate share
    (c) To distribute the members' capital accounts to them in their proportionate share
    (d) To distribute any remaining assets to them in their proportionate share

40. This Operating Agreement may be amended in any manner by majority vote of the members.

41. This Articles of Organization may be amended in any manner by majority vote of the members.

42. The following additional provisions are part of this agreement: none.

43. No modification of this agreement shall be effective unless it is in writing and approved by the required number of members set forth in this agreement. This agreement binds and benefits all members and any successors, inheritors, assigns, or representatives of the members. Time is of the essence of this agreement. This document is the entire agreement between the members. Any attached papers that are referred to in this agreement are part of this agreement. Any alleged oral agreements shall have no force or effect. This agreement is governed by the laws of the State of Superior . If any portion of this agreement is held to be invalid, void, or unenforceable by any court of law of competent jurisdiction, the rest of the agreement shall remain in full force and effect.

Dated June 9, 2008

Signature of Member	Printed Name of Member
Mary Celeste	Mary Celeste
John Celeste	John Celeste
Tom Celeste	Tom Celeste
Cathy Celeste	Cathy Celeste
Pat Celeste	Pat Celeste
Debbie Andrews-Celeste	Debbie Andrews-Celeste
Michael Celeste	Michael Celeste

CHAPTER 11
Members Meetings

The members of a limited liability company transact business as a group. Each individual member has no authority to bind the limited liability company (unless the members as a group have previously authorized him or her to exercise that power). Although it is not required, it is a good idea to hold official meetings to transact company business.

Members should, at a minimum, hold an annual meeting to handle any of the following business:

- Select managers for the coming year, if the company is to be run by managers
- Decide if any changes are necessary to the Articles of Organization or Operating Agreement
- Make any other annual decisions regarding the financial matters of the business
- Generally, review the operation of the company

All of the documents necessary to conduct and record a first and an annual members meeting are contained in this chapter.

First Members Meeting Checklist

The following information should be covered and documented in the minutes of the first members meeting:

- ☐ Name of limited liability company

- ☐ Date of meeting

- ☐ Location of meeting

- ☐ Members at meeting

- ☐ Others present at meeting

- ☐ Name of temporary chairperson presiding over meeting

- ☐ Name of temporary secretary acting at meeting

- ☐ Calling of meeting to order and determination of quorum present

- ☐ Articles of Organization filed with state

- ☐ Date of filing of Articles of Organization

- ☐ Effective date of organization of limited liability company

- ☐ Approval and ratification of any acts of organizers taken on behalf of limited liability company prior to effective date of organization of limited liability company

- ☐ Election of managers of limited liability company

- ☐ Decisions on annual salaries of managers

- ☐ Direction that any organizational expenses be reimbursed to organizers

- ☐ Authorization to open company bank account

- ☐ Approval of Operating Agreement

- ☐ Contributions of members

- ☐ Designation of fiscal-year dates

- ☐ Designation of accounting basis (cash or accrual)

- ☐ Documentation of any other necessary business

- ☐ Adjournment of meeting

- ☐ Dating and signing of minutes by secretary

Minutes of First Members Meeting of

_____

The first meeting of the members of this limited liability company was held on
_____ , 20 _____ , at _____ o'clock ____ . m., at the offices of the company
located at _____ .

Present at the meeting were the following people: _____
_____
_____
_____ ,
all of whom are designated as members of this limited liability company in the Articles of
Organization of this company.

The following other persons were also present: _____
_____
_____
_____ .

1. _____ was elected as the temporary chairperson
   of the meeting.

   _____ was elected as the temporary secretary
   of the meeting.

2. The chairperson announced that the meeting had been duly called by the organizer(s) of
   the limited liability company, called the meeting to order, and determined that a quorum
   was present.

3. The chairperson reported that the Articles of Organization of the company had been duly
   filed with the State of _____ on _____ , 20 _____ , and
   that the organization of the company was effective as of _____ , 20 _____ .

   Upon motion made and carried, a copy of the Articles of Organization of the company was
   ordered to be attached to the minutes of this meeting.

4. Upon motion made and carried, the members
   AGREED that:

The joint and individual acts of _____ and
_____ , the organizer(s) of this limited liability
company, that were taken on behalf of the limited liability company are approved, ratified,
and adopted as acts of the limited liability company.

5. The following persons were elected as managers of the limited liability company to serve
until the first annual members meeting:

Name	Address
_____	_____
_____	_____
_____	_____
_____	_____
_____	_____

6. Upon motion made and carried, the annual salaries of the managers were fixed at the following rates until the next annual meeting of the members:

Name	Salary
_____	_____
_____	_____
_____	_____
_____	_____
_____	_____

7. Upon motion made and carried, it was agreed that the organizer(s) of the company be
reimbursed, from company funds, the following amounts for organizational expenses:

Name	Reimbursement
_____	_____
_____	_____
_____	_____
_____	_____
_____	_____

8. Upon motion made and carried, it was agreed that the company would open a business
checking account at the following banking institution _____
_____ .

9. A copy of the proposed Operating Agreement of the limited liability company was presented
at the meeting and read by each member.

Upon motion made and carried, the members
AGREED that:

The proposed Operating Agreement of this limited liability company is approved and adopted. A copy of this Operating Agreement is ordered to be attached to the minutes of this meeting.

10. The following persons have offered to transfer the property or money listed below to the limited liability company in exchange for the following shares of ownership in the limited liability company:

Name	Property or Money	Ownership
_____	_____	_____
_____	_____	_____
_____	_____	_____
_____	_____	_____
_____	_____	_____

Upon motion made and carried, the members
AGREED that:

The assets proposed for transfer are good and sufficient consideration.

11. Upon motion made and carried, the members
AGREED that:

The fiscal year of this limited liability company shall begin on _____ , 20 _____ , and end on _____ , 20 _____ . This limited liability company shall report its income and expenses on a(n) _____ basis.

12. The following other business was conducted:

There being no further business, upon motion made and carried, the meeting was adjourned.

Dated _____ , 20 _____

_____
Signature of Secretary of Company

_____
Printed Name of Secretary of Company

Annual Members Meeting Checklist

The following information should be covered and documented in the minutes of the annual members meeting:

- ☐ Name of limited liability company

- ☐ Date of meeting

- ☐ Location of meeting

- ☐ Members present at meeting

- ☐ Others present at meeting

- ☐ Name of temporary chairperson presiding over meeting

- ☐ Name of temporary secretary presiding over meeting

- ☐ Calling of meeting to order and determination of quorum present

- ☐ Distribution and approval of minutes of previous meeting

- ☐ Presentation of annual financial report

- ☐ Election of managers of limited liability company

- ☐ Decision on annual salaries of managers

- ☐ Other business (see next page for possible business discussions)

- ☐ Adjournment of meeting

- ☐ Dating and signing of minutes by secretary

Other Possible Business Discussions

- ☐ Date last state and Federal Tax returns filed

- ☐ Date last state annual report filed

- ☐ Date any other required reports/returns filed

- ☐ Date of last Financial Statement

- ☐ Review current employment agreements

- ☐ Review current insurance coverage

- ☐ Review current Financial Statement

- ☐ Review current year-to-date income and expenses

- ☐ Review current salaries

- ☐ Review current pension/profitsharing plans

- ☐ Review accounts receivable

- ☐ Determination of necessity of collection procedures

- ☐ Review status of any outstanding loans

- ☐ Ascertainment of net profit

- ☐ Discussion of any major items requiring member action

- ☐ Major purchases or leases (real estate or personal property)

- ☐ Lawsuits

- ☐ Loans

Minutes of Annual Members Meeting of

_____

The annual meeting of the members of this limited liability company was held on
_____ , 20 _____ , at _____ o'clock ___ . m., at the offices of the company
located at _____ .

Present at the meeting were the following people: _____
_____
_____
_____
_____ ,
all of whom are members of this limited liability company.

The following other persons were also present: _____
_____
_____
_____
_____ .

1. _____ was elected as the temporary chairperson
   of the meeting.

   _____ was elected as the temporary secretary
   of the meeting.

2. The chairperson announced that the meeting had been duly called by the organizer(s) of
   the limited liability company, called the meeting to order, and determined that a quorum
   was present.

3. The secretary distributed copies of the minutes of the previous meeting of the members
   that had been held on _____ , 20 _____ .

   Upon motion made and carried, these minutes were approved.

4. An Annual Financial Report was presented that stated that as of _____ ,
   20 _____ , the limited liability company had a net profit of $ _____ .

   Upon motion made and carried, the Annual Financial Report was approved and the secretary was directed to attach a copy of the Annual Financial Report to these minutes.

5. Upon motion made and carried, the following persons were elected as managers of this limited liability company for a term of one year:

Name	*Address*
_____	_____
_____	_____
_____	_____
_____	_____
_____	_____

6. Upon motion made and carried, the salaries of the managers were fixed for the term of one year at the following rates:

Name		*Rate*
_____	$	_____
_____	$	_____
_____	$	_____
_____	$	_____
_____	$	_____

7. The following other business was conducted:

There being no further business, upon motion made and carried, the meeting was adjourned.

Dated _____ , 20 _____

_____
Signature of Secretary of Company

_____
Printed Name of Secretary of Company

CHAPTER 12

Amendments to Articles of Organization or Operating Agreement

At some time in the course of your limited liability company, changed conditions may require that you *amend* (or alter) certain portions of your Articles of Organization or Operating Agreement. In general, members may agree to alter or amend these documents in any manner, as changed conditions may dictate. However, state law in all states restricts the right to change certain general conditions and rules of limited liability company law and liability. Contact the state office in your state to obtain information regarding amendments to the Articles of Organization. They may even provide fill-in-the-blank forms for your use. There will generally be a fee required for filing Amendments to Articles of Organization. To make amendments to your original Articles of Organization or Operating Agreement, use one of the following forms for amending these limited liability company documents.

Amendment to Articles of Organization of

_____

This Amendment to Articles of Organization is made on _____ , 20 _____ .
It is intended to permanently amend the Articles of Organization, filed on
_____ , 20 _____ , on behalf of _____ , a
limited liability company organized under the laws of the State of _____ .

The above-noted Articles of Organization are hereby amended to read as follows:

All other portions of the original Articles of Organization dated _____ ,
20 _____ , not changed by this Amendment to Articles of Organization, remain in full force
and effect and are ratified and confirmed.

Signature of Member   *Printed Name of Member*

_____   _____

_____   _____

_____   _____

_____   _____

_____   _____

_____   _____

_____   _____

Amendment to Operating Agreement of

_____

.

This Amendment to Operating Agreement is made on _____ , 20 _____ .
It is intended to permanently amend the Operating Agreement of
_____ , a limited liability company
organized under the laws of the State of _____ .

The above noted Operating Agreement is hereby amended to read as follows:

All other portions of the original Operating Agreement dated _____ ,
20 _____ , not changed by this Amendment to Operating Agreement, remain in full force and
effect and are ratified and confirmed.

Signature of Member   _Printed Name of Member_

_____   _____

_____   _____

_____   _____

_____   _____

_____   _____

_____   _____

_____   _____

CHAPTER 13
Termination of Limited Liability Company

In many limited liability companies, there will come a time when the members will desire that the company cease to exist. In order for the dissolution of the limited liability company to proceed as amicably as possible, it is wise to carefully consider all aspects of the impending end of the company and to draft a comprehensive Termination of Limited Liability Company Agreement that will cover each aspect of dissolution of the business to each member's satisfaction. The termination of a business limited liability company is, perhaps, one of the most difficult business situations to confront. The following worksheet is designed to assist you in understanding the factors that will be important as you proceed to terminate your business limited liability company. Following the worksheet is a Termination of Limited Liability Company Agreement that you may use as an outline to prepare your own customized agreement. Please note that in most states, you will also need to file Articles of Dissolution of a Limited Liability Company with your state's registration office. Please check your state's official website (as noted in the appendix) for information on your state's requirements.

Termination Worksheet

Date proposed for termination: _____

Reason for termination: _____
_____
_____

Valuation of limited liability company business: $ _____

Appraisal of limited liability company property: $ _____

Who will appraise the limited liability company property? _____
_____

Does anyone hold a right of first refusal or option to purchase the business?
_____
_____

Is an outside purchase or lease of the business involved? _____
_____

If so, what are the proposed terms of the outside purchaser's offer to buy or lease the business? _____
_____
_____

Are these terms unanimously acceptable to the members? _____

Is the business to be sold or leased to an existing member? _____

If so, what are the proposed terms of the existing purchaser's offer to buy or lease the business? _____
_____
_____

Are these terms unanimously acceptable to the members? _____

Will the limited liability company business be discontinued with no purchase of limited liability company assets? _____

What disposition will be made of the limited liability company name? _____
_____
_____

What date is set for the sale/lease/liquidation of the limited liability company? _____
_____

What are the proportionate shares of profits and losses of each member? _____
_____
_____

What is the liquidation or sale value of all of the limited liability company assets?
_____
_____

What is the value of all of the limited liability company liabilities, other than to the members? _____
_____

What will be the remaining limited liability company assets after all limited liability company liabilities have been met? _____
_____

How much will be distributed to each member's income account? _____

How much will be distributed to each member's capital account? _____

How much additional limited liability company funds will be distributed to each member?
_____
_____

Who will wind up the limited liability company business? _____
_____

What is the estimated date for the distribution of the final limited liability company assets?
_____

Termination of Limited Liability Company of

_____

This Termination of Limited Liability Company Agreement is made on
_____ , 20 _____ , by and between
_____ , of:

and _____ , of:

It is intended to permanently terminate the limited liability company created by the Articles of Organization between the above parties that was dated _____ , 20 _____ , and filed with the State of _____ , on _____ , 20 _____ .

The above noted members agree to terminate their limited liability company under the following terms and conditions:

1. After _____ , 20 _____ , no member shall engage in any further limited liability company business nor incur any further limited liability company obligations, other than to liquidate the assets of the limited liability company and, in general, wind up the limited liability company's affairs.

2. The members agree that each asset of the limited liability company has a present fair market value equal to the asset's value as shown on the financial records of the limited liability company. However, if an asset is sold, the members agree that asset shall be deemed to have a fair market value equal to its sale price.

3. The members agree that their proportionate shares of the assets and liabilities of the limited liability company are as follows:

4. The limited liability company shall proceed to have an accounting made of all of the assets and liabilities of the limited liability company. The equities of the limited liability company creditors and members shall be determined on the date of the accounting, that shall be no later than _____ , 20 _____ . Any liabilities incurred or funds received by the limited liability company after this date shall be distributed to the members according to their proportionate shares.

5. Any limited liability company assets shall be sold. Any member shall have the right to purchase any limited liability company asset before any sale to an outside purchaser. The proceeds from the sale of the limited liability company assets, along with any limited liability company funds, shall be applied to the limited liability company liabilities in the following order:

   a. To pay all the debts and obligations of the limited liability company
   b. To the members' income accounts to the members in their proportionate share
   c. To the members' capital accounts to the members in their proportionate share
   d. To any remaining assets to the members in their proportionate share

6. Every member hereby represents that he or she has not obligated the limited liability company in any way that does not appear on the records of the limited liability company, nor has he or she received any funds or assets that do not appear on the records of the limited liability company.

7. The limited liability company name shall be disposed of as follows:

8. No modification of this agreement shall be effective unless it is in writing and signed by a majority of the members. This agreement binds and benefits all members and any successors, inheritors, assigns, or representatives of the members. Time is of the essence of this agreement. This document is the entire agreement between the members. Any attached papers that are referred to in this agreement are part of this agreement. Any alleged oral agreements shall have no force or effect. This agreement is governed by the laws of the State of _____ . If any portion of this agreement is held to be invalid, void, or unenforceable by any court of law of competent jurisdiction, the rest of the agreement shall remain in full force and effect.

Dated _____ , 20 _____

Signature of Member   *Printed Name of Member*

_____   _____

_____   _____

_____   _____

_____   _____

CHAPTER 14

Employee Documents

The legal forms in this chapter cover a variety of situations that arise in the area of employment. From hiring an employee to subcontracting work on a job, written documents that outline each person's responsibilities and duties are important for keeping an employment situation on an even keel. The employment contract contained in this chapter may be used and adapted for virtually any employment situation. Of course, it is perfectly legal to hire an employee without a contract at all. In many businesses, this is common practice. However, as job skills and salaries rise and employees are allowed access to sensitive and confidential business information, written employment contracts are often a prudent business practice. An independent contractor may also be hired to perform a particular task. As opposed to an employee, this type of worker is defined as one who maintains his or her own independent business, uses his or her own tools, and does not work under the direct supervision of the person who has hired him or her. A contract for hiring an independent contractor is provided in this chapter.

General Employment Contract: This form may be used for any situation in which an employee is hired for a specific job. The issues addressed by this contract are as follows:

- That the employee will perform a certain job and any incidental further duties
- That the employee will be hired for a certain period and for a certain salary
- That the employee will be given certain job benefits (for example: sick pay, vacations, etc.)
- That the employee agrees to abide by the employer's rules and regulations
- That the employee agrees to sign agreements regarding confidentiality and inventions
- That the employee agrees to submit any employment disputes to mediation and arbitration

The information necessary to complete this form is as follows:

- The names and addresses of the employer and employee
- A complete description of the job
- The date the job is to begin and the length of time that the job will last
- The amount of compensation and benefits for the employee (salary, sick pay, vacation, bonuses, and retirement and insurance benefits)
- Any additional documents to be signed

- Any additional terms
- The state whose laws will govern the contract
- Signatures of employer and employee

Independent Contractor Agreement: This form should be used when hiring an independent contractor. It provides a standard form for the hiring out of specific work to be performed within a set time period for a particular payment. It also provides a method for authorizing extra work under the contract. Finally, this document provides that the contractor agrees to *indemnify* (reimburse or compensate) the owner against any claims or liabilities arising from the performance of the work. To complete this form, fill in a detailed description of the work; dates by which certain portions of the job are to be completed; the pay for the job; the terms and dates of payment; and the state whose laws will govern the contract.

Contractor/Subcontractor Agreement: This form is intended to be used by an independent contractor to hire a subcontractor to perform certain work on a job that the contractor has agreed to perform. It provides for the "farming out" of specific work to be performed by the subcontractor within a set time period for a particular payment. It also provides a method for authorizing extra work under the contract. Finally, this document provides that the subcontractor agrees to indemnify the contractor against any claims or liabilities arising from the performance of the work. To complete this form, fill in a detailed description of the work; dates by which portions of the job are to be completed; the pay for the job; the terms and dates of payment; and the state whose laws will govern the contract.

General Employment Contract

This contract is made on _____ , 20 _____ , between
_____ , employer, of
_____ , City of _____ ,
State of _____ , and _____ ,
employee, of _____ , City of
_____ , State of _____ .

For valuable consideration, the employer and employee agree as follows:

1. The employee agrees to perform the following duties and job description:

   The employee also agrees to perform further duties incidental to the general job description. This is considered a full-time position.

2. The employee will begin work on _____ , 20 _____ . This position shall continue for a period of _____ .

3. The employee will be paid the following:

   Weekly salary: $ _____

   The employee will also be given the following benefits:

   Sick pay: $ _____
   Vacations: $ _____
   Bonuses: $ _____
   Retirement benefits: $ _____
   Insurance benefits: $ _____

4. The employee agrees to abide by all rules and regulations of the employer at all times while employed.

5. This contract may be terminated by:

   (a) Breach of this contract by the employee
   (b) The expiration of this contract without renewal
   (c) Death of the employee
   (d) Incapacitation of the employee for over _____ days in any one (1) year

6. The employee agrees to sign the following additional documents as a condition to obtaining employment:

7. Any dispute between the employer and employee related to this contract will be settled by voluntary mediation. If mediation is unsuccessful, the dispute will be settled by binding arbitration using an arbitrator of the American Arbitration Association.

8. Any additional terms of this contract:

9. No modification of this contract will be effective unless it is in writing and is signed by both the employer and employee. This contract binds and benefits both parties and any successors. Time is of the essence of this contract. This document is the entire agreement between the parties. This contract is governed by the laws of the State of _____ .

Dated: _____ , 20 _____

_____
Signature of Employer

_____
Printed Name of Employer

_____
Signature of Employee

_____
Printed Name of Employee

Independent Contractor Agreement

This agreement is made on _____ , 20 _____ , between
_____ , owner, of
_____ , City of _____ ,
State of _____ , and _____ ,
contractor, of _____ , City of
_____ , State of _____ .

For valuable consideration, the owner and contractor agree as follows:

1. The contractor agrees to furnish all of the labor and materials to do the following work for the owner as an independent contractor:

2. The contractor agrees that the following portions of the total work will be completed by the dates specified:

   Work:

   Dates: _____

3. The contractor agrees to perform this work in a workmanlike manner according to standard practices. If any plans or specifications are part of this job, they are attached to and are part of this agreement.

4. The owner agrees to pay the contractor as full payment $ _____ , for doing the work outlined above. This price will be paid to the contractor on satisfactory completion of the work in the following manner and on the following dates:

   Work:

   Dates: _____

5. The contractor and the owner may agree to extra services and work, but any such extras must be set out and agreed to in writing by both the contractor and the owner.

6. The contractor agrees to indemnify and hold the owner harmless from any claims or liability arising from the contractor's work under this agreement.

7. No modification of this agreement will be effective unless it is in writing and is signed by both parties. This agreement binds and benefits both parties and any successors. Time is of the essence of this agreement. This document, including any attachments, is the entire agreement between the parties. This agreement is governed by the laws of the State of _____ .

Dated: _____ , 20 _____

_____
Signature of Owner

_____
Printed Name of Owner

_____
Signature of Contractor

_____
Printed Name of Contractor

Contractor/Subcontractor Agreement

This agreement is made on _____ , 20 _____ , between
_____ , contractor, of
_____ , City of _____ ,
State of _____ , and _____ ,
subcontractor, of _____ , City of
_____ , State of _____ .

1. The subcontractor, as an independent contractor, agrees to furnish all of the labor and materials to do the following portions of the work specified in the agreement between the contractor and the owner dated _____ , 20 _____ .

2. The subcontractor agrees that the following portions of the total work will be completed by the dates specified:

   Work:

   Dates: _____

3. The subcontractor agrees to perform this work in a workmanlike manner according to standard practices. If any plans or specifications are part of this job, they are attached to and are part of this agreement.

4. The contractor agrees to pay the subcontractor as full payment $ _____ , for doing the work outlined above. This price will be paid to the subcontractor on satisfactory completion of the work in the following manner and on the following dates:

   Work:

   Dates: _____

5. The contractor and subcontractor may agree to extra services and work, but any such extras must be set out and agreed to in writing by both the contractor and the subcontractor.

6. The subcontractor agrees to indemnify and hold the contractor harmless from any claims or liability arising from the subcontractor's work under this agreement.

7. No modification of this agreement will be effective unless it is in writing and is signed by both parties. This agreement binds and benefits both parties and any successors. Time is of the essence of this agreement. This document, including any attachments, is the entire agreement between the parties. This agreement is governed by the laws of the State of _____ .

Dated: _____ , 20 _____

_____
Signature of Contractor

_____
Printed Name of Contractor

_____
Signature of Subcontractor

_____
Printed Name of Subcontractor

CHAPTER 15

Business Financial Recordkeeping

Each year, thousands of small businesses fail because their owners have lost control of their finances. Many of these failures are brought on by the inability of the business owners to understand the complex accounting processes and systems that have become relatively standard in modern business. Accounting and bookkeeping have, in most businesses, been removed from the direct control and, therefore, understanding of the business owners themselves. If business owners cannot understand the financial situation of their own businesses, they have little chance of succeeding.

Keeping accurate and clear business financial records can, for many business owners, be the most difficult part of running a business. For most business owners, understanding those records is, at best, a struggle. And yet maintaining a set of clear and understandable financial records is perhaps the single most important factor that separates successful businesses from those that fail. The purpose of the next few chapters is to provide the small business owner with a clear understanding of how to develop a concise and easily-understood financial recordkeeping system, keep the books for a business, and, perhaps most importantly, actually understand those records.

Modern business practices have tended to complicate many areas of business when, in many cases, simplification is what most business owners need. In law, in management, and in accounting, many important business functions have been obscured from their owners by intricate systems and complex terminology. Business owners must then turn the handling of these affairs over to specialized professionals in a particular field. The result, in many cases, is that business owners lose crucial understanding of those portions of their business. With this loss of understanding comes the eventual and almost inevitable loss of control.

This is particularly true for small business owners and their financial records. It is absolutely vital that emerging small business owners intimately understand their financial position. Daily decisions must be made that can make or break a fledgling business. If the financial records of a small business are delegated to an outside accountant or bookkeeper, it is often difficult, if not impossible, for a novice business owner to understand the current financial position of the business on a day-to-day basis. Critical business decisions are then made on the basis of incomplete or often unknown financial information.

The basic aspects of the accounting outlined in this book have been used successfully by millions of businesses in the past. The system presented in this book is designed to be set up and initially used by the business owners themselves. This will insure that the system is both thoroughly understood by the owner and provides the type of information that the owner actually wants. As a business grows and becomes more complex, and a business owner becomes more comfortable with financial recordkeeping, other more sophisticated and complex accounting systems may become appropriate. There are numerous computer-based accounting programs on the market, such as QuickBooks, that can provide the framework for a company accounting system. However, in order to understand and use any of the computer accounting systems, it is necessary to first have an understanding of the basics of financial recordkeeping.

Understanding Financial Records

The purpose of any business financial recordkeeping system is to provide a clear vision of the relative health of the business, both on a day-to-day basis and periodically. Business owners themselves need to know whether they are making a profit, why they are making a profit, which parts of the business are profitable, and which are not. This information is only available if the business owner has a clear and straight-forward recordkeeping system. Business owners also need to be able to produce accurate financial statements for income tax purposes, for loan proposals, and for the purpose of selling the business. Clear, understandable, and accurate business records are vital to the success of any small business. In order to design a good recordkeeping system for a particular business, an understanding of certain fundamental ideas of accounting is necessary. For those unfamiliar with the terms and concepts of accounting, grasping these basic ideas may be the most difficult part of accounting, even simplified accounting.

First, let's get some of the terminology clarified. *Accounting* is the design of the recordkeeping system that a business uses and the preparation and interpretation of reports based on the information that is gathered and put into the system. *Bookkeeping* is the actual inputting of the financial information into the recordkeeping system. The purpose of any business recordkeeping system is to allow the business owner to easily understand and use the information gathered. Certain accounting principles and terms have been adopted as standard over the years to make it easier to understand a wide range of business transactions. In order to understand what a recordkeeping system is trying to accomplish, it is necessary to define some of the standard ways of looking at a business. There are two standard reports that are the main sources of business financial information: the *balance sheet* and the *profit-and-loss statement*.

The Balance Sheet

The purpose of the balance sheet is to look at what the business owns and owes on a specific date. By seeing what a business owns and owes, anyone looking at a balance sheet can tell the relative financial position of the business at that point in time. If the business owns more than it owes, it is in good shape financially. On the other hand, if it owes more than it owns, the business may be in trouble. The balance sheet is the universal financial document used to view this aspect of a business. It provides this information by laying out the value of the assets and the liabilities of a business. One of the most critical financial tasks that a small business owner must confront is keeping track of what the business owns and owes. Before the business buys or sells anything or makes a profit or loss, the business must have some assets.

The *assets* of a business are anything that the business owns. These can be cash on hand or in a bank account; personal property, like office equipment, vehicles, tools, or supplies; inventory, or material that will be sold to customers; real estate, buildings, and land; and money that is owed to the business. Money that is owed to a business is called its *accounts receivable*, basically the money that the business hopes to eventually receive. The total of all of these things that a business owns are the business's assets.

The *liabilities* of a business are anything that the business owes to others. These consist of long-term debts, such as a mortgage on real estate or a long-term loan. Liabilities also consist of any short-term debts, such as money owed for supplies or taxes. Money that a business owes to others is called its *accounts payable*, basically the money that the business hopes to eventually pay. In addition to money owed to others, the *equity* of a business is also considered a liability. The equity of a business is the value of the ownership of the business. It is the value that would be left over if all of the debts of the business were paid off. If the business is a partnership or a sole proprietorship, the business equity is referred to as the *net worth* of the business. If the business is a corporation, the owner's equity is called the *capital surplus* or *retained capital*. All of the debts of a business and its equity are together referred to as the business's liabilities.

The basic relationship between assets and liabilities is shown in a simple equation:

$$\text{Assets} = \text{Liabilities}$$

This simple equation is the basis of business accounting. When the books of a business are said to *balance*, it is this equation that is in balance: the assets of a business must equal the liabilities of a business. Since the liabilities of a business consist of both equity and debts, the equation can be expanded to read:

$$\text{Assets} = \text{Debts} + \text{Equity}$$

Rearranging the equation can provide a simple explanation of how to arrive at the value of a business to the owner, or its equity:

$$Equity = Assets - Debts$$

A basic tenet of recordkeeping is that both sides of this financial equation must always be equal. The formal statement of the assets and liabilities of a specific business on a specific date is called a *balance sheet*. A balance sheet is usually prepared on the last day of a month, quarter, or year. A balance sheet simply lists the amounts of the business's assets and liabilities in a standardized format.

On a balance sheet, the assets of a business are generally broken down into two groups: *current assets* and *fixed assets*. Current assets consist of cash, accounts receivable (remember, money that the business intends to receive; basically, bills owed to the business), and inventory. Current assets are generally considered anything that could be converted into cash within one year. Fixed assets are more permanent-type assets and include vehicles, equipment, machinery, land, and buildings owned by the business.

The liabilities of a business are broken down into three groups: *current liabilities*, *long-term liabilities*, and *owner's equity*. Current liabilities are short-term debts, generally those that a business must pay off within one year. This includes accounts payable (remember, money that the business intends to pay; basically, bills the business owes), and taxes that are due. Long-term liabilities are long-term debts such as mortgages or long-term business loans. Owner's equity is whatever is left after debts are deducted from assets. Thus, the owner's equity is what the owner would have left after all of the debts of the business were paid off. Owner's equity is the figure that is adjusted to make the equation of assets and liabilities balance.

Let's look at a simple example: a basic sales business.

Smith's Gourmet Foods has the following assets: Smith has $500.00 in a bank account, is owed $70.00 by customers who pay for their food monthly, has $200.00 worth of food supplies, and owns food preparation equipment worth $1,300.00.

These are the assets of Smith's Gourmet Foods and they are shown on a balance sheet as follows:

Cash	$	500.00
+ Accounts owed to it	$	70.00
+ Inventory	$	200.00
+ Equipment	$	1,300.00
= Total assets	$	2,070.00

Smith also has the following debts: $100.00 owed to the supplier of the food, $200.00 owed to the person from whom she bought the food equipment, and $100.00 owed to the state for sales taxes that have been collected on food sales. Thus, the debts of Smith's Gourmet Foods are shown as follows:

Accounts it owes	$ 100.00
+ Loans it owes	$ 200.00
+ Taxes it owes	$ 100.00
= Total debts	$ 400.00

To find what Smith's equity in this business is, we need to subtract the amount of the debts from the amount of the assets. Remember: assets − debts = equity. Thus, the owner's equity in Smith's Gourmet Foods is as follows:

Total assets	$ 2,070.00
− Total debts	$ 400.00
= Owner's equity	$ 1,670.00

That's it. The business of Smith's Gourmet Foods has a net worth of $1,670.00. If Smith paid off all of the debts of the business, there would be $1,670.00 left. This basic method is used to determine the net worth of businesses worldwide, from the smallest to the largest: assets = debts + equity, or assets − debts = equity. Remember, both sides of the equation always have to be equal.

The Profit and Loss Statement

The other main business report is the *profit and loss statement*. This report is a summary of the income and expenses of the business during a certain period. Profit and loss statements are sometimes referred to as *income statements* or *operating statements*. You may choose to prepare a profit and loss statement monthly, quarterly, or annually, depending on your particular needs. You will, at a minimum, need to have an annual profit and loss statement in order to streamline your tax return preparation.

A profit and loss statement, however, provides much more than assistance in easing your tax preparation burdens. It allows you to clearly view the performance of your business over a particular time period. As you begin to collect a series of profit and loss statements, you will be able to conduct various analyses of your business. For example, you will be able to compare monthly performances over a single year to determine which month was the best or worst for your business. Quarterly results will also be able to be contrasted. The comparison of several annual expense and revenue figures will allow you to judge the growth or shrinkage of your business over time. Numerous other comparisons are possible, depending on your particular business. How have sales been influenced by advertising expenses? Are production costs higher this quarter than last? Do seasons have an impact on sales? Are certain expenses becoming a burden on the business? The profit and loss statement is one of the key financial statements for the analysis of your business.

Generally, *income* for a business is any money that it has received or will receive during a certain period. *Expenses* are any money that it has paid or will pay out during a certain period. Simply put, if the business has more income than expenses during a certain period, it has made a profit. If it has more expenses than income, then the business has a loss for that period of time.

Income can be broken down into two basic types: service income and sales income. The difference between the two types of income lies in the need to consider inventory costs. *Service income* is income derived from performing a service for someone (cutting hair, for example). *Sales income* is revenue derived from selling a product of some type. With service income, the profit can be determined simply by deducting the expenses that are associated with making the income. With sales income, however, in addition to deducting the expenses of making the income, the cost of the product that was sold must also be taken into account. This is done through inventory costs. Thus, for sales income, the income from selling a product is actually the sales income minus the cost of the product to the seller. This inventory cost is referred to as the *cost of goods sold*.

A profit and loss statement begins with a sale. Back to the food business as an example: Smith had the following transactions during the month of July: $250.00 worth of food was sold, the wholesale cost of the food that was sold was $50.00, the cost of napkins, condiments, other supplies, and rent amounted to $100.00, and interest payments on the equipment loan were $50.00. Thus, Smith's profit and loss statement would be prepared as follows:

Gross sales income	$ 250.00
– Cost of food	$ 50.00
= Net sales income	$ 200.00
Operating expenses	$ 100.00
+ Interest payments	$ 50.00
= Net expenses	$ 150.00

Thus, for the month of July, Smith's business performed as follows:

Net sales income	$ 200.00
– Net expenses	$ 150.00
= Net profit	$ 50.00

Again, this simple setup reflects the basics of profit and loss statements for all types of businesses, no matter what their size. For a pure service business, with no inventory of any type sold to customers: income – expenses = net profit. For a sales-type business or a sales/service combined business: income – cost of goods sold – expenses = profit.

These two types of summary reports—the balance sheet and the profit and loss statement—are the basic tools for understanding the financial health of any business. The figures on them can be used for many purposes to understand the operations of a business. The balance sheet shows what proportion of a business's assets are actually owned by the business owner and what proportion is owned or owed to someone else.

Looking at Smith's balance sheet, we can see that the owner's equity is $1,670.00 of assets of $2,070.00. Thus, we can see that the owner has more than 80 percent ownership of the business, a very healthy situation. There are numerous ways to analyze the figures on these two financial statements. Understanding what these figures mean and how they represent the health of a business are keys to keeping control of the finances of any business.

Accounting Methods

There are a few more items that must be understood regarding financial recordkeeping. First is the method for recording the records. There are two basic methods for measuring transactions: the *cash method* and the *accrual method*. Cash-method accounting is a system into which income is recorded when it is received and expenses are recorded when they are paid. With cash accounting, there is no effective method to accurately reflect inventory costs. Thus, Internal Revenue Service regulations require that the cash method of accounting may only be used by those few businesses that are solely service businesses and do not sell any materials to their customers at all, even a few spare parts. If a business sells any type of product or material whatsoever, it must use the accrual method of accounting. (An exception to this general rule is allowed for any corporation or partnership with annual gross receipts of under $5 million.)

The accrual method of accounting counts income and expenses when they are due to the business. Income is recorded when the business has a right to receive the income. In other words, accounts receivable (bills owed to the business) are considered as income that has already been received by the business. Expenses are considered and recorded when they are due, even if they are not yet paid. In other words, accounts payable (bills owed by the business) are considered expenses to the business when they are received, not when they are actually paid. The vast majority of businesses will wish to use the accrual method of accounting. A business must choose to keep its records either on the accrual basis or on the cash basis. Once this decision is made, approval from the IRS must be obtained before the method can be changed. After you select the type of accounting you will use, please consult a tax professional if a change in the system must be made.

Accounting Systems

In addition, there are two basic types of recordkeeping systems: *single-entry* and *double-entry*. Both types are able to be used to keep accurate records, although the double-entry system has more ways available to double-check calculations. Double-entry recordkeeping is, however, much more difficult to master, in that each and every transaction must be entered in two separate places in the records. The system that is used in this book is a modified form of single-entry accounting. The benefits of ease of use of a single-entry system far outweigh the disadvantages of this system. The IRS recommends single-entry records for beginning small businesses, and states that this type of system can be "relatively simple...used effectively...and is adequate for income tax purposes." Many accountants will disagree with this and insist that only double-entry accounting is acceptable. For the small business owner who wishes to understand his or her own company's finances, the advantages of single-entry accounting far outweigh the disadvantages.

Accounting Periods

A final item to consider is the accounting period for your business. A business is allowed to choose between a *fiscal-year* accounting period and a *calendar-year* period. A fiscal year consists of 12 consecutive months that do not end on December 31st. A calendar year consists of 12 consecutive months that do end on December 31st. There are complex rules relating to the choice of fiscal-year accounting. Partnerships and S-corporations may generally choose to report on a fiscal-year basis only if there is a valid business purpose that supports the use of a fiscal year. This generally complicates the reporting of income and should be avoided unless there is an important reason to choose a fiscal-year accounting period. If a fiscal-year period is considered necessary, please consult a tax or accounting professional as there are complicated rules to comply with.

For the majority of small businesses, the choice of a calendar-year period is perfectly adequate and, in most cases, will simplify the tax reporting and accounting recordkeeping. In the year in which a business is either started or ended, the business year for reporting may not be a full year. Thus, even for those who choose to use a calendar year, the first year may actually start on a date other than January 1st.

The simplified small business accounting system that is explained in this book is a modified single-entry accounting system. It is presented as a system for accrual-basis accounting for small businesses. The records are designed to be used on a calendar-year basis. Within these basic parameters, the system can be individually tailored to meet the needs of most small businesses.

The backbone of the recordkeeping system is the Chart of Accounts for your business. A chart of accounts will list each of the income, expense, asset, or debt categories that you wish to keep track of. Every business transaction that you make and every financial record that you create will fit into one of these four main categories. Your transactions will either be money coming in (income) or money going out (expenses). Your records will also track things the business owns (assets) or things the business owes (debts). The chart of accounts that you create in the next chapter will allow you to itemize and track each of these four broad categories in detail.

Following is a checklist for setting up your business financial recordkeeping using this book:

Financial Recordkeeping Checklist

- ☐ Set up your business chart of accounts
- ☐ Open a business checking account
- ☐ Prepare a check register
- ☐ Set up a business petty cash fund
- ☐ Prepare a petty cash register
- ☐ Set up asset accounts
- ☐ Prepare current asset account records
- ☐ Prepare fixed asset account records
- ☐ Set up expense account records
- ☐ Set up income account records
- ☐ Set up a payroll system
- ☐ Prepare payroll time sheets
- ☐ Prepare payroll depository records
- ☐ Determine proper tax forms for use in business

CHAPTER 16
Business Accounts

The financial recordkeeping system that you will set up using this book is designed to be adaptable to any type of business. Whether your business is a service business, a manufacturing business, a retail business, a wholesale distributorship, or a combination of any of these, you will be able to easily adapt this simplified system to work with your particular situation. A key to designing the most useful recordkeeping system for your particular needs is to examine your type of business in depth. After a close examination of the particular needs and operations of your type of business, you will need to set up an array of specific accounts to handle your financial records. This set of general accounts is called a Chart of Accounts.

A Chart of Accounts will list all of the various categories of financial transactions that you will need to track. There will be an account for each general type of expense that you want to keep track of. You will also have a separate account for each type of income your business will receive. Accounts will also be set up for your business assets and liabilities. Setting up an account for each of these categories consists of the simple task of deciding which items you will need to categorize, selecting a name for the account, and assigning a number to the account.

Before you can set up your accounts, you need to understand the reason for setting up these separate accounts. It is possible, although definitely not recommended, to run a business and merely keep track of your income and expenses without any itemization at all. However, you would be unable to analyze how the business is performing beyond a simple check to see if you have any money left after paying the expenses. You would also be unable to properly fill in the necessary information for business income tax returns. A major reason for setting up separate accounts for many business expense and income transactions is to separate and itemize the amounts spent in each category so that this information is available at tax time. This insures that a business is taking all of its allowable business deductions. The main reason, however, to set up individual accounts is to allow the business owner to have a clear view of the financial health of the business. With separate accounts for each type of transaction, a business owner can analyze the proportional costs and revenues of each aspect of the business. Is advertising costing more than labor expenses? Is the income derived from sale items worth the discount of the sale? Only by using the figures obtained from separate itemized accounts can these questions be answered.

In the following sections, you will select and number the various accounts for use in your business Chart of Accounts. You will select various income accounts, expense accounts, asset accounts, and liability accounts. You will also assign a number to each account. For ease of use, you should assign a particular number value to all accounts of one type. For example, all income accounts may be assigned #10 to 29. Sales income may be Account #11; service income may be Account #12, interest income may be Account #13. Similarly, expenses may be assigned #30 to 79. Balance Sheet accounts for assets and liabilities may be #80 to 99. Be sure to leave enough numbers for future expansion of your list of accounts. There will normally be far more expense accounts than any other type of account.

If you have income or expenses from many sources, you may wish to use a three-digit number to identify each separate category. For example, if your business consists of renting out residential houses and you have 10 properties, you may wish to set up a separate income and expense account for each property. You may wish to assign Accounts #110 to 119 to income from all properties. Thus, for example, you could then assign rental income from Property #1 to Account #111, rental income from Property #2 to Account #112, rental income from Property #3 to Account #113, and so on. Similarly, expenses can be broken down into separate accounts for individual properties. All advertising expenses could be Accounts #510 to 519; thus, advertising expenses for Property #1 could then be assigned Account #511, advertising expenses for Property #2 would be assigned Account #512, etc.

How your individual Chart of Accounts will be organized will be specific to your particular business. If you have a simple business with all income coming from one source, you will probably desire a two-digit number from, for example, 10 to 29, assigned to that income account. On the other hand, a more complex business with many sources of income and many different types of expenses may wish to use a system of three-digit numbers. Take some time to analyze your specific business to decide how you wish to set up your accounts. Ask yourself what type of information you will want to extract from your financial records. Do you need more details of your income sources? Then you should set up several income accounts for each type and possibly even each source of your income. Would you like more specific information on your expenses? Then you would most likely wish to set up clear and detailed expense accounts for each type of expense that you must pay.

Be aware that you may wish to alter your Chart of Accounts as your business grows. You may find that you have set up too many accounts and unnecessarily complicated your recordkeeping tasks. You might wish to set up more accounts once you see how your Balance Sheets and Profit and Loss Statements look. You can change, add, or delete accounts at any time. Remember, however, that any transactions that have been recorded in an account must be transferred to any new account or accounts that take the place of the old account.

Income Accounts

These are accounts that are used to track the various sources of your company's income. There may be only a few sources of income for your business or you may wish to track your income in more detail. The information which you collect in your income accounts will be used to prepare your Profit and Loss Statements periodically. Recall that a Profit and Loss Statement is also referred to as an Income and Expense Statement.

On the Chart of Accounts that is used in this book, income is separated into several categories. You can choose the income account categories which best suit your type of business. If your business is a service business, you may wish to set up accounts for labor income and for materials income. Or you may wish to set up income accounts in more detail, for example: sales income, markup income, income from separate properties, or income from separate sources in your business, etc. Nonsales income, such as bank account interest income or income on the sale of business equipment, should be placed in separate individual income accounts. You may also wish to set up separate income accounts for income from different ongoing projects or income from separate portions of your business.

Following is a list of various general income accounts. Decide how much detail you will want in your financial records regarding income and then choose the appropriate accounts. You may wish to name and create different accounts than are listed here. After you have chosen your income accounts, assign a number to each account.

Income Chart of Accounts

Account #	Account Name and Description
	Income from sale of goods
	Income from services
	Income from labor charges
	Income from sales discounts
	Income from interest revenue
	Income from consulting
	Miscellaneous income

Expense Accounts

These are the accounts that you will use to keep track of your expenses. Each separate category of expense should have its own account. Many of the types of accounts are dictated by the types of expenses which should be itemized for tax purposes. You will generally have separate accounts for advertising costs, utility expenses, rent, phone costs, etc. One or more separate accounts should also be set up to keep track of inventory expenses. These should be kept separate from other expense accounts as they must be itemized for tax purposes.

Following is a list of various general expense accounts. Please analyze your business and determine which accounts would be best suited to select for your particular situation. You will then number these accounts, as you did the income accounts. The categories presented are general categories that match most Internal Revenue Service tax forms. You may, of course, set up separate accounts that are not listed to suit your particular needs. Try not to set up too many accounts or you will have a hard time trying to remember all of them. Also note that you may add or delete accounts as you need them. If you delete an account, however, you must shift any transactions that you have recorded in that account to a new account.

Expense Chart of Accounts

Account #	Account Name and Description
	Advertising expenses
	Auto expenses
	Cleaning and maintenance expenses
	Charitable contributions
	Dues and publications
	Office equipment expenses
	Freight and shipping expenses
	Business insurance expenses
	Business interest expenses
	Legal expenses
	Business meals and lodging
	Miscellaneous expenses
	Postage expenses
	Office rent expenses
	Repair expenses
	Office supplies
	Sales taxes paid
	Federal unemployment taxes paid
	State unemployment taxes paid
	Telephone expenses
	Utility expenses
	Wages and commissions

Asset and Liability Accounts

Asset and liability accounts are collectively referred to as *Balance Sheet Chart of Accounts*. This is because the information collected on them is used to prepare your business Balance Sheets. You will set up current and fixed asset accounts and current and long-term liability accounts. Types of current asset accounts are cash, short-term notes receivable, accounts receivable, inventory, and prepaid expenses. Fixed assets may include equipment, vehicles, buildings, land, long-term notes receivable, and long-term loans receivable.

Types of current liability accounts are *short-term notes payable* (money due within one year), *short-term loans payable* (money due on a loan within one year), unpaid taxes, and unpaid wages. Long-term liability accounts may be *long-term notes payable* (money due more than one year in the future) or *long-term loans payable* (money due on a loan more than one year in the future). Finally, you will need an owner's equity account to tally the ownership value of your business.

Choose the asset and liability accounts that best suit your business and assign appropriate numbers to each account.

Balance Sheet Chart of Accounts

Account #	Account Name and Description
	Accounts receivable (current asset)
	Bank checking account (current asset)
	Bank savings account (current asset)
	Cash on hand (current asset)
	Notes receivable (current asset, if short-term)
	Loans receivable (current asset, if short-term)
	Inventory (current asset)
	Land (fixed asset)
	Buildings (fixed asset)
	Vehicles (fixed asset)
	Equipment (fixed asset)
	Machinery (fixed asset)
	Accounts payable (current debt)
	Notes payable (current, if due within 1 year)
	Loans payable (current, if due within 1 year)
	Notes payable (long-term debt, if over 1 year)
	Loans payable (long-term debt, if over 1 year)
	Mortgage payable (long-term debt, if over 1 year)
	Retained capital

Chart of Accounts

After you have selected and numbered each of your accounts, you should prepare your Chart of Accounts. Simply type the number and name of each account in a numerical list. You will refer to this chart often as you prepare your financial records. Following is a sample completed Chart of Accounts. This sample chart is set up to reflect the business operations of our sample company, Smith's Gourmet Foods. This is a company that prepares and packages food products and delivers the products directly to consumers in their homes. The chart reflects that the income will primarily come from one source: direct customer payments for the products that are sold. The expense accounts are chosen to cover most of the standard types of business expenses that a small business will encounter. The Balance Sheet accounts reflect that the business will have as assets only a bank account, some accounts receivable, inventory, and some equipment. The only liabilities that this business will have, at least initially, will be a loan for equipment and accounts payable. Although this sample Chart of Accounts is fairly brief, it covers all of the basic accounts that the business will need as it begins. There is sufficient room in the numbering system chosen to add additional accounts as the business expands.

Sample Chart of Accounts

Account #	Account Name and Description
11	Income from sale of goods
12	Miscellaneous income
31	Advertising expenses
32	Auto expenses
33	Cleaning and maintenance expenses
34	Office equipment expenses
35	Business insurance expenses
36	Business meals and lodging
37	Miscellaneous expenses
38	Postage expenses
39	Repair expenses
40	Office supplies
41	Sales taxes paid
42	Telephone expenses
43	Office rent expense
51	Cash on hand (current asset)
52	Accounts receivable (current asset)
53	Bank checking account (current asset)
54	Inventory (current asset)
61	Equipment (fixed asset)
71	Accounts payable (current debt)
81	Loans payable (long-term debt)
91	Retained capital

Tracking Business Assets

After setting up a Chart of Accounts the next financial recordkeeping task for a business will consist of preparing a method to keep track of the assets of the business. Recall that the assets of a business are everything that is owned by the business and are either current assets that can be converted to cash within a year or fixed assets that are more long-term in nature. Each of these two main categories of assets will be discussed separately.

Current Assets

Following is a list of typical current assets for a business:

- Business bank checking account
- Business bank savings account
- Cash (petty cash fund and cash on hand)
- Accounts receivable (money owed to the company)
- Inventory

A company may have other types of current assets such as notes or loans receivable, but the five listed above are the basic ones for most small businesses. In complex double-entry accounting systems, the current asset account balances are constantly being changed. In a double-entry system, each time an item of inventory is sold, for example, the account balance for the inventory account must be adjusted to reflect the sale. In single-entry systems, all asset and liability accounts are updated only when the business owner wishes to prepare a Balance Sheet. This may be done monthly, quarterly, or annually. At a minimum, this updating must take place at the end of the year in order to have the necessary figures available for tax purposes.

Current Asset Account

The main form for tracking your current business assets will be a Current Asset Account sheet. A copy of this form follows this discussion. On this form, you will periodically track the value of the current asset that you are following, except for your inventory. (For inventory, you will use specialized inventory records.) You should prepare a separate Current Asset Account sheet for each asset. For example, if your current assets consist of a business checking account, cash on hand, and accounts receivable, you will have three separate Current Asset Accounts, one for each category of asset. These forms are very simple to use. Follow the instructions below:

1. Simply fill in the account number for the Current Asset Account for which you are setting up the form. You will get this number from your Chart of Accounts. Fill in also a description of the account. For example: Account #53—Business Banking Account.

2. You must then decide how often you will be preparing a Balance Sheet and updating your Balance Sheet account balances. If you wish to keep close track of your finances, you may wish to do this on a monthly basis. For many businesses, a quarterly Balance Sheet may be sufficient. All businesses, no matter how small, must prepare a Balance Sheet at least annually at the end of the year. Decide how often you wish to update the balances and enter the time period in the space provided.

3. Next, enter the date that you open the account. Under description, enter "Opening Balance." In the "Balance" column, enter the opening value. The amount to enter for an opening balance will be as follows:

   • For a bank account, this will be the opening balance of the account
   • For cash on hand, this will be the opening balance of the petty cash fund and cash on hand for sales, such as the cash used in a cash register
   • For accounts receivable, this will be the total amount due from all accounts

4. After you have entered the balances on the appropriate Current Asset Account sheet, you will transfer the balances to your Balance Sheet.

Current Asset Account

Account #:
Account Name: Period:

Date	Description of Asset	Balance	

Inventory

Any business that sells an item of merchandise to a customer must have a system in place to keep track of inventory. *Inventory* is considered any merchandise or materials that are held for sale during the normal course of your business. Inventory costs include the costs of the merchandise or products themselves and the costs of the materials and paid labor that go into creating a finished product. Inventory does not include the costs of the equipment or machinery that you need to create the finished product.

There are several reasons you will need a system of inventory control. First, if you are stocking parts or supplies to sell, you will need to keep track of what you have ordered, what is in stock, and when you will need to reorder. You will also need to keep track of the cost of your inventory for tax purposes. The amount of money that you spend on your inventory is not fully deductible in the year spent as a business deduction. The only portion of your inventory cost that will reduce your gross profit for tax purposes is the actual cost of the goods that you have sold during the tax year.

The basic method for keeping track of inventory costs for tax purposes is to determine the cost of goods sold. First, you will need to know how much inventory is on hand at the beginning of the year. To this amount, you add the cost of any additional inventory you purchased during the year. Finally, you determine how much inventory is left at the end of the year. The difference is essentially the cost (to you) of the inventory that you sold during the year. This amount is referred to as the *cost of goods sold*. Every year at tax time, you will need to figure the cost of goods sold. Additionally, you may need to determine your cost of goods sold monthly or quarterly for various business purposes.

Using our sample company, Smith's Gourmet Foods, we will start the owner's first year in business with an inventory of $0.00. When her business begins, there is no inventory. During the first year, she purchases $17,500.00 worth of products that are for selling to customers. At the end of the year, she counts all of the items that are left in her possession and determines her cost for these items. The cost of the items left unsold at the end of the year is $3,700.00.

The calculation of the cost of goods sold for the first year in business is as follows:

	Inventory at beginning of first year	$ 00.00
+	Cost of inventory added during year	$ 17,500.00
=	Cost of inventory	$ 17,500.00
−	Inventory at end of first year	$ 3,700.00
=	Cost of Goods Sold for first year	$ 13,800.00

For the second year in business, the figure for the inventory at the beginning of the year is the value of the inventory at the end of the previous year. Thus, if Smith's Gourmet Foods added $25,000.00 additional inventory during the second year of operation and the value of the inventory at the end of the second year was $4,800.00, the cost-of-goods-sold calculations for the second year would be as follows:

	Inventory at beginning of second year	$ 3,700.00
+	Cost of inventory added during year	$ 25,000.00
=	Cost of inventory	$ 28,700.00
−	Inventory at end of second year	$ 4,800.00
=	Cost of goods sold for second year	$ 23,900.00

Thus, for the second year in operation the cost of goods sold would be $23,900.00. This amount would be deducted from the gross revenues that Smith's Gourmet Foods took in for the year to determine the gross profit for the second year in business.

Physical Inventory Report

This form should be used to record the results of an actual physical counting of the inventory at the end of the year and at whatever other times during the year you decide to take a physical inventory. If you decide that you will need to track your inventory monthly or quarterly, you may need to prepare this form for those time periods. To prepare this form, take the following steps:

1. The form should be dated and signed by the person doing the inventory.

2. The quantity and description of each item of inventory should be listed, along with an item number if applicable.

3. The cost (to you) of each item should be then listed under "Unit Price." A total per item cost is then calculated by multiplying the quantity of units by the unit price. This total per item cost should be listed in the far right-hand column. You will need to extract this per item unit price from your Periodic or Perpetual Inventory Records (explained next).

4. The total inventory cost should be figured by adding all of the figures in the far right-hand column.

Physical Inventory Report

Date: Taken by:

Quantity	Description	Item #	Unit Price		Total	
			TOTAL			

Periodic Inventory Record

This is the form that you will use to keep continual track of your inventory if you have a relatively small inventory. You will use the Periodic Inventory Record for the purpose of keeping track of the costs of your inventory and of any orders of additional inventory. You will refer to this record when you need to order additional inventory, determine when an order should be received, and determine the cost of your inventory items at the end of the year or at other times if desired. If you have an extensive inventory, you will need to consult an accounting professional to assist you in setting up a perpetual-type inventory system. Or you may be able to set up a complex inventory system using commercial accounting software that is available.

1. Prepare a separate Periodic Inventory Record for each item of inventory. Identify the type of item that is being tracked by description and by item number, if applicable. You may also wish to list the supplier of the item.

2. The first entry on the Periodic Inventory Record should be the initial purchase of inventory. On the right-hand side of the record, list the following items:

   - Date purchased
   - Quantity purchased
   - Price per item
   - Total price paid
   - *Note*: Shipping charges should not be included in the prices entered. Only the actual costs of the goods should be listed.

3. When you are running low on a particular item and place an order, on the left-hand side of the record enter the following information:

   - Date of the order
   - The order number
   - The quantity ordered
   - The date the order is due to arrive

4. When the order arrives, enter the actual details about the order on the right-hand side of the page. This will allow you to keep track of your order of inventory items and also allow you to keep track of the cost of your items of inventory.

Periodic Inventory Record

Item: Item #:

Supplier:

INVENTORY ORDERED			
Date	Order #	Quantity	Due

INVENTORY RECEIVED			
Date	Quantity	Price	Total

Cost of Goods Sold Report

The final record for inventory control is the Cost of Goods Sold Report. It is on this report that you will determine the actual cost to your business of the goods that were sold during a particular time period. There are numerous methods to determine the value of your inventory at the end of a time period. The three most important are the specific identification method, the first-in first-out (FIFO) method, and the last-in first-out (LIFO) method. Specific identification is the easiest to use if you have only a few items of inventory, or one-of-a-kind type merchandise. With this method, you actually keep track of each specific item of inventory. You keep track of when you obtained the item, its cost, and when you sold the specific item. With the FIFO method, you keep track only of general quantities of your inventory. Your inventory costs are calculated as though the oldest inventory merchandise was sold first. The first items that you purchased are the first items that you sell. With the LIFO method, the cost values are calculated as though you sold your most-recently purchased inventory first. It is important to note that you do not necessarily have to actually sell your first item first to use the FIFO method and that you don't have to actually sell your last item first to use the LIFO method of calculation.

Although there may be significant advantages in some cases to using the LIFO method, it is also a far more complicated system than the FIFO. The specific identification method allows you to simply track each item of inventory and deduct the actual cost of the goods that you sold during the year. The FIFO method allows you to value your inventory on hand at the end of a time period based on the cost of your most recent purchases.

1. At the end of your chosen time period (monthly, quarterly, or annually), take an actual physical inventory count on your Physical Inventory Report.

2. Using the most recent purchases as listed on your Periodic Inventory Record, determine the unit price of the items left in your inventory and enter this in the Unit Price column on your Physical Inventory Report.

3. Once all of your items of inventory have been checked, counted, and a unit price determined, simply total each item and then total the value of the entire inventory. If you are conducting your final annual inventory, this figure is your inventory value at year's end.

4. On the Cost of Goods Sold Report, enter this number on the line titled "Inventory Value at End of Period." If this is your first year in business, enter "zero" as the Inventory Value at Beginning of Period. For later periods, the Inventory Value at Beginning of Period will be the Inventory Value at End of Period from the previous time period.

5. Using your Periodic Inventory Records, total the amount of orders during the period that are listed in the "Inventory Received" column. This total will be entered on the "Inventory Added During Period" line. Now simply perform the calculations. You will use the figures on this report at tax time to prepare your taxes.

Note: This type of inventory calculation is not intended for manufacturing companies that manufacture finished goods from raw materials or for those with gross annual receipts more than $10 million. For those types of companies, an additional calculation is necessary because of uniform capitalization rules. This tax rule requires that manufacturing inventory values include the overhead associated with the manufacturing process. Please consult an accounting professional if your business falls into this category.

Cost of Goods Sold Report

Period Ending:

Inventory Value at Beginning of Period		
+ Inventory Added during Period		
= Total Inventory Value		
− Inventory Value at End of Period		
= Cost of Goods Sold		

Beginning Inventory Value for Next Period
(Take from Inventory Value at End of This Period)

Fixed Assets

The final category of assets that you will need to track are your *fixed assets*. Fixed assets are the more permanent assets of your business, generally the assets that are not for sale to customers. The main categories of these fixed assets are:

- Buildings
- Land
- Machinery
- Tools
- Furniture and Equipment
- Vehicles

There are many more types of fixed assets, such as patents, copyrights, and goodwill. However, the six listed above are the basic ones for most small businesses. If your business includes other types of fixed assets, please consult an accounting professional. For those with basic fixed assets, you will need to keep track of the actual total costs to you to acquire them. These costs include sales taxes, transportation charges, installation costs, etc. The total cost of a fixed asset to you is referred to as the asset's *cost basis*. With a major exception explained below, the costs of fixed assets are, generally, not immediately deductible as a business expense. Rather, except for land, their costs are deductible proportionately over a period of time. This proportionate deduction is referred to as *depreciation*. Since these assets generally wear out over time (except for land), each year you are allowed to deduct a portion of the initial cost as a legitimate business expense. Each type of fixed asset is given a specific time period for dividing up the cost into proportional amounts. This time period is called the *recovery period* of the asset. Depreciation is a very complex subject and one whose rules change nearly every year. The full details of depreciation are beyond the scope of this book. What follows is only a general outline of depreciation rules. It will allow you to begin to set up your fixed asset records. However, you will need to consult either an accounting or tax professional or consult specific tax preparation manuals for details on how your specific assets should be depreciated.

The major exception to depreciation rules is that, under the rules of Internal Revenue Service Code Section 179, every year a total of $112,000.00 (beginning in the tax year 2007, this amount will be adjusted annually for inflation) of your fixed asset costs can be immediately used as a business deduction. This means that if your total purchases of equipment, tools, vehicles, etc., during a year amounted to less than $112,000.00, you can deduct all of the costs as current expenses. If your total fixed asset costs are more than $112,000.00, you can still deduct the first $112,000.00 in costs and then depreciate the remaining costs over time. Here are some basic rules relating to depreciation:

1. The depreciation rules that were in effect at the time of the purchase of the asset will be the rules that apply to that particular asset.

2. The actual cost to you of the asset is the cost basis that you use to compute your depreciation amount each year.

3. Used assets that you purchase for use in your business can be depreciated in the same manner as new assets.

4. Assets that you owned prior to going into business and that you will use in your business can be depreciated. The cost basis will be the lower of their actual market value when you begin to use them in your business or their actual cost to you. For example, you start a carpentry business and use your personal power saw in the business. It cost $150.00 new, but is now worth about $90.00. You can depreciate $90.00 (or deduct this amount as an expense if the total of your fixed asset deductions is less than $112,000.00).

5. You may depreciate proportionately those assets that you use partially for business and partially for personal use. In the above example, if you use your saw 70 percent of the time in your business and 30 percent for personal use, you may deduct or depreciate 70 percent of $90.00, which is $63.00.

The tax depreciation rules set up several categories of asset types for the purpose of deciding how long a period you must use to depreciate the asset. Cars, trucks, computer equipment, copiers, and similar equipment are referred to as five-year property. Most machinery, heavy equipment, and office furniture are referred to as seven-year property. This means that for these types of property the actual costs are spread out and depreciated over five or seven years—that is, the costs are deducted over a period of five or seven years.

There are also several different ways to compute how much of the cost can be depreciated each year. There are three basic methods: straight-line, MACRS, and ACRS. Straight-line depreciation spreads the deductible amount equally over the recovery period. Thus for the power saw that is worth $90.00 and is used 70 percent of the time in a business, the cost basis that can be depreciated is $63.00. This asset has a recovery period of seven years. Spreading the $63.00 over the seven-year period allows you to deduct a total of $9.00 per year as depreciation of the saw. After the first year, the saw will be valued on your books at $54.00. Thus, after seven years, the value of the saw on your books will be zero. It will have been fully depreciated. You will have finally been allowed to fully deduct its cost as a business expense. Of course, if you have fixed asset costs of less than $112,000.00 for the year you put the saw in service, you will be allowed to claim the entire $63.00 deduction that first year. See the glossary for an explanation of MACRS and ACRS depreciations.

Other methods of depreciation have more complicated rules that must be applied. For full details, please refer to a tax preparation manual or consult a tax or accounting professional.

Following are listed various types of property that are depreciable or deductible. Consult this list to determine which of your business purchases may be depreciated and which of them may be written off as an immediately deductible expense. Recall that up to $112,000.00 of depreciable assets may be immediately deductible as a special Section 179 deduction. Of course, also remember that tax laws are always subject to change.

DEDUCTIBLE EXPENSES

Advertising	Legal and professional fees
Bad debts	Maintenance
Bank charges	Office equipment worth less than $100
Books and periodicals	Office furniture worth less than $100
Car and truck expenses:	Office supplies
Gas, repairs, licenses, insurance, maintenance	Pension plans
Commissions to salespersons	Postage
Independent contractor costs	Printing costs
Donations	Property taxes
Dues to professional groups	Rent
Educational expenses	Repairs
Entertainment of clients	Refunds, returns, and allowances
Freight costs	Sales taxes collected
Improvements worth less than $100	Sales taxes paid on purchases
Insurance	Telephone
Interest costs	Tools worth less than $100
Laundry and cleaning	Uniforms
Licenses for business	Utilities
	Wages paid

DEPRECIABLE PROPERTY

Business buildings (not land)	Business machinery
Office furniture worth over $100	Tools worth over $100
Office equipment worth over $100	Vehicles used in business

Fixed Asset Account

Recall that fixed assets are business purchases that are depreciable, unless you elect to deduct fixed asset expenses up to $112,000.00 per year. For recordkeeping purposes, you will prepare a Fixed Asset Account record for each fixed asset that you have if you have acquired more than $112,000.00 in a calendar year. If you have acquired less than $112,000.00 worth in a year, you may put all of your fixed asset records on one Fixed Asset Account record.

To prepare your Fixed Asset Account record, follow these instructions:

1. List the date on which you acquired the property. If the property was formerly personal property, list the date on which you converted it to business property.

2. Then list the property by description. Enter the actual cost of the property. If the property is used, enter the lower amount of the cost of the property or the actual market value of the property. If the property is part business and part personal, enter the value of the business portion of the property.

3. If you will have more than $112,000.00 worth of depreciable business property during the year, you will additionally need to enter information in the next three columns on the record. First, you will need to enter the recovery period for each asset. For most property other than buildings, this will be either five or seven years. Please consult a tax manual or tax professional.

4. You will need to enter the method of depreciation. Again, check a tax manual or tax professional.

5. Finally, you will need to determine the amount of the deduction for the first year (*Hint:* consult a tax manual or tax professional).

6. Once you have set up a method for each fixed asset, each year you will determine the additional deduction and update the balance. You will then use that figure on your business tax return and in the preparation of your Balance Sheet.

Fixed Asset Account

Date	Item	Cost		Years	Method	Annual	Balance	

Tracking Business Debts

Business debts are also referred to as *business liabilities*. However, technically, business liabilities also include the value of the owner's equity in the business. Business debts can be divided into two general categories. First are *current debts*, those that will normally be paid within one year. The second general category is *long-term debts*. These are generally debts that will not be paid off within one year. Current debts for most small businesses consist primarily of accounts payable and taxes that are due during the year. For small businesses, the taxes that are due during a year fall into three main categories: estimated income tax payments, payment of collected sales taxes, and payroll taxes. Since the collection and payment of sales taxes are handled differently in virtually every state, you will need to contact your state's department of revenue or similar body to determine the specific necessary recordkeeping requirements for that business debt. Payroll taxes will be explained in the next chapter and estimated taxes will be dealt with in Chapter 18.

That leaves us only with accounts payable to track as a current debt. You will have only one simple form to use to keep track of this important category. *Accounts payable* are the current bills that your business owes. They may be for equipment or supplies that you have purchased on credit or for items that you have ordered on account. Regardless of the source of the debt, you will need a clear system to record the debt and keep track of how much you still owe on the debt.

Long-term debts are, generally, debts based on business loans for equipment, inventory, business-owned vehicles, or business property. In the accounting system outlined in this book, you will only keep track of the current principal and interest for these debts. For long-term debts of your business, you will fill in the Long-Term Debt Record, that is explained later in this chapter. You will find an Accounts Payable Record on the following form. You will enter any bills or short-term debts that you do not pay immediately on this record. If you pay the bill off upon receipt of the bill, you need not enter the amount on this record. Your records for expenses will take care of the necessary documentation for those particular debts. If your business has many accounts payable that must be tracked, it may be a good idea to prepare an individual Accounts Payable Record for each account.

Accounts Payable Record

Follow these instructions to prepare and fill in this particular form:

1. For those debts that you do not pay off immediately, you will need to record the following information in the left-hand column of the record:

   - The date the debt was incurred
   - To whom you owe the money
   - Payment terms (for instance: due within 30, 60, or 90 days)
   - The amount of the debt

2. In the right-hand column of the Accounts Payable Record, you will record the following information:

   - The date of any payments
   - To whom the payments were made
   - The amount of any payments made

3. By periodically totaling the left- and right-hand columns, you will be able to take a look at the total amount of your unpaid accounts payable. You may wish to do this weekly, monthly, or quarterly. You will also need this figure for your total unpaid accounts payable for the preparation of your Balance Sheet.

4. When you have totaled your accounts payable at the end of your chosen periodic interval, you should start a new record and carry the unpaid accounts over to it. Using this simple record, you will be able to check your accounts payable at a glance and also have enough information available to use in preparing a Balance Sheet for your business.

Accounts Payable Record

Period from: to:

UNPAID ACCOUNTS

Date	Due to	Terms	Amount	
		TOTAL		

PAYMENTS

Date	Paid to	Amount	
	TOTAL		

Total Unpaid Accounts

− Total Payments

= Total Accounts Payable

Long-Term Debt Record

If your business has any outstanding loans that will not be paid off within one year, you will prepare a Long-Term Debt Record for each loan. You will track the principal and interest paid on each long-term debt of your business. This information will enable you to have long-term debt figures for use in preparing your Balance Sheet and interest-paid figures for use in preparing your Profit and Loss Statements. On the following page, you will find a Long-Term Debt Record to be used for this purpose. In order to fill in this record, follow these directions:

1. You will need to enter the following information for each company to whom a loan is outstanding:

    - Company name
    - Address
    - Contact person
    - Phone number
    - Loan account number
    - Loan interest rate
    - Original principal amount of the loan
    - Term of the loan

2. You will need a loan payment book or amortization schedule in order to obtain the necessary information regarding the portions of each of your payments that are principal and interest. As you make a payment, enter the following information:

    - Date of payment
    - Total payment made
    - Amount of principal paid
    - Amount of interest paid
    - Balance due (the previous balance minus principal)

3. Total the balance due after each payment. Using this method of tracking accounts payable will allow you to always have a running total of your long-term liability for each long-term debt.

4. To prepare a Balance Sheet entry for long-term debts, you will simply need to total all of the various account balances for all of your long-term debts.

5. You should also periodically total all of the columns on your Long-Term Debt Record. You will need the totals of the interest paid for your Annual Expense Summaries.

Long-Term Debt Record

Company:
Address:
Contact Person   Phone:
Loan Account #:   Loan Interest Rate:
Original Loan Amount: Term:

Date	Payment		Principal		Interest		Balance	
TOTALS								

Tracking Business Expenses

The expenses of a business are all of the transactions of the business where money is paid out of the business, with one general exception. Money paid out of the business to pay off the principal of a loan is not considered an expense of a business. Because of the tax deductibility of the cost of most business expenses, it is crucial for a business to keep careful records of what has been spent to operate the business. But even beyond the need for detailed expense records for tax purposes, a small business needs a clear system that will allow a quick examination of where money is being spent. The tracking of business expenses will allow you to quickly see where your money is flowing.

In order to track your business expenses, you will use a Weekly Expense Record and a Monthly Expense Summary. You may also need to use a number of additional specialized forms if your business needs dictate their use. There is also an Annual Expense Summary for totaling your expense payments.

On your Weekly Expense Record, you will record all of your business expenses in chronological order. The expense transactions will generally come from three main sources: your business bank account check register, your monthly business credit card statements, and your petty cash register. You will transfer all of the expenses from these three sources to the main expense record. This will provide you with a central listing of all of the expenditures for your business.

From this record, you will transfer your expenses to a Monthly Expense Summary. On the Monthly Expense Summary, you will enter a line for each expense type that you have listed on your business Chart of Accounts. You will then go through your Weekly Expense Records for each month and total the expenses for each account. You will enter this total in the column for the specific type of expense.

Finally, on a monthly basis, you will transfer the totals for your various expense categories to the Annual Expense Summary record. On this record, you collect and record the total monthly expenses. With these figures, you will be able to easily total your expense amounts to ascertain your quarterly and annual expenses.

By recording your business expenses in this manner, you should have little difficulty being able to keep track of the money flowing out of your business on a daily, weekly, monthly, quarterly, and annual basis. You will have all of the information that you will need to easily provide the necessary expenditure figures for preparing a Profit and Loss Statement. Remember that you must tailor the forms to fit your particular business.

Weekly Expense Record

1. Fill in the date or dates that the form will cover where indicated at the top.

2. Beginning with your bank account check register, transfer the following information from the register to the Weekly Expense Record:

   - The date of the transaction
   - The check number
   - To whom the amount was paid
   - The expense account number (from your Chart of Accounts)
   - The amount of the transaction

3. Next, transfer the following information from your records that you have kept regarding your petty cash to the expense record:

   - The date of the transaction
   - In the "Check #" column, put "PC" indicating it was a petty cash expense
   - To whom the amount was paid
   - The expense account number (off your Chart of Accounts)
   - The amount of the transaction
   - *Note*: Do not list the checks that you make out to "Petty Cash" as an expense

4. For credit card transactions, follow these rules:

   - Do not list payment to a credit card company as an expense
   - List the monthly amount on the credit card bill for interest as an interest expense
   - Individually, list each business purchase on the credit card as a separate expense item, assigning an account number to each separate business charge. Make a notation for the date, to whom the expense was paid, and the amount. In the "Check #" column, provide the type of credit card, for example, "V" for Visa
   - Do not list any personal charge items as business expenses
   - If a charged item is used partially for business and partially for personal reasons, list only that portion that is used for business reasons as a business expense

5. At the end of the period, total the Amount column. You will use this weekly total expense amount to cross-check your later calculations.

6. It is a good idea to keep all of your various business expense receipts for at least three years after the tax period to which they relate. You may wish to buy envelopes for each weekly period, label each appropriately, and file your weekly business expense receipts in them. This will make it easy to find each specific receipt, if necessary.

Weekly Expense Record

Week of:

Date	Check #	To Whom Paid	Account #	Amount	
				TOTALS	

Monthly Expense Summary

Using this record, you will compile and transfer the total expense amount for each expense category. In this way, you will be able to keep a monthly total of all of the expenses, broken down by category of expense. To fill in this form, do the following:

1. Indicate the month that the Monthly Expense Summary will cover where shown.

2. In the first column on the left-hand side, list all of your expense account names and numbers from your business Chart of Accounts.

3. In the next column, using your Weekly Expense Records, transfer the amounts for each expense. If you have more than four expense amounts for any account, use a second Monthly Expense Summary to record additional amounts.

4. In the Total column, list the total expenses in each category for the month.

5. At the bottom of the page, total the amount for all of the categories for the month. Don't forget to include any amounts from any additional records in your totals.

6. To double-check your transfers and your calculations, total all of your Weekly Expense Record total amounts. This figure should equal your Monthly Expense Summary total for that month. If there is a discrepancy, check each of your figures until you discover the error.

Monthly Expense Summary

Month of:

Account Name/#	Amount		Amount		Amount		Amount		Total	
								TOTAL		

Annual Expense Summary

1. Fill in the year. Fill in your account numbers from your Chart of Accounts across the top row. If you have more than nine expense accounts, use a second and third page, if necessary.

2. On a monthly basis, carry the totals from all of the rows on your Monthly Expense Summaries to the appropriate column of the Annual Expense Summary.

3. At the end of each quarter, total all of the monthly entries to arrive at your quarterly totals for each category.

4. To double-check your monthly calculations, total your categories across each month and put this total in the final column. Compare this total with the total on your Monthly Expense Records. If there is a discrepancy, check each of your figures until you discover the error. Don't forget to include your extra records if you have more than nine expense accounts to list.

5. To double-check your quarterly calculations, total your monthly totals in the final quarterly column. This figure should equal the total of the quarterly category totals across the quarterly row. If there is a discrepancy, check each of your figures until you discover the error.

6. Finally, total each of your quarterly amounts to arrive at the annual totals. To cross-check your calculations, total the quarterly totals in the final column. This figure should equal the total for all of the annual totals in each category across the Annual Total row. If there is a discrepancy, check each of your figures until you discover the error.

Annual Expense Summary

Year of:

Account # ⇨												Total
January												
February												
March												
1st Quarter												
April												
May												
June												
2nd Quarter												
July												
August												
September												
3rd Quarter												
October												
November												
December												
4th Quarter												
Annual TOTAL												

Tracking Business Income

The careful tracking of your business income is one of the most important accounting activities you will perform. It is essential for your business that you know intimately where your income comes from. Failure to accurately track income and cash is one of the most frequent causes of business failure. You must have in place a clear and easily understood system to track your business income. There are three separate features of tracking business income that must be incorporated into your accounting system. You will need a system in place to handle cash, a system to track all of your sales and service income, and a system to handle credit sales.

The first system you will need is a clear method for handling cash on a weekly basis. This is true no matter how large or small your business may be and regardless of how much or how little cash is actually handled. You must have a clear record of how much cash is on hand and how much cash is taken in during a particular time period. You will also need to have a method to tally this cash flow on a monthly basis. For these purposes, two forms are provided: a Weekly Cash Report and a Monthly Cash Report Summary.

The second feature of your business income tracking system should be a method to track your actual income from sales or services. This differs from your cash tracking. With these records you will track taxable and nontaxable income whether the income is in the form of cash, check, credit card payment, or payment on an account. Please note that when *nontaxable income* is referred to, it means only that income which is not subject to any state or local sales tax (generally, this will be income from the performance of a service). These records will also track your intake of sales taxes, if applicable. For this segment of your income tracking, you will have a Weekly Income Record. You will also track your income on income summaries that will provide you with monthly, quarterly, and annual reports of your taxable income, nontaxable income, and sales tax collection.

The third feature of your business income tracking consists of a method to track and bill credit sales. With this portion of income tracking, you will list and track all of your sales to customers that are made on account or on credit. The accounts that owe you money are referred to as your *accounts receivable*. These are the accounts from whom you hope to receive payment. The tracking of these credit sales will take place on a Monthly Credit Sales Record. You will also use a Credit Sales Aging Report to see how your customers are doing over time. The actual billing of these credit sales will require you to prepare and incorporate an invoice, statement, and past due statement, all of which are explained at the end of this chapter.

Tracking Cash

Most businesses will have to handle cash in some form. Here we are not talking about the use of petty cash. *Petty cash* is the cash that a business has on hand for the payment of minor expenses that may crop up and for which the use of a business check is not convenient. The cash handling discussed in this section is the daily handling of cash used to take money in from customers or clients and the use of a cash drawer or some equivalent. You must have some method to accurately account for the cash used in your business in this regard.

Weekly Cash Report

1. You must decide how much cash you will need to begin each period with sufficient cash to meet your needs and make change for cash sales. Usually $100.00 should be sufficient for most needs. Choose a figure and begin each period with that amount in your cash drawer. Excess cash that has been collected should be deposited in your business bank account. Each period, fill in the date and the cash on hand on your Weekly Cash Report.

2. As you take in cash and checks throughout the period, record each item of cash taken in, checks taken in, and any instances of cash paid out. *Cash out* does not mean change that has been made, but rather cash paid out for business purposes (for example, a refund).

3. Your business may have so much daily cash flow that it will be burdensome to record each item of cash flow on your sheet. In that case, you will need a cash register of some type. Simply total the cash register at the end of the day and record the total cash in, checks in, and cash out in the appropriate places on the Weekly Cash Report.

4. At the end of each period, total your Cash In and Checks In. Add these two amounts to your Cash on Hand at the beginning of the period. This equals your Total Receipts for the period. Subtract any Cash Out from this amount for the Balance on Hand. Make a bank deposit for all of the checks and for all of the cash in excess of the amount that you will need to begin the next period. Subtract the Bank Deposit from the Balance. This figure should equal your actual cash on hand at the end of the period.

5. In the space for deposits, note the following: a deposit number, if applicable; the date of the deposit; the deposit amount; and the name and signature of the person who made the deposit. Don't forget to also record your deposit in your business bank account check register.

Weekly Cash Report

Week of: _____   Cash on Hand Beginning: _____

Week	CASH IN Name	Amount		CHECKS IN Name	Amount		CASH OUT Name	Amount	
1									
2									
3									
4									
5									
6									
7									
8									
9									
10									
11									
12									
TOTAL									

Deposit #:	
Deposit Date:	
Deposit Amount:	
Deposited by:	
Signed:	

Total Cash in

+ Total Checks in

+ Cash on Hand Beginning

= Total Receipts

− Total Cash Out

= Balance on Hand

− Bank Deposit

= Cash on Hand Ending

Monthly Cash Report Summary

This form will be used to keep a monthly record of your Weekly Cash Reports. It serves as a monthly listing of your cash flow and of your business bank account deposits. You will, of course, also record your bank deposits in your business bank account check register. To use this form, follow these instructions:

1. On a weekly basis, collect your Weekly Cash Reports. From each Report, record the following information on the monthly summary:

   - Cash on hand at the beginning of the period
   - Cash taken in
   - Checks taken in
   - Cash paid out
   - The amount of the weekly bank deposit
   - Cash on hand at the end of the period and after the bank deposit

2. You can total the Deposit column as a cross-check against your bank account check register record of deposits.

Monthly Cash Report Summary

Month:

Date	On Hand		Cash in		Checks in		Cash out		Deposit		On Hand	
1												
2												
3												
4												
5												
6												
7												
8												
9												
10												
11												
12												
13												
14												
15												
16												
17												
18												
19												
20												
21												
22												
23												
24												
25												
26												
27												
28												
29												
30												
31												

Tracking Income

The second feature of your business income tracking system should be a method to keep track of your actual income. This portion of the system will provide you with a list of all taxable and nontaxable income and of any sales taxes collected, if applicable. For sales tax information, please contact your state's sales tax revenue collection agency. If your state has a sales tax on the product or service that you provide, you will need accurate records to determine your total taxable and nontaxable income and the amount of sales tax that is due. For this purpose and for the purpose of tracking all of your income for your own business analysis, you should prepare a Weekly Income Record. The information from these reports will then be used to prepare Monthly and Annual Income Summaries.

Weekly Income Record

1. You will need to contact your state taxing agency for information on how to determine if a sale or the provision of a service is taxable or nontaxable. You will also need to determine the appropriate rates for sales tax collection.

2. For each item, record the following information:

   - Invoice number
   - Taxable income amount
   - Sales tax amount
   - Nontaxable income amount
   - Total income (Taxable, sales tax, and nontaxable amounts combined)

3. On a weekly basis, total the amounts in each column to determine the totals for the particular time period. These figures will be carried over to the Monthly and Annual Income Summaries, that will be explained next.

Weekly Income Record

Week of:

Invoice #	Taxable Income		Sales Tax		Nontaxable Income		Total Income	
Weekly TOTAL								

Monthly Income Summary

1. Fill in the appropriate month.

2. Using your Weekly Income Records, record the following information for each week:

    -   Invoice number
    -   Total taxable income amount
    -   Total sales tax amount
    -   Total nontaxable income amount
    -   Total income (taxable, sales tax, and nontaxable amounts combined)

3. On a monthly basis, total the amounts in each column to determine the totals for the particular month. These figures will be carried over to the Annual Income Summary, that will be explained next.

Monthly Income Summary

Month of:

Invoice #	Taxable Income		Sales Tax		Nontaxable Income		Total Income	
Monthly TOTAL								

Annual Income Summary

1. On a monthly basis, carry the totals from all of the columns on your Monthly Income Summary to the appropriate columns of the Annual Income Summary.

2. At the end of each quarter, total all of the monthly entries to arrive at your quarterly totals for each category.

3. To double-check your monthly calculations, total your categories across each month and put this total in the final column. Compare this total with the total on your Monthly Income Summaries. If there is a discrepancy, check each of your figures until you discover the error.

4. To double-check your quarterly calculations, total your monthly totals in the final column. This figure should equal the total of the quarterly category totals across the quarterly row. If there is a discrepancy, check each of your figures until you discover the error.

5. Finally, total your quarterly amounts to arrive at the annual totals. To cross-check your calculations, total the quarterly totals in the final column. This figure should equal the total for all of the annual totals across the Annual Total row. If there is a discrepancy, check each of your figures until you discover the error.

Annual Income Summary

Year of: _____

Date	Taxable Income		Sales Tax		Nontaxable Income		Total Income	
January								
February								
March								
1st Quarter								
April								
May								
June								
2nd Quarter								
July								
August								
September								
3rd Quarter								
October								
November								
December								
4th Quarter								
Annual TOTAL								

Tracking Credit Sales

The final component of your business income tracking system will be a logical method to track your credit sales. You will use a Monthly Credit Sales Record to track the actual sales on credit, and Credit Sales Aging Report to track the payment on these sales. In addition, several forms are provided for the billing of these credit sales: an Invoice, Statement, Past Due Statement, and Credit Memo.

Monthly Credit Sales Record

1. Fill in the appropriate date or time period.

2. For each sale that is made on credit, fill in the following information from the customer Invoice (see Invoice instructions later in this chapter):

   - Invoice number
   - Date of the sale
   - Customer name
   - Total sale amount

3. The final column is for recording the date that the credit sale has been paid in full.

4. The information from your Monthly Credit Sales Record will also be used to prepare your Credit Sales Aging Report on a monthly basis.

Monthly Credit Sales Record

Month of:

Invoice #	Sale Date	Customer	Sale Total		Date Paid

Credit Sales Aging Report

This report is used to track the current status of your credit sales or accounts receivables. Through the use of this form you will be able to track whether or not the people or companies that owe you money are falling behind on their payments. With this information, you will be able to determine how to handle these accounts: sending past due notices, halting sales to them, turning them over to a collection agency, etc. To use this form, do the following:

1. Decide on which day of the month you would like to perform your credit sales aging calculations.

2. For each credit sales account, enter the name of the account from your Monthly Credit Sales Record.

3. In the "Total" column, enter the total current amount that is owed to you. If this figure is based on credit sales during the current month, enter this figure again in the "Current" column. Do this for each credit account.

4. Each month you will prepare a new Credit Sales Aging Report on a new sheet. On the same date in the next month, determine how much of the originally owed balance has been paid off. Enter the amount of the unpaid balance from the previous month in the "30–60 days" column. Enter any new credit sales for the month under the "Current" column. The figure in the "Total" column should be the total of all of the columns to the right of the "Total" column.

5. Each month, determine how much was paid on the account, deduct that amount from the oldest amount due, and shift the amounts due over one column to the right. Add any new credit sales to the "Current" column and put the total of the amounts in the "Total" column.

6. After entering the information for each month, total each of the columns across the "Total" line at the bottom of the report. The "Total" column is 100 percent of the amount due. Calculate the percentage for each of the other columns to determine how much of your accounts receivable are 30, 60, 90, or more than 90 days overdue.

Credit Sales Aging Report

Account Name	Total		Current		30–60 Days		60–90 Days		90 Days +	
TOTALS										
PERCENT	100%									

Invoices and Statements

For credit sales, you will need to provide each customer with a current Invoice. You will also need to send a Statement if the balance is not paid within the first 30 days. In addition, you will need to send a Past Due Statement if the balance becomes overdue. Finally, a Credit Memo form is provided to record instances when a customer is given credit for a returned item. You will need to produce two copies of each of these forms: one for your records and one for the customer.

Invoice

The invoice is your key credit sales document. To prepare and track invoices, follow these directions:

1. Make a number of copies of the Invoice form. You can insert your business card in the upper-left corner before copying. Number each form consecutively. Make a photocopy of the form when the form is sent out to the customer or print two copies if using the Forms-on-CD.

2. For each order, fill in the following information:

   - Date
   - Invoice number
   - Name and address of who will be billed for the order
   - Name and address where the order will be shipped
   - Item number of the product or service sold
   - Quantity ordered
   - Description of the item
   - Per unit price of the item
   - Total amount billed (quantity times per unit price)

3. Subtotal all of the items where shown. Add any sales taxes and shipping costs and total the balance.

4. Record the pertinent information from the Invoice on the Monthly Credit Sales Record.

5. Record the pertinent information from the Invoice on the Monthly Income Summary.

6. Send one copy of the Invoice to the customer with the order and file the other copy in a file for your invoices.

Invoice

Date:

Invoice No.:

Bill to:	Ship to:

Item #	Qty.	Description	Price Each		Total	

	Subtotal	
	Tax	
	Shipping	
	BALANCE	

Statement and Past Due Statement

Statements are used to send your credit customers a notice of the amount that is currently due. Statements are generally sent at 30-day intervals, beginning either 30 days after the Invoice is sent, at the beginning of the next month, or at the next cycle for sending statements. Follow these instructions for preparing your statements:

1. You should decide on a statement billing cycle. Generally, this is a specific date each month (for example: the 1st, 10th, or 15th of each month).

2. Make a copy of the Statement form using your business card in the upper-left corner. Fill in the date and the account name and address in the "Account" box.

3. In the body of the form, enter information from any Invoice that is still unpaid as of the date you are completing the Statement. You should enter the following items for each unpaid Invoice:

    *   The date of the Invoice
    *   A description of the Invoice (including Invoice number)
    *   Any payments received since the last statement or since the sale
    *   The amount still owed on that Invoice

4. When all of the invoice information for all the customer's invoices has been entered, total the "Amount Due" column and enter the balance at the bottom. The information on the Statement can then be used to enter information on your Credit Sales Aging Report.

5. The Past Due Statement is simply a version of the basic Statement that includes a notice that the account is past due. This Past Due Statement should be sent when the account becomes overdue. Fill it out in the same manner used for statements.

Statement

Date:

Account:

Date	Description	Payment		Amount Due	

Please pay this BALANCE

Past Due Statement

Date:

Account:

This account is now past due. Please pay upon receipt to avoid collection costs

Date	Description	Payment	Amount Due

Please pay this BALANCE

Credit Memo

The final form for tracking your business income is the Credit Memo. This form is used to provide you and your customer with a written record of any credit given for goods that have been returned by the customer. You will need to set a policy regarding when such credit will be given (for example, for only a certain time period after the sale, for defects, or for other limitations). To use the Credit Memo, follow these instructions:

1. Fill in the date, the number of the original Invoice, and the customer's name and address in the "Credit" box.

2. Fill in the following information in the body of the Credit Memo:

   - Item number of item returned
   - Quantity of items returned
   - Description of item returned
   - Per unit price of item returned
   - Total amount of credit (quantity x per unit price)

3. Subtotal the credit for all items. Add any appropriate sales tax credit and total those amounts for the credit. This is the amount that will be credited or refunded to the customer.

4. In the lower left corner of the form, indicate the reason for the return, any necessary approval, and the date of the approval.

5. Handle the Credit Memo like a negative Invoice. Record the amount of credit as a negative on the Weekly Income Record.

6. Record the pertinent information from the Credit Memo as a negative amount on the appropriate Monthly Credit Sales Record, if the Credit Memo applies to a previous sale on credit that was recorded on a Monthly Credit Sales Record.

Credit Memo

Date:

Invoice #:

Credit to:

GOODS RETURNED

Item #	Qty.	Description	Price Each		Total	

Reason for return: Subtotal

Approved by: Tax

Date: CREDIT

CHAPTER 17
Business Payroll

One of the most difficult and complex accounting functions that small businesses face is their payroll. Because of the various state and Federal taxes that must be applied and the myriad government forms that must be prepared, the handling of a business payroll often causes accounting nightmares. Even if there is only one employee, there is a potential for problems.

First, let's examine the basics. If your business is a corporation, all pay must be handled as payroll, even if you are the only employee. The corporation is a separate entity and the corporation itself will be the employer. You and any other people that you hire will be the employees. A business payroll entails a great deal of paperwork and has numerous government tax filing deadlines. You will be required to make payroll tax deposits, file various quarterly payroll tax returns, and make additional end-of-the-year reports.

Initially, you must take certain steps to set up your payroll and official status as an employer. The following information contains the instructions only for meeting Federal requirements. Please check with your particular state and local governments for information regarding any additional payroll tax, state unemployment insurance, or workers' compensation requirements.

Setting up Your Payroll

1. The first step in becoming an employer is to file Internal Revenue Service Form SS-4: *Application for Employer Identification Number*. This will officially register your business with the Federal government as an employer. This form and instructions are included on the Forms-on-CD.

2. Next, each employee must fill in an IRS Form W-4: *Employee's Withholding Allowance Certificate*. This will provide you with the necessary information regarding withholding allowances to enable you to prepare your payroll.

3. You must then determine the gross salary or wage that each employee will earn. For each employee, complete an Employee Payroll Record and prepare a Quarterly Payroll Time Sheet as explained later in this chapter.

4. You will then need to consult the tables in IRS Circular E: *Employer's Tax Guide.* From the tables in this publication, you will be able to determine the proper deductions for each employee for each pay period. If your employees are paid on an hourly basis and the number of hours worked is different each pay period, you will have to perform these calculations for each pay period.

5. Before you pay your employee, you should open a separate business bank account for handling your business payroll tax deductions and payments. This will allow you to immediately deposit all taxes due into this separate account and help prevent the lack of sufficient money available when the taxes are due.

6. Next you will pay your employee and record the deduction information on the Employee Payroll Record.

7. When you have completed paying all of your employees for the pay period, you will write a separate check for the total amount of all of your employees' deductions and any employer's share of taxes. You will then deposit this check into your business payroll tax bank account that you set up following the instructions above.

8. At the end of every month, you will need to transfer the information regarding employee deductions to your Payroll Depository Record and Annual Payroll Summary. Copies of these forms and instructions are included later in this chapter. You will then calculate your employer share of Social Security and Medicare taxes. Each month (or quarter if your tax liability is less than $2,500.00 per quarter), you will need to deposit the correct amount of taxes due to the Federal government. This is done either by making a monthly payment to your bank for the taxes due using IRS Form 8109: *Federal Tax Deposit Coupon* or by making the payment on a quarterly basis when you file IRS Form 941: *Employer's Quarterly Federal Tax Return.* Copies of these forms are contained on the Forms-on-CD.

9. On a quarterly or annual basis, you will also need to make a tax payment for Federal Unemployment Tax, using IRS Form 940: *Employer's Annual Federal Unemployment (FUTA) Tax Return.* This tax is solely the responsibility of the employer and is not deducted from the employee's pay. Also on a quarterly basis, you will need to file IRS Form 941: *Employer's Quarterly Federal Tax Return.* If you have made monthly deposits of your taxes due, there will be no quarterly taxes to pay, but you will still need to file these forms quarterly.

10. Finally, to complete your payroll, at the end of the year you must do the following:

- Prepare IRS Form W-2: *Wage and Tax Statement* for each employee
- File IRS Form W-3: *Transmittal of Wage and Tax Statements*

Remember that your state and local tax authorities will generally have additional requirements and taxes that will need to be paid. In many jurisdictions, these requirements are tailored after the Federal requirements and the procedures and due dates are similar.

Quarterly Payroll Time Sheet

On the following page is a Quarterly Payroll Time Sheet. If your employees are paid an hourly wage, you will prepare a sheet like this for each employee for each quarter during the year. On this sheet you will keep track of the following information:

- Number of hours worked (daily, weekly, and quarterly)
- Number of regular and overtime hours worked

The information from this Quarterly Payroll Time Sheet will be transferred to your individual Employee Payroll Record in order to calculate the employee's paycheck amounts. This is explained following the Quarterly Payroll Time Sheet.

Quarterly Payroll Time Sheet

Employee:

Week of	Sun	Mon	Tue	Wed	Thu	Fri	Sat	Reg	OT	Total
Quarterly TOTAL										

Employee Payroll Record

You will use this form to track each employee's payroll information.

1. For each employee, fill in the following information at the top of the form:

   - Name and address of employee
   - Employee's Social Security number
   - Number of exemptions claimed by employee on Form W-4
   - Regular and overtime wage rates
   - Pay period (ie., weekly, biweekly, monthly, etc.)
   - Date check is written
   - Payroll check number

2. For each pay period, fill in the number of regular and overtime ("OT") hours worked by the employee from his or her Quarterly Payroll Time Sheet. Multiply this amount by the employee's wage rate to determine the *gross pay*. For example: 40 hours at the regular wage of $8.00/hour = $320.00; plus five hours at the overtime wage rate of $12.00/hour = $60.00. Gross pay for the period is $320.00 + $60.00 = $380.00.

3. Determine the Federal withholding tax deduction for the pay amount by consulting the withholding tax tables in IRS Circular E: *Employer's Tax Guide*. Enter this figure on the form in the "Fed. W/H" column.

4. Determine the employee's share of Social Security and Medicare deductions. As of 2000, the employee's Social Security share rate is 6.2 percent and the employee's Medicare share rate is 1.45 percent. Multiply these rates times the employee's gross wages and enter the figures in the appropriate places; the "S/S Ded." and "Medic. Ded." columns. For example: for $380.00, the Social Security deduction would be $380.00 x .062 = $23.56 and the Medicare deduction would be $380.00 x .0145 = $5.51.

5. Determine any state taxes and enter in the appropriate column.

6. Subtract all of the deductions from the employee's gross wages to determine the employee's *net pay*. Enter this figure in the final column and prepare the employee's paycheck using the deduction information from this sheet. Also prepare a check to your payroll tax bank account for a total of the Federal withholding amount and two times the Social Security and Medicare amounts. This includes your employer share of these taxes. The employer's share of Social Security and Medicare taxes is equal to the employee's share.

Employee Payroll Record

Employee: Social Security #:

Address: Number of Exemptions:

                                  Rate of Pay: Overtime Rate:

                                  Pay Period:

Date	Check #	Pay Period	Reg. Hours	OT Hours	Gross Pay	Fed. W/H	S/S Ded.	Medic. Ded.	State Taxes	Net Pay
Pay Period TOTAL										

Payroll Depository Record

You will be required to deposit taxes with the IRS on a monthly or quarterly basis (unless your total employment taxes totaled more than $50,000.00 for the previous year, in which case you should obviously consult an accountant). If your employment taxes total less than $2,500.00 per quarter, you may pay your payroll tax liability when you quarterly file your Federal Form 941: *Employer's Quarterly Federal Tax Return*. If your payroll tax liability is more than $2,500.00 per quarter, you must deposit your payroll taxes on a monthly basis with a bank using IRS Form 8109: *Federal Tax Deposit Coupon*. Copies of these two Federal forms are contained on the Forms-on-CD. To track your payroll tax liability, use the Payroll Depository Record which follows these instructions:

1. On a monthly basis, total each column on all of your Employee Payroll Records. This will give you a figure for each employee's Federal withholding, Social Security, and Medicare taxes for the month.

2. Total all of the Federal withholding taxes for all employees for the month and enter this figure in the appropriate column on the Payroll Depository Record.

3. Total Social Security and Medicare taxes for all of your employees for the entire month and enter this figure in the appropriate columns on the Payroll Depository Record. Note that "SS/EE" refers to Social Security/Employee's Share and that "MC/EE" refers to Medicare/Employee's Share.

4. Enter identical amounts in the SS/ER and MC/ER columns as you have entered in the SS/EE and MC/EE columns. "ER" refers to the employer's share. The employer's share of Social Security and Medicare is the same as the employee's share, but is not deducted from the employee's pay.

5. Total all of the deductions for the month. This is the amount of your total monthly Federal payroll tax liability. If necessary, write a check to your local bank for this amount and deposit it using IRS Form 8109: *Federal Tax Deposit Coupon*.

6. If you must file only quarterly, total all three of your monthly amounts on a quarterly basis and pay this amount when you file your IRS Form 941: *Employer's Quarterly Federal Tax Return*. On a yearly basis, total all of the quarterly columns to arrive at your total annual Federal payroll tax liability.

Payroll Depository Record

Month	Fed. W/H		SS/EE		SS/ER		MC/EE		MC/ER		Total	
January												
February												
March												
1st Quarter												

1st Quarter Total Number of Employees: Total Wages Paid:

Month	Fed. W/H		SS/EE		SS/ER		MC/EE		MC/ER		Total	
April												
May												
June												
2nd Quarter												

2nd Quarter Total Number of Employees: Total Wages Paid:

Month	Fed. W/H		SS/EE		SS/ER		MC/EE		MC/ER		Total	
July												
August												
September												
3rd Quarter												

3rd Quarter Total Number of Employees: Total Wages Paid:

Month	Fed. W/H		SS/EE		SS/ER		MC/EE		MC/ER		Total	
October												
November												
December												
4th Quarter												

4th Quarter Total Number of Employees: Total Wages Paid:

Yearly TOTAL												

Yearly Total Number of Employees: Total Wages Paid:

Annual Payroll Summary

The final payroll form is used to total all of the payroll amounts for all employees on a monthly, quarterly, and annual basis. Much of the information on this form is similar to the information that you compiled for the Payroll Depository Record. However, the purpose of this form is to provide you with a record of all of your payroll costs, including the payroll deduction costs. This form will be useful for both tax and planning purposes as you examine your business profitability on a quarterly and annual basis. Follow these directions to prepare this form:

1. For each month, total all of your employees' gross and net pay amounts from their individual Employee Payroll Records and transfer these totals to this form.

2. For each month, transfer the amounts for Federal withholding from the Payroll Depository Record to this form.

3. For each month, total both columns on your Payroll Depository Record for SS/EE ("Social Security/Employee") and SS/ER ("Social Security/Employer") and transfer this total to the "S/S Taxes" column on this summary. Total the MC/EE ("Medicare/Employee") and MC/ER ("Medicare/Employer") columns also and enter the total in the "Medicare Taxes" column on this form.

4. On a quarterly basis, total the columns to determine your quarterly payroll costs. Annually, total the quarterly amounts to determine your annual costs.

Annual Payroll Summary

	Gross Pay	Federal W/H	S/S Taxes	Medicare Taxes	State Taxes	Net Pay
January						
February						
March						
1st Quarter Total						
April						
May						
June						
2nd Quarter Total						
July						
August						
September						
3rd Quarter Total						
October						
November						
December						
4th Quarter Total						
Yearly TOTAL						

Payroll Checklist

☐ File IRS Form SS-4: *Application for Employer Identification Number* and obtain Federal Employer Identification Number (FEIN)

☐ Obtain IRS Form W-4: *Employee's Withholding Allowance Certificate* for each employee

☐ Set up Quarterly Payroll Time Sheets and Employee Payroll Records for employees

☐ Open separate business payroll tax bank account

☐ Consult IRS Circular E: *Employer's Tax Guide* and use tables to determine withholding tax amounts

☐ Obtain information on any applicable state or local taxes

☐ List Federal withholding, Social Security, Medicare, and any state or local deductions on Employee Payroll Record

☐ Pay employees and deposit appropriate taxes in payroll tax bank account

☐ Fill in Payroll Depository Record and Annual Payroll Summary

☐ Pay payroll taxes

   ☐ Monthly, using IRS Form 8109: *Federal Tax Deposit Coupon*, if your payroll tax liability is more than $2,500 per quarter

   ☐ Quarterly, using IRS Form 941: *Employer's Quarterly Federal Tax Return*, if your payroll tax liability is less than $2,500 per quarter

   ☐ Annually, file IRS Form 940: *Employer's Annual Federal Unemployment (FUTA) Tax Return*

☐ Annually, prepare and file IRS Form W-2: *Wage and Tax Statement* and IRS Form W-3: *Transmittal of Wage and Tax Statement* for each employee

CHAPTER 18

Taxation of Limited Liability Company

There may be certain tax advantages to the operation of a business as a limited liability company. There are three methods by which a limited liability company can be taxed at the Federal level. The choice of method is, for the most part, up to the member(s) of the company. The checklists provided in this chapter are separated into these three general divisions.

Taxation As a Partnership

All limited liability companies that have more than one member will be taxed at the Federal level as a partnership, *unless* the members elect otherwise. The partnership taxation is automatic and does not require any election or filing of any form for the election. If, however, a limited liability company elects to be taxed as a regular corporation, the members must vote to make this election and they must file Internal Revenue Service Form 8832: *Entity Classification Election.* If corporate taxation is elected, see below under "Taxation As a Corporation."

If the limited liability company is to be taxed as a partnership, the profits generated by the limited liability company may be distributed directly to the members without incurring any "double" tax liability, as is the case with the distribution of corporate profits in the form of dividends to the shareholders. Income from a limited liability company is taxed at the personal income tax rate of each individual member. Note, however, that depending on the individual tax situation of each member, this aspect could prove to be a disadvantage. The losses of a limited liability company are also distributed directly to each member at the end of each fiscal year and may be written off as deductions by each individual member. Tax credits are also handled in a similar fashion. A list of necessary tax forms for limited liability companies being taxed as partnerships is included at the end of this chapter.

Taxation As a Corporation

All limited liability companies, whether they have only one member or many, may elect to be taxed at the Federal level as a corporation. This corporate taxation is not automatic and requires the filing of IRS Form 8832: *Entity Classification Election.* The company should complete this form, checking the box stating "Initial classification by a newly-formed entity (or change in current classification of an existing entity to take effect on January 1, 1997)." Under "Form of Entity" on this form, the limited liability company should check the box in front of the statement: "A domestic eligible entity electing to be classified as an association taxable as a corporation." This will cause the limited liability company to be taxed as a corporation.

If the limited liability company is to be taxed as a corporation, the profits generated by the limited liability company will not pass through directly to the member, as with taxation of sole proprietorships or partnerships. Indeed, taxation of corporations opens the company up to "double" tax liability, in that any corporate profits are first taxed at the corporate level, and then the distribution of corporate profits in the form of dividends to the shareholders (or members) is taxed at the individual level at the personal income tax rates of the members. Note, however, that depending on the individual tax situation of the member, this aspect could prove to be an advantage. For a limited liability company that elects to be taxed as a corporation, the business losses are also not distributed directly to the member as individual deductions, but rather serve as deductions only for the company against company income. Tax credits are also handled in a similar fashion. A list of necessary tax forms for limited liability companies being taxed as corporations is included at the end of this chapter.

Taxation As a Sole Proprietorship

All limited liability companies that have only one member will be taxed at the Federal level as a sole proprietorship, *unless* the sole member elects otherwise. The sole proprietorship taxation requires the filing of IRS Form 8832: *Entity Classification Election*. The single-member company should complete this form, checking the box stating "Initial classification by a newly-formed entity (or change in current classification of an existing entity to take effect on January 1, 1997)." Under "Form of Entity" on this form, the single-member limited liability company should check the box in front of the statement: "A domestic eligible entity with a single owner electing to be disregarded as a separate entity." This will cause the single-member limited liability company to be taxed as a sole proprietorship. If, however, a single-member limited liability company elects to be taxed as a regular corporation, the member must also file IRS Form 8832: *Entity Classification Election*. If corporate taxation is elected, see above under "Taxation As a Corporation."

If the limited liability company is to be taxed as a sole proprietorship, the profits generated by the limited liability company pass through directly to the sole member without incurring any "double" tax liability, as is the case with the distribution of corporate profits in the form of dividends to the shareholders. Income from a limited liability company is taxed at the personal income tax rate of the sole member. Note, however, that depending on the individual tax situation of the member, this aspect could prove to be a disadvantage. The losses of a limited liability company are also distributed directly to the member as individual deductions. Tax credits are also handled in a similar fashion. A list of necessary tax forms for limited liability companies being taxed as sole proprietorships is included at the end of this chapter.

For a detailed understanding of the individual tax consequences of operating your business as a limited liability company, a competent tax professional should be consulted. The Federal tax forms that are mentioned in this chapter are contained on the Forms-on-CD. Check with the Forms-on-CD listing that follows the Table of Contents. A brief study of the tax forms will provide you with an overview of the method by which limited liability companies are taxed. The financial records that you will compile using the forms in this book and Forms-on-CD will make your tax preparation much easier, whether it is handled by you or by a tax professional. A basic comprehension of the information required on Federal tax forms will help you understand why certain financial records are necessary. Understanding tax reporting will also assist you as you decide how to organize your business financial records.

Various checklists of tax forms are provided that detail which IRS forms may be necessary for each method of taxation of limited liability companies. In addition, various schedules of tax filing are also provided to assist you in keeping your tax reporting timely.

Limited Liability Company Tax Forms Checklist

Taxed As a Partnership

☐ IRS Form 1040: *U.S. Individual Income Tax Return* must be filed by all members. Do not use IRS Form 1040A or IRS Form 1040EZ: *Income Tax Return for Single and Joint Filers With No Dependents*

☐ IRS Form 1065: *U.S. Return of Partnership Income* must be completed by all limited liability companies which are taxed as partnerships

☐ IRS Schedule K-1 (Form 1065): *Partner's Share of Income, Credits, Deductions, etc.* must be filed by all members

☐ IRS Form 1040-SS: *U.S. Self-Employment Tax Return.* Required for any member who shows $400+ income from his or her business on Schedule K-1

☐ IRS Form 1040-ES: *Estimated Tax for Individuals* must be used by all members who expect to make a profit requiring estimated taxes

☐ IRS Form SS-4: *Application for Employer Identification Number* must be filed by all companies that will hire one or more employees

☐ IRS Form W-2: *Wage and Tax Statement* must be filed by all companies that have one or more employees

☐ IRS Form W-3: *Transmittal of Wage and Tax Statements* must be filed by all companies that have one or more employees

☐ IRS Form W-4: *Employee's Withholding Allowance Certificate* must be provided to employees of companies. Not filed with the IRS

☐ IRS Form 940: *Employer's Annual Federal Unemployment (FUTA) Tax Return* must be filed by all companies that have employees

☐ IRS Form 941: *Employer's Quarterly Federal Tax Return* must be filed by all partnerships that have one or more employees

☐ IRS Form 8109: *Federal Tax Deposit Coupon*. Used by all companies with quarterly employee tax liability over $2,500. (Obtain from IRS)

☐ Any required state and local income and sales tax forms. Please check with the appropriate tax authority for more information

Taxed As a Corporation

☐ IRS Form 8832: *Entity Classification Election*. This form must be completed and filed by all limited liability companies electing to be treated as a corporation

☐ IRS Form 1040: *U.S. Individual Income Tax Return* must be filed by all members. Do not use IRS Form 1040A or IRS Form 1040EZ: *Income Tax Return for Single and Joint Filers With No Dependents*

☐ IRS Form 1120: *U.S. Corporation Income Tax Return* or 1120-A: *U.S. Corporation Short-Form Income Tax Return*. One of these forms must be filed by all limited liability companies electing to be treated as a corporation

☐ IRS Form 1120-W (Worksheet): *Estimated Tax for Corporations* must be completed by all limited liability companies expecting a profit requiring estimated tax payments

☐ IRS Form SS-4: *Application for Employer Identification Number* must be filed by all limited liability companies

☐ IRS Form W-2: *Wage and Tax Statement* must be filed by all limited liability companies

☐ IRS Form W-3: *Transmittal of Wage and Tax Statements* must be filed by all limited liability companies

☐ IRS Form W-4: *Employee's Withholding Allowance Certificate* must be provided to employees of limited liability companies. It is not filed with the IRS

☐ IRS Form 940: *Employer's Annual Federal Unemployment (FUTA) Tax Return* must be filed by all limited liability companies

☐ IRS Form 941: *Employer's Quarterly Federal Tax Return* must be filed by all limited liability companies

☐ IRS Form 8109: *Federal Tax Deposit Coupon.* Used by companies with quarterly employee monthly tax liability over $2,500. (Obtain from IRS)

☐ Any required state and local income and sales tax forms. Please check with the appropriate tax authority for more information

Taxed As a Sole Proprietorship

☐ IRS Form 8832: *Entity Classification Election.* This form must be completed and filed by all limited liability companies electing to be treated as a corporation

☐ IRS Form 1040: *U.S. Individual Income Tax Return.* Do not use IRS Form 1040A or IRS Form 1040EZ: *Income Tax Return for Single and Joint Filers With No Dependents*

☐ IRS Schedule C (Form 1040): *Profit or Loss From Business (Sole Proprietorship)* must be filed with IRS Form 1040 by all limited liability companies electing to be treated as sole proprietorships, unless Schedule IRS Schedule C-EZ: *Net Profit From Business (Sole Proprietorship)* is filed

☐ IRS Schedule C-EZ (Form 1040): *Net Profit From Business (Sole Proprietorship)* may be filed if expenses are under $5,000 and other qualifications are met (see schedule C-EZ)

☐ IRS Form 1040-SS: *U.S. Self-Employment Tax Return.* Required for any sole proprietor who shows $400+ income from his or her limited liability company business on IRS Schedule C or IRS Schedule C-EZ

- [ ] IRS Form 1040-ES: *Estimated Tax for Individuals* must be used by all companies that expect to make a profit requiring estimated taxes

- [ ] IRS Form SS-4: *Application for Employer Identification Number* must be filed by all companies who will hire one or more employees

- [ ] IRS Form W-2: *Wage and Tax Statement* must be filed by all companies that have one or more employees

- [ ] IRS Form W-3: *Transmittal of Wage and Tax Statements* must be filed by all companies that have one or more employees

- [ ] IRS Form W-4: *Employee's Withholding Allowance Certificate* must be provided to employees of companies. Not filed with the IRS

- [ ] IRS Form 940: *Employer's Annual Federal Unemployment (FUTA) Tax Return* must be filed by all companies that have employees

- [ ] IRS Form 941: *Employer's Quarterly Federal Tax Return* must be filed by all companies that have one or more employees

- [ ] IRS Form 8109: *Federal Tax Deposit Coupon.* Used by all companies with quarterly employee tax liability over $2,500. (Obtain from IRS)

- [ ] IRS Form 8829: *Expenses for Business Use of Your Home.* Filed with annual IRS Form 1040, if necessary

- [ ] Any required state and local income and sales tax forms

Limited Liability Company Tax Schedules Checklist

Monthly Tax Schedule

☐ If you have employees, and your quarterly payroll tax liability is over $2,500 monthly, you must make monthly tax payments using IRS Form 8109: *Federal Tax Deposit Coupon*

☐ If required, file and pay any necessary state or local sales tax

Quarterly Tax Schedule

☐ Pay any required estimated taxes using vouchers from IRS Form 1040-ES: *Estimated Tax for Individuals*

☐ If you have employees, file IRS Form 941: *Employer's Quarterly Federal Tax Return* and make any required payments of FICA and withholding taxes

☐ If you have employees and your unpaid quarterly FUTA tax liability is over $500, make FUTA deposit using IRS Form 8109: *Federal Tax Deposit Coupon*

☐ If required, file and pay any necessary state or local sales tax

Annual Tax Schedule

☐ If you have employees, prepare IRS Form W-2: *Wage and Tax Statement* for each employee and provide to employees by January 31; and file IRS Form W-3: *Transmittal of Wage and Tax Statements* and copies of all W-2 Forms with IRS by January 31

☐ If you have paid any independent contractors over $600 annually, prepare IRS Form 1099-MISC: *Miscellaneous Income* and provide to recipient by January 31; and file IRS Form 1096: *Annual Summary and Transmittal of U.S. Information Returns* and copies of all 1099 Forms with IRS by January 31

☐ Make required unemployment tax payment and file IRS Form 940 or 940-EZ: *Employer's Annual Federal Unemployment (FUTA) Tax Return*

☐ File IRS Form 1040-SS: *U.S. Self-Employment Tax Return* with your annual IRS Form 1040: *U.S. Individual Income Tax Return*

☐ File IRS Form 1065: *U.S. Return of Partnership Income* and Schedule K-1 (Form 1065): *Partner's Share of Income, Credits, Deductions, etc.* (treatment as a partnership)

☐ File IRS Form 1120: *U.S. Corporation Income Tax Return* (treatment as a corporation)

☐ File IRS Schedule C (Form 1040): *Profit or Loss From Business (Sole Proprietorship)* and IRS Form 1040: *U.S. Individual Income Tax Return* (treatment as a sole proprietorship)

☐ If you are required, file and pay any necessary state or local sales, income, or unemployment taxes

Appendix of State Limited Liability Company Information

This appendix contains a summary of the laws relating to limited liability companies for all states and the District of Columbia (Washington D.C.). This appendix has been compiled directly from the most recently available statute books and legislation for each state. It has been abridged for clarity and succinctness. Every effort has been made to assure that the information contained in this appendix is accurate and complete. However, laws are subject to constant change. Therefore, prior to reliance on any legal points which are particularly important in a certain situation, the current status of a specific law should be checked in the appropriate law book. In the listings, after each section of information, the chapter and section number of the specific place in the state statute is noted. The following information is listed for each state:

Address of state office for filing: This listing notes the address of the correct state office for filing the organizational documents.

State web address: This listing notes the internet web address of each state's online website. For most state sites, you will arrive at the main index for the state and will need to locate the specific site for the state's statute/legislative information by using the references in the listing "State law reference" below.

Download state forms: This listing provides a direct link to the state website from which you should be able to download any specific state forms. Generally, this is the Secretary of State's office website for a state.

State law reference: This listing specifies the correct state statute book(s) which contain limited liability company law. The specific section numbers for the statutes are listed after each appropriate appendix listing.

Title of filing: Here is listed the correct terminology to use for the title of the main limited liability company organizational document.

Forms available online: Listed here are the forms that are available on each state's website.

Forms provided on CD: This listing provides the names of the forms that are provided on the CD that accompanies this book. Unlike most state forms, these Nova-prepared forms have been formated to be fillable on your computer.

Filing Fee: Here is noted the proper registration fee and whether any additional fees are required for organizational document registration.

Name requirements: The proper method for designating an official company name and the requirements to reserve the name are noted here.

Organizer requirements: The number and type of persons or entities that must organize the limited liability company are the subject of this listing.

Articles of Organization requirements: What information must be included in the organizational documents is noted here.

Annual report requirement: Whether an annual (or biennial) report to the state is required is noted in this listing.

Publication requirement: A few states require newspaper publication of notice of formation of a limited liability company. Those requirements are listed under this heading.

Effective date of limited liability company organization: The date upon which the company takes effect and, thus, the limit on liability for the owners, is noted here.

Membership requirements: In most states, the minimum number of members required is one. However, a few states require at least two members. The members may, generally, be a natural person or a business entity.

Other Provisions: This listing explains any other state-specific requirements or information.

Alabama

Address of state office for filing:
Alabama Secretary of State
Corporations Division
PO Box 5616
Montgomery AL 36103-5616
Telephone: 334-242-5324
State web address: http://www.alabama.gov/
Download state forms: http://www.sos.state.al.us/downloads/dl1.cfm
State law reference: Alabama Code, Section 10-12.
Title of filing: Articles of Organization.
Forms available online: Articles of Organization, Change of Registered Agent or Registered Office, Articles of Amendment to Articles of Organization, .
Forms provided on CD: Articles of Organization
Filing Fee: $40 to Secretary of State, plus $35 to Probate Court Judge for recordation of Articles of Organization.
Name requirements: The official name must contain the words "limited liability company" or the abbreviation "LLC" or "L.L.C." (Section 10-12-5).
Organizer requirements: A limited liability company may be organized by one person. The organizer need not be a natural person, nor a member. (Sections 10-12-9, 10-12-2).
Articles of Organization requirements: Articles of Organization must contain the following: (1) name of company, (2) duration of company, if less than perpetual, (3) company purpose, (4) registered agent name and office address, (5) initial members' names and mailing addresses, (6) reservation of right to admit new members, (7) right of company to continue following an act of dissolution or dissociation, (8) whether company will be managed by managers or members and the names and addresses of the managers if managed by managers, and (9) any additional matters. (Section 10-12-10).
Annual report requirement: A company must file an annual report complying with Section 10-2B-16.22 when it files its annual Alabama business privilege tax return and pays the applicable taxes. (Section 40-14A-25).
Publication requirement: No.
Effective date of limited liability company organization: On the date of official approval of Articles of Organization, the company becomes a legal entity and the members are shielded from personal liability. (Section 10-12-14).
Membership requirements: Minimum number required is one. The member may be a natural person or business entity. (Sections 10-12-9, 10-12-2).
Other provisions: Alabama does not provide for Name Reservation of Limited Liability Companies.

Alaska

Address of state office for filing:
Alaska Department of Commerce, Community, and Economic Development
Corporations Section
Box 110808
Juneau AK 99811-0808
Telephone: (907) 465-2530
State web address: http://www.state.ak.us/
Download state forms: www.commerce.state.ak.us/bsc/cforms.htm
State law reference: Alaska Statutes, Chapter 10.50.
Title of filing: Articles of Organization.
Forms available online: Articles of Organization, Business or Corporation Name Reservation Application, Articles of Amendment, Restated Articles of Organization, Notice of Change of Members or Managers, Statement of Change of Registered Agent or Registered Agent Address, Registered Agent Notice of Resignation, NAICS Codes for Business Activity for the State of Alaska.
Forms provided on CD: Articles of Organization, Business or Corporation Name Reservation Application
Filing Fee: $250
Name requirements: The official name must contain the words "limited liability company" or the abbreviation "LLC" or "L.L.C." The word "Limited" may be abbreviated to "Ltd." and the word "Company" may be abbreviated to "Co." In addition, the name may not contain the words "city," "borough," "village" or imply that the company is a municipality, but the name of a city, borough, or village may be used in the company name. (Section 10.50.020). A company name may be reserved for 120 days for a fee of $25. (Section 10.50.035).
Organizer requirements: A limited liability company may be organized by one person. The organizer need not be a natural

person, nor a member. (Section 10.50.070).

Articles of Organization requirements: Articles of Organization must contain the following: (1) name of company, (2) company purpose, (3) registered agent name and office address, (4) duration of company, (5) whether company will be managed by a manager, and (6) any additional matters. Past and future contributions, the identity of those who manage the company, the company's power to continue business, and the limited liability company's power to avoid dissolution need not be stated. (Section 10.50.075).

Annual report requirement: Yes, however, the report is biennial, not annual. (Section 10.50.750).

Publication requirement: No.

Effective date of limited liability company organization: On the date of official approval of Articles of Organization, the company becomes a legal entity and the members are shielded from personal liability. (Section 10.50.080).

Membership requirements: Minimum required is one. May be a natural person or a business entity. (Section 10.50.155).

Other provisions: Articles of Organization must include a statement of codes from the NAICS Codes for Business Activity for the State of Alaska describing business type.

Arizona

Address of state office for filing:
Arizona Corporation Commission
Corporations Division
1300 West Washington Street
Phoenix AZ 85007-2929

Telephone: 1-800-345-5819

State law reference: Arizona Revised Statutes Annotated, Title 29, Chapter 4.

State web address: http://www.azleg.gov/

Download state forms: http://www.azcc.gov/divisions/corporations/filings/forms/index.htm

Title of filing: Articles of Organization.

Forms available online: Articles of Organization, Application for Reservation of a Corporate Name, General Filing Instructions for Limited Liability Companies, Corporations Division Submission Cover Sheet, Notice for Publication, Articles of Amendment, Statement of Change of Known Place of Business or Statutory Agent, or Change of Address of Statutory Agent, Member, or Manager, Statement of Resignation of Statutory Agent, Articles of Correction

Forms provided on CD: Articles of Organization, Application for Reservation of a Corporate Name

Filing Fee: $50

Name requirements: The official name must contain the words "Limited Liability Company," "Limited Company," or the abbreviations "LLC," "L.L.C.," "L.C," or "LC" and may not contain the words "association," "corporation," "incorporated" or an abbreviation of those words. (Section 29-602). A name may be reserved for 120 days for a $10 fee. (Section 29-603).

Organizer requirements: A limited liability company may be organized by one person or entity. Organizer need not be a member. (Section 29-631).

Articles of Organization requirements: Articles of Organization must contain the following: (1) name of company, (2) registered agent name and office address, (3) company address, if different from that of registered agent, (4) duration of company, if less than perpetual, (5) whether company will be managed by managers or members, (6) the names and addresses of the managers if managed by managers, or the names and addresses of members if managed by members, and (7) any additional matters. Past and future contributions, the limited liability company's power to continue business, and the limited liability company's power to avoid dissolution need not be stated. (Section 29-632).

Annual report requirement: Yes.

Publication requirement: Yes. Within 60 days of filing of the Articles of Organization, a Notice of Filing must be published 3 times in a newspaper of general circulation in the county where the limited liability company has its place of business. Within 90 days of filing of the Articles of Organization, an Affidavit of Publication must be filed with the Arizona Corporation Commission. There is no fee for filing the Affidavit. There will be a charge for the actual publication of the Notice of Filing, which will be determined by the particular newspaper. (Section 29-635).

Effective date of limited liability company organization: On the date of official approval of Articles of Organization, the company becomes a legal entity and the members are shielded from personal liability. This date is retroactive to the date of submission of the Articles and may be delayed to a later date that is stated in the Articles. (Section 29-635).

Membership requirements: Minimum number required is one. The member may be a natural person or a business entity. (Section 29-601).

Other: If the company is managed by managers, the Articles of Organization must indicate the names and addresses of the managers and members who own a 20% or greater interest in the capital or profits of the company.

Arkansas

Address of state office for filing:
Arkansas Secretary of State
Business and Commercial Services Division
1401 West Capitol Ave.
Suite 250
Little Rock AR 72201
Telephone: 501-682-3409
State web address: http://www.arkleg.state.ar.us/
Download state forms: http://www.sos.arkansas.gov/business_entity_fees_forms_pro.html
State law reference: Arkansas Code, Title 4, Chapter 32.
Title of filing: Articles of Organization.
Forms available online: Application for Reservation of Entity Name, Articles of Organization, Limited Liability Company Franchise Tax Registration, Certificate of Amendment to Articles of Organization, Notice of Change of Registered Office or Registered Agent or Both
Forms provided on CD: Application for Reservation of Entity Name, Articles of Organization
Filing Fee: online, $45; paper, $50
Name requirements: The official name must contain the words "Limited Liability Company," "Limited Company," or the abbreviations "LLC," "LC," "L.L.C.," or "L.C." The word "Limited" may be abbreviated as "Ltd.," and the word "Company" may be abbreviated as "Co." If the company provides professional services, the company name must include the term "Professional" or the abbreviation "P." or "P" if the company name is abbreviated, and may not contain the name of a non-member, unless that person is a former member or a member of a predecessor organization. (Section 4-32-103). In addition, a company name may be reserved for 120 days for a $25 fee. (Section 4-32-104).
Organizer requirements: A limited liability company may be organized by one person. The organizer need not be a natural person, nor a member. (Sections 4-32-201, 4-32-102).
Articles of Organization requirements: Articles of Organization must contain the following: (1) name of company, (2) registered agent name and office address, and (3) if company will be managed by managers, a statement to that effect. Past and future contributions, and the limited liability company's power to avoid dissolution need not be stated. (Section 4-32-202).
Annual report requirement: Yes, Franchise Tax Report plus applicable taxes due annually to Secretary of State.
Publication requirement: No.
Effective date of limited liability company organization: On the date of official approval of Articles of Organization, the company becomes a legal entity and the members are shielded from personal liability. This date is retroactive to the date of submission and may be delayed to a date stated in the Articles. (Section 4-32-206).
Membership requirements: Minimum number required is one. The member may be a natural person or a business entity. (Section 4-32-102).
Other: Limited Liability Company Franchise Tax Registration form should be filed at time of organization. Articles of Organization must contain the address of the company's principal place of business.

California

Address of state office for filing:
California Secretary of State
1500 11th Street
Sacramento CA 95814
Attention: Document Filing Support Unit
Telephone: (916) 657-5448
State web address: http://www.state.ca.us/
Download state forms: http://www.sos.ca.gov/business/business.htm
State law reference: California Corporations Code, Sections 17000+.
Title of filing: Articles of Organization.
Forms available online: Name Reservation Request, Articles of Organization, Statement of Information, Certificate of Amendment, Certificate of Correction, Resignation of Registered Agent.
Forms provided on CD: Name Reservation Request, Articles of Organization
Filing Fee: $70
Name requirements: The official name must contain the words "Limited Liability Company" or the abbreviation "LLC" or

"L.L.C." The words "Limited" and "Company" may be abbreviated as "Ltd. and "Co." (Section 17052(a)). A company name may be reserved for 60 days for a $10 fee. (Section 17053).

Organizer requirements: A limited liability company may be organized by one or more persons. The organizer need not be a natural person, nor a member. (Section 17050(a)).

Articles of Organization requirements: Articles of Organization must contain the following: (1) name of company, (2) the statement, "The purpose of the limited liability company is to engage in any lawful act or activity for which a limited liability company may be organized under the Beverly-Killea Limited Liability Company Act." (3) registered agent name and office address, unless a corporate agent is designated, in which case only the name of the agent shall be set forth, (4) if the company will be managed by one or more managers and not by all its members, a statement to that effect, under Section 17151, (5) if the company will be managed by only one manager, a statement to that effect, and (6) any additional matters. (Section 17051).

Annual report requirement: Yes, initial Statement of Information is due to the Secretary of State within 90 days of the filing of the Articles of Organization and biennially thereafter. Filing fee is $20.

Publication requirement: No.

Effective date of limited liability company organization: On the date of official approval of Articles of Organization, the company becomes a legal entity and the members are shielded from personal liability. (Section 17050(c)).

Membership requirements: Minimum number required is one. The member may be a natural person or a business entity. (Section 17050(b)).

Other: If the company is to be managed by members, the Articles should include a statement to that effect. The Articles must be signed and dated by the organizer who executed the Articles.

Colorado

Address of state office for filing:
    Colorado Secretary of State
    Corporations Section
    1700 Broadway, Suite 200
    Denver CO 80290

Telephone: 303-894-2200

State web address: http://www.leg.state.co.us/

Download state forms: http://www.sos.state.co.us/biz/FileDoc.do

State law reference: Colorado Revised Statutes, Title 7, Articles 80 and 90.

Title of filing: Articles of Organization.

Forms available online: Form 400 – Articles of Organization

Forms provided on CD: No forms are available on the CD. Colorado provides for LLC formation forms to be completed and filed online. (File LLC online save $100.00) File at: www.sos.state.co.us/biz/FileDoc.do

Filing Fee: $25 online filing fee, $125 paper filing fee

Name requirements: The official name must contain the words "Limited Liability Company" or "Limited," or the abbreviations "L.L.C." or "LLC." The word "Limited" may be abbreviated as "Ltd." and the word "Company" may be abbreviated as "Co." (Section 7-90-601). Names may be reserved for 120 days (renewable). (Section 7-90-602). $25 fee for online filing, $125 fee for paper filing.

Organizer requirements: A limited liability company may be organized by one person. The organizer need not be a natural person, nor a member. (Section 7-80-203).

Articles of Organization requirements: Articles of Organization must contain the following: (1) name of company, (2) initial principal office of company, (3) registered agent name and office address, (4) organizers' names and mailing addresses, (5) whether company will be managed by managers or members, (6) a statement that the company has at least one member, and (7) any additional matters. (Section 7-80-204).

Annual report requirement: Yes, to Secretary of State. (Sections 7-90-501, 7-80-301). $10 online filing fee, $100 paper filing fee.

Publication requirement: No.

Effective date of limited liability company organization: On the date of official approval of Articles of Organization, the company becomes a legal entity and the members are shielded from personal liability. (Section 7-80-207).

Membership requirements: Minimum number required is one. The member may be a natural person or a business entity. (Sections 7-80-102(9), 7-80-204).

Other: None.

Connecticut

Address of state office for filing:
Connecticut Secretary of State
30 Trinity Street
Hartford CT 06016
Telephone: 860-509-6000
State web address: http://www.ct.gov
Download state forms: http://www.sots.ct.gov/downloadforms.htm
State law reference: Connecticut General Statutes, Title 34, Chapter 613 (Section 34-100+).
Title of filing: Articles of Organization
Forms available online: Application for Reservation of Name, Articles of Organization, Transfer of Reserved Name, Articles of Amendment, Cancellation of Reserved Name, Interim Notice of Change of Member or Manager, Change of Address, Change of Statutory Agent, Change of Statutory Agent's Address
Forms provided on CD: Application for Reservation of Name, Articles of Organization
Filing Fee: $60
Name requirements: The official name must contain the words "Limited Liability Company" or the abbreviations "LLC," or "L.L.C." The word "Limited" may be abbreviated to "Ltd.," and the word "Company" may be abbreviated to "Co." (Section 34-102). A company name may be reserved for a period of 120 days for a $30 fee. (Section 34-103).
Organizer requirements: A limited liability company may be organized by one person. The organizer need not be a natural person, nor a member. (Section 34-120).
Articles of Organization requirements: Articles of Organization must contain the following: (1) name of company, (2) if company will be managed by managers, a statement to that effect, ((3) company purpose, except that it is sufficient to state that the purpose of the company is to engage in any lawful act or activity for which limited liability companies may be formed, (4) principal office address of the company, (5) registered agent name and office address, and (6) any additional matters. (Section 34-121).
Annual report requirement: Yes, to Secretary of State. (Section 34-106).
Publication requirement: No.
Effective date of limited liability company organization: On the date of official approval of Articles of Organization, the company becomes a legal entity and the members are shielded from personal liability. (Sections 34-110 & 34-123).
Membership requirements: Minimum number required is one. The member may be a natural person or a business entity. (Section 34-101).
Other: The organizer or organizers must file with the Secretary of State the name and business and home address of one member or manager. (Section 34-120).

Delaware

Address of state office for filing:
Delaware Department of State
Division of Corporations
401 Federal Street, Suite 4
Dover, DE 19901
Telephone: 302-739-3073
State web address: http://www.delaware.gov/
Download state forms: http://www.corp.delaware.gov/forms.shtml
State law reference: Delaware Code, Title 6, Chapter 18.
Title of filing: Certificate of Formation.
Forms available online: Certificate of Formation, Certificate of Amendment, Certificate of Change of Agent, Application for Reservation of Limited Liability Name.
Forms provided on CD: Certificate of Formation, Application for Reservation of Limited Liability Name
Filing Fee: $90.
Name requirements: The official name must contain the words "Limited Liability Company" or the abbreviation "LLC or "L.L.C." (Section 18-102). A company name may be reserved for 120 days for a $75 fee. (Section 18-103).
Organizer requirements: A limited liability company may be organized by one person. The organizer need not be a natural person, nor a member. (Section 18-201).
Certificate of formation requirements: Certificates of Formation must contain the following: (1) name of company, (2) registered agent name and office address, and (3) any additional matters. (Section 18-201).

Annual report requirement: No, but company must pay an annual tax of $200. (Section 18-1107).

Publication requirement: No.

Effective date of limited liability company organization: On the date of official approval of Certificate of Formation, the company becomes a legal entity and the members are shielded from personal liability. (Section 18-201(b)).

Membership requirements: Minimum number required is one. The member may be a natural person or a business entity. (Section 18-101).

Other: The Certificate of Formation must specify the duration of company, if less than perpetual.

District of Columbia (Washington D.C.)

Address of state office for filing:
   Department of Consumer and Regulatory Affairs
   Business and Professional Licensing Administration
   Corporations Division
   941 North Capitol Street NE
   Washington DC 20002

Telephone: (202) 442-4400

State web address: http://dccouncil.washington.dc.us/

Download state forms: http://dcra.dc.gov/dcra/site/

State law reference: District of Columbia Code Annotated, Title 29, Chapter 10.

Title of filing: Articles of Organization.

Forms available online: Application for Name Reservation, Guidelines for Articles of Amendment to Articles of Organization, Guidelines for Articles of Organization, Instructions for Filing Articles of Organization, Guidelines for Articles of Correction to Articles of Organization, Statement of Resignation of Registered Agent, Blanket Statement of Change of Registered Office, Statement of Change of Registered Office or Registered Agent or Both, Written Consent to Act as Registered Agent

Forms provided on CD: Application for Name Reservation, Articles of Organization (prepared by Nova)

Filing Fee: $150

Name requirements: The official name must contain the words "Limited Liability Company" or the abbreviation "LLC" or "L.L.C." If the company is to be used for a profession, the word "Professional" or the abbreviation "P." or "P" must precede the name. (Section 29-1004). A company name may be reserved for 60 days for a $35 fee. (Section 29-1005).

Organizer requirements: A limited liability company may organized by one person. The organizer need not be a natural person, nor a member. (Section 29-1002).

Articles of Organization requirements: Articles of Organization must contain the following: (1) name of company, (2) registered agent's name and office address, and (3) evidence of the registered agent's consent. (Section 29-1006).

Annual report requirement: Yes, to Department of Consumer and Regulatory Affairs. The report is due by June 16 the year after incorporation, and by June 16 every two years thereafter. (Section 29-1064).

Publication requirement: No.

Effective date of limited liability company organization: On the date of official approval of Articles of Organization, the company becomes a legal entity and the members are shielded from personal liability. This date is retroactive to the date of submission and may also be delayed to a later date stated in the Articles of Organization. (Section 29-1006).

Membership requirements: Minimum number required is one. The member may be a natural person or a business entity. (Section 29-1001(16), (22)).

Other: An executed "Written Consent to Act as Registered Agent" form must accompany the Articles of Organization at the time of filing.

Florida

Address of state office for filing:
   Department of State
   Division of Corporations
   P.O. Box 6327
   Tallahassee FL 32314

Telephone: (850) 245-6052

State web address: http://www.leg.state.fl.us/

Download state forms: http://www.dos.state.fl.us/doc/form_download.html

State law reference: Florida Statutes, Title 36, Chapter 608.

Title of filing: Articles of Organization.

Forms available online: Articles of Organization, Registration of Fictitous Name, Articles of Amendment to Articles of Organization, Resignation of Registered Agent, Resignation of Member, Managing Member, or Manager, Statement of Change of Registered Office or Registered Agent or Both, Articles of Correction

Forms provided on CD: Articles of Organization, Registration of Fictitous Name

Filing Fee: $125 (includes filing fee for Articles of Organization and Designation of Registered Agent).

Name requirements: The official name must contain the words "Limited Liability Company," "Limited Company" or the abbreviations "LLC," "L.L.C.," "L.C." or "LC." The word "Limited" may be abbreviated to "Ltd.," and the word "Company" may be abbreviated to "Co." (Section 608.406). Name reservations are not available. A preliminary name availability search may be conducted online at www.sunbiz.org. Fictitious Name Fee $50 (Fee on form).

Organizer requirements: One or more persons or entities (need not be) members. (Section 608.405, 608.402).

Articles of Organization requirements: Articles of Organization must contain the following: (1) name of company, (2) the mailing address and street address of the company's principal office, (3) registered agent name and office address, (4) signature of registered agent accepting the appointment and stating that he or she is familiar with and accepts the obligations of that position, and (5) any other matters. (Sections 608.407, 608.415).

Annual report requirement: Yes, to Department of State. (Section 608.4511).

Publication requirement: No.

Effective date of limited liability company organization: On the date of official approval of Articles of Organization, the company becomes a legal entity and the members are shielded from personal liability. The effective date is retroactive to the date of submission of the Articles if approved within five days. In addition, the effective date may be delayed to a date stated in the Articles, but that date may not be more than 90 days after the date of filing. (Sections 608.407, 608.409).

Membership requirements: Minimum number required is one. The member may be a natural person or a business entity. (Sections 608.405, 608.402).

Other: The Articles of Organization should include the name and address of each manager or managing member, but need not specify whether the company is to be managed by managers. (Section 608.407).

Georgia

Address of state office for filing:

Georgia Secretary of State
Corporations Division
Suite 315 West Tower
2 Martin Luther King Drive
Atlanta GA 30334-1530

Telephone: 404-656-2817

State web address: http://www.legis.state.ga.us/

Download state forms: http://www.sos.state.ga.us/corporations/

State law reference: Official Code of Georgia Annotated, Title 14, Chapter 11.

Title of filing: Articles of Organization.

Forms available online: Guidelines for Articles of Organization, Transmittal Information Form

Forms provided on CD: Guidelines for Articles of Organization, Transmittal Information Form, Articles of Organization. Note: Georgia has online filing located at: http://corp.sos.state.ga.us/business/

Filing Fee: $100

Name requirements: The official name must contain the words "Limited Liability Company," "Limited Company," or the abbreviations "LLC," " L.L.C.," "LC," or "L.C." The word "Limited" may be abbreviated to "Ltd." and the word "Company" may be abbreviated to "Co." The name must contain 80 characters or less. (Section 14-11-207). Names are reservablefor 30 days for $25. The same or a different applicant may renew the reservation for an additional 30 days and $25 fee if the Articles of Organization have not been filed. (Section 14-11-208).

Organizer requirements: A limited liability company may be organized by one person. The organizer need not be a natural person, nor a member. (Section 14-11-203).

Articles of Organization requirements: Articles of Organization must contain the following: (1) name of company, (2) name and address of each organizer, (3) registered agent name and office address (including county), and (4) the mailing address of the company's principal place of business. (Sections 14-11-203, 14-11-204).

Annual report requirement: Yes, annual registration with the Secretary of State. (Section 14-11-1103). Filing fee of $30.

Publication requirement: No.

Effective date of limited liability company organization: On the date of official approval of Articles of Organization, the company becomes a legal entity and the members are shielded from personal liability. The effective date may be delayed to a date stated in the Articles of Organization up to 90 days after official approval. (Sections 14-11-203, 14-11-206).

Membership requirements: Minimum number required is one. The member may be a natural person or a business entity. (Section 14-11-101(16), 14-11-101(19)).

Other: None.

Hawaii

Address of state office for filing:
State of Hawaii
Department of Commerce and Consumer Affairs
Business Registration Division
PO Box 40
Honolulu Hawaii 96810

Telephone: 808-586-2727

State web address: http://www.capitol.hawaii.gov

Download state forms: http://www.hawaii.gov/dcca/areas/breg/registration/

State law reference: Hawaii Revised Statutes, Title 23A, Chapter 428.

Title of filing: Articles of Organization.

Forms available online: Application for Reservation of Name, Transfer of Name Reservation, Statement of Change of Registered Agent, Statement of Change of Registered Agent's Business Address, Statement of Resignation of Registered Agent, Articles of Correction, Instructions for Filing Articles of Organization for Limited Liability Company, Articles of Amendment to Change Limited Liability Company Name, Articles of Amendment of Limited Liability Company, Restated Articles of Organization, Amended and Restated Articles of Organization.

Forms provided on CD: Application for Name Reservation, Articles of Organization (prepared by Nova)

Filing Fee: $50.

Name requirements: The official name must contain the words "Limited Liability Company" or the abbreviation "LLC" or "L.L.C." The word "Limited" may be abbreviated to "Ltd." and the word "Company" may be abbreviated to "Co." (Section 428-105). A company name may be reserved for 120 days for a fee of $10. (Section 428-106).

Organizer requirements: A limited liability company may be organized by one person or entity. The organizer need not be a member. (Section 428-202).

Articles of Organization requirements: Articles of Organization must contain the following: (1) name of company, (2) mailing address of company's initial principal office, (3) registered agent name and office address, (4) organizers' names and addresses, (5) duration of company, if less than perpetual, (6) whether the company is to be managed by managers, (7) if the company is to be managed by managers, the name and address of each initial manager, and the number of initial members, or if the company is to be managed by members, the name and address of each initial member, (7) whether the members of the company are to be liable for its debts and obligations under Section 428-303(c), and (8) any additional matters. (Section 428-203).

Annual report requirement: Yes, to Department of Commerce and Consumer Affairs. (Section 428-210). $15 filing fee.

Publication requirement: No.

Effective date of limited liability company organization: On the date of official approval of Articles of Organization, the company becomes a legal entity and the members are shielded from personal liability. (Section 428-202).

Membership requirements: Minimum number required is one. The member may be a natural person or a business entity. (Section 428-202).

Other: None.

Idaho

Address of state office for filing:
Idaho Secretary of State
Corporation Division
700 West Jefferson
PO Box 83720
Boise ID 83720-0080

Telephone: 208-334-2301

State web address: http://www.state.id.us/

Download state forms: http://www.idsos.state.id.us/corp/corindex.htm

State law reference: Idaho Code, Title 53, Chapter 6.

Title of filing: Articles of Organization.

Forms available online: Application for Reservation of Legal Entity Name, Articles of Organization, Articles of Amendment to Articles of Organization, Amended and Restated Articles of Organization, Statement of Change of Registered Office or Registered Agent or Both, Statement of Change of Business Address

Forms provided on CD: Application for Reservation of Legal Entity Name, Articles of Organization

Filing Fee: $100 if Articles are typed and there are no attachments; $120 if Articles are not typed or there are attachments.

Name requirements: The official name must contain the words "Limited Liability Company," "Limited Company," or the abbreviations "LLC," "L.L.C.," "L.C.," or "LC." The word "Limited" may be abbreviated to "Ltd." and the word "Company" may be abbreviated to "Co." If the company will offer professional services, the company name must end with the words "Professional Company" or the abbreviations "PLLC" or "P.L.L.C." (Section 53-602). A company name may be reserved for four months for a fee of $20.

Organizer requirements: A limited liability company may be organized by one person. The organizer need not be a natural person, nor a member. (Section 53-607).

Articles of Organization requirements: Articles of Organization must contain the following: (1) name of company, (2) registered agent name and office address, (3) whether the company will be managed by managers or members, (4) the names and addresses of one or more of the managers if managed by managers, or the names and addresses of one or more of the members if managed by members, (6) if the company will render professional services, the principal profession which members are duly authorized or licensed to practice, and (7) any additional matters. (Section 53-608).

Annual report requirement: Yes, to Secretary of State. (Section 53-613).

Publication requirement: No.

Effective date of limited liability company organization: On the date of official approval of Articles of Organization, the company becomes a legal entity and the members are shielded from personal liability. (Sections 53-611, 53-612).

Membership requirements: Minimum number required is one. The member may be a natural person or a business entity. (Sections 53-601(10), 53-601(12)).

Other: None.

Illinois

Address of state office for filing:

Illinois Secretary of State

Department of Business Services

Limited Liability Division

Michael J. Howlett Bldg., Rm. 351

501 S. Second St.

Springfield IL 62756

Telephone: (217) 782-6961

State web address: http://www.illinois.gov/government/

Download state forms: http://www.cyberdriveillinois.com/departments/business_services/

State law reference: Illinois Revised Statutes Annotated, Chapter 805, Section 180/1-1+.

Title of filing: Articles of Organization.

Forms available online: Resignation of Registered Agent, Statement of Change of Registered Agent or Registered Office or Both, Articles of Organization, Articles of Amendment, Restated Articles of Organization, Application for, Cancellation of, or Transfer of Reserved Name.

Forms provided on CD: Articles of Organization, Application for, Cancellation of, or Transfer of Reserved Name.

Filing Fee: $500

Name requirements: The official name must contain the words "Limited Liability Company" or the abbreviations "LLC or "L.L.C." The abbreviations "Ltd." and "Co." are not allowed. (Section 180/1-10). A company name may be reserved for 90 days for a $300 fee. (Section 180/1-15).

Organizer requirements: A limited liability company may be organized by one person. The organizer need not be a natural person, nor a member. (Section 180/5-1).

Articles of Organization requirements: Articles of Organization must contain the following: (1) name of company, (2) the address of the company's principal place of business, (3) company purpose (general "all purpose" clause is acceptable), (4) registered agent name and office address, (5) the names and addresses of the initial managers if managed by managers, (6) the names and addresses of the initial members if managed by members, (7) the latest date (if any) on which the company is to dissolve, (8) the names and addresses of the organizers, and (9) any additional matters. (Section 180/5-5(a)).

Annual report requirement: Yes, to Secretary of State. (Section 180/50-1). $250 filing fee.

Publication requirement: No.

Effective date of limited liability company organization: On the date of official approval of Articles of Organization, the company becomes a legal entity and the members are shielded from personal liability. The effective date may be delayed up to 60 days if stated in the Articles of Organization. (Section 180/5-5(b)).

Membership requirements: Minimum number required is one. The member may be a natural person or a business entity. (Section 180/5-1(b)).

Other: None.

Indiana

Address of state office for filing:
Indiana Secretary of State
Corporations Division
302 West Washington
Room E018
Indianapolis IN 46204

Telephone: 317-232-6576

State web address: http://www.state.in.us/

Download state forms: http://www.in.gov/sos/business/forms.html

State law reference: Indiana Code, Title 23, Article 18.

Title of filing: Articles of Organization.

Forms available online: Articles of Organization, Articles of Amendment, Application for Reservation of Exclusive Use of Corporate Name

Forms provided on CD: Articles of Organization, Application for Reservation of Exclusive Use of Corporate Name

Filing Fee: $90

Name requirements: The official name must contain the words "Limited Liability Company" or the abbreviations "LLC" or "L.L.C." The name may contain the name of a member or manager. (Section 23-18-2-8). A name may be reserved for 120 days for a $20 fee. The reservation is renewable. (Section 23-18-2-9).

Organizer requirements: A limited liability company may be organized by one person. The organizer need not be a natural person, nor a member. (Section 23-18-2-4, 23-18-1-17).

Articles of Organization requirements: Articles of Organization must contain the following: (1) name of company, (2) registered agent name and office address, (3) duration of company, if less than perpetual, and (4) whether the company will be managed by managers or members. (Section 23-18-2-4).

Annual report requirement: Yes, biennial report to Secretary of State. (Section 23-18-12-11). $30 filing fee if filed in writing, $21 filing fee if filed electronically.

Publication requirement: No.

Effective date of limited liability company organization: On the date of official approval of Articles of Organization, the company becomes a legal entity and the members are shielded from personal liability. (Section 23-18-2-7).

Membership requirements: Minimum number required is one. The member may be a natural person or a business entity. (Section 23-18-6-0.5).

Other: None.

Iowa

Address of state office for filing:
Iowa Secretary of State
Business Services
First Floor, Lucas Building
321 E. Twelfth St.
Des Moines IA 50319

Telephone: 515-281-5204

State web address: http://www.legis.state.ia.us/

Download state forms: http://www.sos.state.ia.us/business/form.html

State law reference: Iowa Code, Chapter 490A.

Title of filing: Articles of Organization.

Forms available online: Statement of Change of Registered Office or Registered Agent or Both, Statement of Resignation of Registered Agent, Application for Reservation of Name

Forms provided on CD: Application for Reservation of Name, Articles of Organization (prepared by Nova)

Filing Fee: $50

Name requirements: The official name must contain the words "Limited Liability Company" or "Limited Company" or the abbreviation "L.L.C." or "L.C." (Section 490A.401). A company name may be reserved for 120 days for a fee of $10.

Organizer requirements: A limited liability company may be organized by one person. The organizer need not be a natural person, nor a member. (Section 490A.301).

Articles of Organization requirements: Articles of Organization must contain the following: (1) name of company, (2) registered agent name and office address, (3) address of the principal office of the company, (4) duration of company, if less than perpetual, and (5) any additional matters. (Section 490A.303).

Annual report requirement: Yes, biennial report to Secretary of State. (Section 490A.131). Filing fee of $5.

Publication requirement: No.

Effective date of limited liability company organization: On the date of official approval of Articles of Organization, the company becomes a legal entity and the members are shielded from personal liability. The effective date may be delayed up to 90 days to a date stated in the Articles of Organization. (Section 490A.122).

Membership requirements: Minimum number required is one. Member may be a natural person or a business entity. (Section 490A.102(17)).

Other: None.

Kansas

Address of state office for filing:
Kansas Secretary of State
Business Services
Memorial Hall, 1st Floor
120 SW 10th Avenue
Topeka KS 66612-1594

Telephone: 785-296-4564

State web address: http://www.kansas.gov/index.php

Download state forms: http://www.kssos.org/business/business.html

State law reference: Kansas Statutes Annotated, Title 17, Article 76.

Title of filing: Articles of Organization.

Forms available online: Articles of Organization, Certificate of Amendment, Corrected Document, Certificate of Correction, Change of Registered Office or Agent, Reservation of Corporate Name

Forms provided on CD: Articles of Organization, Reservation of Corporate Name

Filing Fee: $165 paper filing; $160 online filing

Name requirements: The official name must contain the words "Limited Liability Company," "Limited Company," or the abbreviations "LLC," "L.L.C.," "LC," or "L.C." The name may contain the name of a member or manager. (Section 17-7664). A company name may be reserved for 120 days for a $35 fee. (Sections 17-7402, 17-7665).

Organizer requirements: A limited liability company may be organized by one person. The organizer need not be a natural person, nor a member. (Sections 17-7663(l), 17-7663(m)).

Articles of Organization requirements: Articles of Organization must contain the following: (1) name of company, (2) registered agent name and office address, (3) if the company is organized to exercise the powers of a professional association or corporation, the company's profession; and (4) any additional matters. (Section 17-7673).

Annual report requirement: Yes, to Secretary of State. (17-76,139). $55 filing fee.

Publication requirement: No.

Effective date of limited liability company organization: On the date of official approval of Articles of Organization, the company becomes a legal entity and the members are shielded from personal liability. This date is retroactive to the date of submission if within five days of official approval. In addition, this date may be delayed for up to 90 days if so stated in the Articles of Organization. (Section 17-7673).

Membership requirements: Minimum number required is one. The member may be a natural person or a business entity. (Sections 17-7663(l), 17-7663(m)).

Other: None.

Kentucky

Address of state office for filing:
Secretary of State
P. O. Box 718
Frankfort KY 40602-0718
Telephone: 502-564-2848
State web address: http://www.lrc.state.ky.us/
Download state forms: http://sos.ky.gov/forms.htm
State law reference: Kentucky Revised Statutes, Chapter 275.
Title of filing: Articles of Organization.
Forms available online: Application for Reserved Name, Articles of Organization, Statement of Consent of Registered Agent, Statement of Resignation of Registered Agent, Statement of Resignation of Registered Agent, Statement of Change of Registered Office or Agent or Both, Statement of Change of Principal Office Address
Forms provided on CD: Application for Reserved Name, Articles of Organization
Filing Fee: $40 to Secretary of State.
Name requirements: The official name must contain the words "Limited Liability Company," "Limited Company," or the abbreviations "LLC" or "LC." The word "Limited" may be abbreviated as "Ltd" and the word "Company" may be abbreviated as "Co." If the company will offer professional services, the word "Professional" or the abbreviation "P" must precede the name. (Section 275.100). A company name may be reserved for 120 days for a fee of $15. (Section 275.105).
Organizer requirements: A limited liability company may be organized by one person. The organizer need not be a natural person, nor a member. (Sections 275.020, 275.015(15)).
Articles of Organization requirements: Articles of Organization must contain the following: (1) name of company, (2) registered agent name and office address, (3) the mailing address of the company's principal place of business, (4) whether company will be managed by managers or members, (5) duration of company, if less than perpetual, (6) company purpose, if the company will render professional services, and (7) any other matters. (Section 275.025).
Annual report requirement: Yes, to Secretary of State. (Section 275.190). $15 filing fee.
Publication requirement: No.
Effective date of limited liability company organization: On the date of official approval of Articles of Organization, the company becomes a legal entity and the members are shielded from personal liability. The effective date may be delayed up to 90 days after the official approval date if stated in the Articles of Organization. (Section 275.060).
Membership requirements: Minimum number required is one. The member may be a natural person or a business entity. (Sections 275.015(11), 275.015(16)).
Other: The company must deliver to the Secretary of State the registered agent's written consent to the appointment along with the Articles. (Section 275.025). No member of the company has a vested property right resulting from any provision of the Articles. (Section 275.025).

Louisiana

Address of state office for filing:
Louisiana Secretary of State
Commercial Division
PO Box 94125
Baton Rouge LA 70804-9125
Telephone: 225-925-4704
State web address: http://www.legis.state.la.us/
Download state forms: http://www.sos.louisiana.gov/tabid/66/default.aspx
State law reference: Louisiana Revised Statutes Annotated, Title 12, Sections 1301+.
Title of filing: Articles of Organization.
Forms available online: Articles of Organization, Reservation of Corporate or LLC Name, Supplemental Initial Report for Corporation or LLC, Notice of Change of Registered Office or Agent or Both, Initial Report
Forms provided on CD: Articles of Organization, Reservation of Corporate or LLC Name
Filing Fee: $75
Name requirements: Official name must contain the words "Limited Liability Company" or the abbreviation "L.L.C" or "L.C." (Section 1306). Company name may be reserved for 60 days for a $25 fee. (Section 1307).
Organizer requirements: A limited liability company may be organized by one person. The organizer need not be a natural

person, nor a member. (Sections 1301, 1304, 1305).

Articles of Organization requirements: Articles of Organization must contain the following: (1) name of company, (2) company purpose, and (3) any additional matters. (Section 1305).

Annual report requirement: Yes, to Secretary of State. (Section 1308.1). $25 filing fee.

Publication requirement: No.

Effective date of limited liability company organization: On the date of official approval of Articles of Organization, the company becomes a legal entity and the members are shielded from personal liability. The effective date is also retroactive to the date of submission if filed within five days of its signing, excluding holidays. The organizers may specify a date for the Articles to become effective up to 30 days beyond the date of filing. This must be stated to the Secretary of State upon filing. (Section 1304).

Membership requirements: Minimum number required is one. The member may be a natural person or a business entity. (Section 1301(A)(10), (18)).

Other: An Initial Report must be filed with the Articles of Organization, setting forth (1) the location and street address, if any, of the company's registered office, (2) the name and street address, if any, of the company's registered agents, (3) a notarized affidavit by the registered agent, acknowledging and accepting the appointment, (4) if company is to be managed by managers, the names and street addresses of the initial managers, if they have been selected when the Articles are filed, (5) if company is to be managed by members, the names and street addresses of the initial members, if they have been selected if the Articles are filed. If the initial managers or members have not been selected when the Articles are filed, the company must file a supplementary report with the Secretary of State when the initial managers or members are selected. The supplementary report must be signed by each person who signed the Articles. (Section 1305(E)(4)). Articles of Organization must include company's duration (may be perpetual). Articles of Organization must be notarized.

Maine

Address of state office for filing:
  Maine Secretary of State
  Bureau of Corporations
  Corporate Examining Section
  101 State House Station
  Augusta ME 04333-1010

Telephone: 207-624-7740

State web address: http://janus.state.me.us/legis/

Download state forms: http://www.maine.gov/sos/cec/corp/llc.html

State law reference: Maine Revised Statutes Annotated, Title 31, Chapter 13.

Title of filing: Articles of Organization.

Forms available online: Application for Reservation of Name, Change of Registered Agent or Registered Office or Both, Notice of Resignation of Registered Agent, Articles of Organization, Restated Articles of Organization, Articles of Amendment, Certificate of Correction, Acceptance of Appointment as Registered Agent

Forms provided on CD: Application for Reservation of Name, Articles of Organization

Filing Fee: $175

Name requirements: The official name must contain the words "Limited Liability Company" Or the abbreviations "LLC" or "L.L.C." If the company provides professional services, the name must state "Professional Association," "Chartered," or the abbreviation "P.A." The name must not be obscene, promote abusive or unlawful activity, falsely suggest an association with a public institution, or violate any other law of the state. (Section 603-A). A company name may be reserved for a fee of $20. (Section 604-A).

Organizer requirements: A limited liability company may be organized by one person. The organizer need not be a natural person, nor a member. (Section 621, 602).

Articles of Organization requirements: Articles of Organization must contain the following: (1) name of company, (2) registered agent name and office address, (3) whether company will be managed by managers or members, (4) if managed by managers, the minimum and maximum numbers of managers permitted, (5) if managed by managers and if managers have been selected, the names and addresses of the managers, and (6) any additional matters. (Section 622(1)).

Annual report requirement: Yes, to Secretary of State. (Section 757). Filing fee of $85. (Section 751).

Publication requirement: No.

Effective date of limited liability company organization: On the date of official approval of Articles of Organization, the company becomes a legal entity and the members are shielded from personal liability. (Section 622(2)).

Membership requirements: Minimum number required is one. The member may be a natural person or a business entity. (Section 621, 602).

Other: If the company is to provide professional services, the Articles of Organization must state the type of services to be provided. Also, unless the registered agent signs the Articles, the corporation must deliver to the Secretary of State the registered agent's written consent to the appointment along with the Articles, on the state form titled Acceptance of Appointment as Registered Agent.

Maryland

Address of state office for filing:
State Department of Assessments and
    Taxation
Charter Division
301 W. Preston St., Room 801
Baltimore MD 21201-2392
Telephone: 410-767-1340
State web address: http://mlis.state.md.us/index.html
Download state forms: http://www.dat.state.md.us/sdatweb/charter.html
State law reference: Annotated Code of Maryland, Corp. and Assoc. Articles, Titles 1 and 4A.
Title of filing: Articles of Organization.
Forms available online: Articles of Organization, Articles of Amendment, Trade Name Application, Resolution to Change Principal Office or Resident Agent, Resident Agent's Notice of Change of Address
Forms provided on CD: Articles of Organization, Trade Name Application
Filing Fee: $100
Name requirements: The official name must contain the words "Limited Liability Company" or the abbreviations "LLC," "L.L.C.," "L.C.," or "LC." (Section 1-502(b)). A company name may be reserved for 30 days for a fee of $25. (Section 1-505).
Organizer requirements: A limited liability company may be organized by one person. The organizer must be a natural person. (Sections 4A-206(a)(1), 4A-202(a)).
Articles of Organization requirements: Articles of Organization must contain the following: (1) name of company, (2) company purpose, (3) registered agent name and office address, and (4) any additional matters. (Section 4A-204).
Annual report requirement: Personal Property Return due annually to Department of Assessments and Taxation.
Publication requirement: No.
Effective date of limited liability company organization: On the date of official approval of Articles of Organization, the company becomes a legal entity and the members are shielded from personal liability. In addition, the effective date may be delayed to a date stated in the Articles of Organization. (Section 4A-202(b)).
Membership requirements: Minimum number required is one. The member may be a natural person or a business entity. (Section 4A-101(n)(1)).
Other: Articles of Organization must state purpose for which company is filed.

Massachusetts

Address of state office for filing:
Secretary of the Commonwealth
One Ashburton Place, 17th Floor
Boston MA 02108-1512
Telephone: (617) 727-9640
State web address: www.mass.gov/legis
Download state forms: http://www.sec.state.ma.us/cor/coridx.htm
State law reference: Massachusetts General Laws Annotated, Chapter156C.
Title of filing: Certificate of Organization.
Forms available online: Application of Reservation of Name
Forms provided on CD: Application of Reservation of Name, Articles of Organization (prepared by Nova)
Filing Fee: $500
Name requirements: The official name must contain the words "Limited Liability Company," "Limited Company," or the abbreviations "LLC," "L.L.C.," "L.C.," or "LC." (Section 3). A company name may be reserved for a period of 30 days, renewable once. (Section 4).
Forms provided on CD: Filing Fee: The filing fee is $30.
Organizer requirements: A limited liability company may be organized by one person. The organizers need not be a natural

person, nor a member. (Section 12).

Certificate of Organization requirements: Certificate of Organization must contain the following: (1) name of company, (2) registered agent name and office address, (3) duration of company, if less than perpetual, (4) if the company has managers at the time of its formation, the names and business addresses of the managers, (5), the name of any other person in addition to any manager who is authorized to execute any documents to be filed with the Secretary of the Commonwealth (at least one such person must be named if there are no managers), (6) company purpose, and (7) any additional matters. (Section 12).

Annual report requirement: Yes, to Commonwealth of Massachusetts, Corporation Division. (Section 12(c)). Filing fee of $500. (Section 12(d)).

Publication requirement: No.

Effective date of limited liability company organization: On the date of official approval of Certificate of Organization, the company becomes a legal entity and the members are shielded from personal liability. The effective date may also be delayed to any later date if so stated in the Certificate of Organization. (Section 12(b)).

Membership requirements: Minimum number required is one. The member may be a natural person or a business entity. (Sections 2(5), 2(8), 2(10)).

Other: The Certificate of Organization must include (1) the company's Federal Employer Identification Number (FEIN), if available, (2) the street address in the Commonwealth at which the company's records will be maintained, and (3) if the company is to render professional services, (a) the type of service to be rendered, (b) the name and address of each member or manager who will render a service in the Commonwealth, (c) a statement that the company will abide by the provisions of liability insurance required by Section 65, and (d) a certificate of any applicable regulating board that each member or manager who will render a professional service in the Commonwealth is duly licensed.

Michigan

Address of state office for filing:
Michigan Department of Labor and Economic Growth
Bureau of Commercial Services - Corporation Division
7150 Harris Drive
PO Box 30054
Lansing MI 48909

Telephone: (517) 241-6470

State web address: http://www.legislature.mi.gov

Download state forms: http://www.michigan.gov/businessstartup

State law reference: Michigan Compiled Laws, Corporation Law, Chapter 450, Section 450.4101+.

Title of filing: Articles of Organization.

Forms available online: Articles of Organization, Articles of Organization (Professional Service), Application for Reservation of Name

Forms provided on CD: Articles of Organization, Application for Reservation of Name

Filing Fee: $50

Name requirements: The official name must contain the words "Limited Liability Company" or the abbreviations "LLC," "L.L.C.," "L.C.," or "LC." If the company provides professional services, the name must include the word "Professional" or the abbreviations "P" or "P." before the name. (Section 450.4204). Reservable for six months for $25 fee. Renewable. (Section 450.4205).

Organizer requirements: A limited liability company may be organized by one person. The organizer need not be a natural person, nor a member. (Sections 450.4202(1), 450.4102(r)).

Articles of Organization requirements: Articles of Organization must contain the following: (1) name of company, (2) company purpose (general "all purpose" clause acceptable), (3) registered agent name and office address, (4) if company will be managed by managers, a statement to that effect, (5) duration of company, if less than perpetual, and (6) any additional matters. (Section 450.4203).

Annual report requirement: Yes, to Secretary of State. (Section 450.4207(3)). $25 filing fee.

Publication requirement: No.

Effective date of limited liability company organization: On the date of official approval of Articles of Organization, the company becomes a legal entity and the members are shielded from personal liability. In addition, the effective date may be delayed up to 90 days if so stated in the Articles of Organization. (Sections 450.4104(6), 450.4202(2)).

Membership requirements: Minimum number required is one. The member may be a natural person or a business entity. (Sections 450.4102(2)(o), 450.4102(2)(r)).

Other: Unless the Articles of Organization provide that the company is to be managed by managers, the company is automatically managed by members. (Section 450.4401).

Minnesota

Address of state office for filing:
  Minnesota Secretary of State
  Corporate Division
  180 State Office Building
  100 Rev. Dr. Martin Luther King Jr. Blvd.
  St. Paul MN 55155-1299
Telephone: 651-296-2803
State web address: http://www.leg.state.mn.us/
Download state forms: http://www.sos.state.mn.us/business/forms.html
State law reference: Minnesota Statutes Annotated, Chapter 322B.
Title of filing: Articles of Organization.
Forms available online: Articles of Organization, Amendment of Articles of Organization, Notice of Change of Registered Office or Registered Agent, Request for Reservation of Name.
Forms provided on CD: Articles of Organization, Request for Reservation of Name
Filing Fee: $160
Name requirements: The official name must contain the words "Limited Liability Company" or the abbreviation "LLC." (Section 322B.12). A company name may be reserved for a renewable 12-month period for a fee of $35. (Section 322B.125).
Organizer requirements: A limited liability company may be organized by one person. The organizer must be a natural person. (Section 322B.105)
Articles of Organization requirements: Articles of Organization must contain the following: (1) name of company, (2) registered office address, (3) name of registered agent, if any, (4) names and addresses of organizers, (5) duration of company, if less than perpetual, and (6) any additional matters. (Section 322B.115(1)).
Annual report requirement: Yes, annual renewal is required to be filed with the Secretary of State. Failure to file by December 31 results in termination or revocation of the company. (Section 322B.960).
Publication requirement: No.
Effective date of limited liability company organization: On the date of official approval of Articles of Organization, the company becomes a legal entity and the members are shielded from personal liability. The effective date may be delayed by up to 30 days if so stated in the Articles. (Section 322B.175).
Membership requirements: Minimum number required is one. The member may be a natural person or a business entity. (Sections 322B.11, 322B.03).
Other: A Minnesota limited liability company is required to have a registered office, but naming a registered agent is optional. (Section 322B.13). Also, section 322B.115(2) lists twenty-two different provisions that will govern a limited liability company unless modified in the Articles or a member control agreement. For example, unless stated otherwise in the Articles, cumulative voting for governors is allowed, (Section 322B.115(2)(4)), a member is not subject to expulsion (Section 322B.115(2)(18)), written actions of the board of governors or members taken without a meeting must be signed by all governors or members. (Sections 322B.115(2)(6), 322B.115(2)(16)), and members have no right to receive distributions in kind and the company has only limited rights to make distributions in kind. (Section 322B.115(2)(17). For a complete list of the provisions, see Section 322B.115(2)). Finally, the Articles of Organization must disclose whether the LLC owns, leases, or has any interest in agricultural land or land capable of being farmed.

Mississippi

Address of state office for filing:
  Secretary of State
  P. O. Box 136
  301 North President Street
  Jackson MS 39205-0136
Telephone: 601-359-1333
State web address: http://www.mscode.com/
Download state forms: http://www.sos.state.ms.us/busserv/index.asp
State law reference: Mississippi Code Annotated, Title 79, Chapter 29.
Title of filing: Certificate of Formation.
Forms available online: Certificate of Formation, Certificate of Amendment, Registered Agent or Office Statement of Change, Application for Name Reservation.
Forms provided on CD: Certificate of Formation, Application for Name Reservation

Filing Fee: $50

Name requirements: The official name must contain the words "Limited Liability Company" or the abbreviation "LLC" or "L.L.C." It may contain the name of a member or manager. (Section 79-29-104). A company name may be reserved for 180 days for a fee of $25. (Section 79-29-105).

Organizer requirements: A limited liability company may be organized by one person. The organizer need not be a natural person, nor a member. (Section 79-29-205).

Certificate of Formation requirements: Certificate of Formation in Mississippi must contain the following: (1) name of company, (2) registered agent name and office address, (3) duration of company, if less than perpetual, (4) if company will be wholly or partly managed by managers, a statement to that effect, and (5) any additional matters. (Section 79-29-201(1)).

Annual report requirement: No.

Publication requirement: No.

Effective date of limited liability company organization: On the date of official approval of Certificate of Formation, the company becomes a legal entity and the members are shielded from personal liability. The effective date may be delayed by up to 90 days if so stated in the Certificate of Formation. (Section 79-29-201(2)).

Membership requirements: Minimum number required is one. The member may be a natural person or a business entity. (Section 79-29-103(j), 103(n), 103(q)).

Other: The Certificate of Formation should include the company's federal tax identification number.

Missouri

Address of state office for filing:

Corporations Division
P.O. Box 778
600 W. Main Street, Rm 322
Jefferson City MO 65102

Telephone: 573-751-4153

State web address: www.moga.state.mo.us/

Download state forms: http://www.sos.mo.gov/business/

State law reference: Missouri Revised Statutes, Title 23, Chapter 347.

Title of filing: Articles of Organization.

Forms available online: Statement of Change of Registered Agent or Registered Office or Both, Application for Reservation of Name, Statement of Change of Business Office Address by a Registered Agent, Articles of Organization, Amendment of Articles of Organization, Statement of Correction, Statement of Resignation of Registered Agent.

Forms provided on CD: Application for Reservation of Name, Articles of Organization

Filing Fee: $105

Name requirements: The official name must contain the words "Limited Liability Company," "Limited Company," or the abbreviations "LLC," "LC," "L.L.C." or "L.C." A company name may not contain the abbreviation "Ltd." (Section 347.020). A company name may be reserved for 60 days for a fee of $25. The reservation is renewable twice. (Section 347.025).

Organizer requirements: A limited liability company may be organized by one person. The organizer need not be a natural person, nor a member. (Section 347.037)

Articles of Organization requirements: Articles of Organization must contain the following: (1) name of company, (2) company purpose (general statement of purpose is acceptable), (3) registered agent name and office address, (4) whether company will be managed by managers or members, (5) duration of company, (6) the name and address of each organizer, and (7) any additional matters. (Section 347.039).

Annual report requirement: No.

Publication requirement: No.

Effective date of limited liability company organization: On the date of official approval of Articles of Organization, the company becomes a legal entity and the members are shielded from personal liability. The effective date may be delayed by up to 90 days if so stated in the Articles of Organization. (Section 347.037(2)).

Membership requirements: Minimum number required is one. The member may be a natural person or a business entity. (Sections 347.017, 347.015).

Other: None.

Montana

Address of state office for filing:
Secretary of State
P.O. Box 202801
Helena MT 59620-2801
Telephone: 406-444-3665
State web address: http://leg.mt.gov/css/default.asp
Download state forms: http://www.sos.state.mt.us/BSB/Business_Forms.asp
State law reference: Montana Code Annotated, Title 35, Chapter 8.
Title of filing: Articles of Organization.
Forms available online: Articles of Organization, Reservation of Name, Articles of Amendment, Acceptance of Appointment of Agent.
Forms provided on CD: Articles of Organization, Reservation of Name
Filing Fee: $70
Name requirements: The official name must contain the words "Limited Liability Company," "Limited Company," or the abbreviations "LLC," "L.L.C.," "L.C.," or "LC." The word "Limited" may be abbreviated to "Ltd." and the word "Company" may be abbreviated to 'Co." (Section 35-8-103). If the company will provide professional services, the name must contain the words "professional limited liability company", "professional limited company", "professional l.l.c.", "professional llc", "p.l.l.c.", or "pllc." (Section 35-8-1302). A company name may be reserved for 120 days for a fee of $10. (Section 35-8-104).
Organizer requirements: A limited liability company may be organized by one person. The organizer need not be a natural person, nor a member. (Section 35-8-201).
Articles of Organization requirements: Articles of Organization must contain the following: (1) name of company, (2) duration of company, if less than perpetual, (3) the address of the company's principal place of business, (4) registered agent name and office address, (5) whether company will be managed by managers or members, (6) the names and addresses of the managers if managed by managers, or the names and addresses of the members if managed by members; (7) whether one or more members of the company are to be liable for the company's debts and obligations under Section 35-8-304(3), (8) company purpose, if the company will render professional services, and (9) any additional matters. (Section 35-8-202).
Annual report requirement: Yes, to Secretary of State. (Section 35-8-208). $15 filing fee before April 15; $30 filing fee after April 15.
Publication requirement: No.
Effective date of limited liability company organization: On the date of official approval of Articles of Organization, the company becomes a legal entity and the members are shielded from personal liability. The effective date is also retroactive to the date of submission. (Section 35-8-205).
Membership requirements: Minimum number required is one. The member may be a natural person or a business entity. (Section 35-8-201).
Other: Under Section 35-8-304(3), the Articles of Organization may provide that all or specified members of a company are liable in their capacity as members for all or specified debts, obligations, or liabilities of the company. If one or more members of the company are to be liable for the company's debts and obligations under Section 35-8-304(3), the written consent of each of these members must be filed with the Articles. Also, the registered agent must deliver to the Secretary of State a written statement accepting the appointment. (Section 35-8-105). The state provides a form for this purpose.

Nebraska

Address of state office for filing:
Nebraska Secretary of State
Corporate Division
Box 94608
Lincoln NE 68509
Telephone: (402) 471-4079
State web address: http://www.unicam.state.ne.us/web/public/home
Download state forms: http://www.sos.state.ne.us/business/corp_serv/corp_form.html
State law reference: Revised Statutes of Nebraska, Chapter 21, Sections 2601+.
Title of filing: Articles of Organization.
Forms available online: Articles of Organization, Change of Registered Agent or Registered Office or Both, Amended Articles of Organization, Application for Reservation of Name

Forms provided on CD: Articles of Organization, Application for Reservation of Name

Filing Fee: $100, plus $5 per page and $10 for certificate

Name requirements: The official name must contain the words "Limited Liability Company" or "Limited Company," or the abbreviations "Ltd. Liability Co.," "LLC," or "L.L.C." (Section 21-2604). A company name may be reserved for 120 days for a fee of $15. (Section 21-2604.01).

Organizer requirements: A limited liability company may be organized by one person. The organizer need not be a natural person, nor a member. (Section 21-2605).

Articles of Organization requirements: Articles of Organization must contain the following: (1) name of company, (2) company purpose, (3) company's principal place of business, (4) registered agent name and office address, (5) the total amount of cash contributed to stated capital and a description and agreed value of property other than cash contributed; (6) the total additional contributions agreed to be made by all members and the times at which or events upon the happening of which the contributions will be made; (7) reservation of right to admit new members and the terms and conditions of that admission, (8) whether company will be managed by managers or members, (9) the names and addresses of the managers if managed by managers, or names and addresses of members if managed by members, and (10) any additional matters. (Section 21-2606).

Annual report requirement: Biennial report to Secretary of State. (Section 21-2617.01).

Publication requirement: No.

Effective date of limited liability company organization: On the date of official approval of Articles of Organization, the company becomes a legal entity and the members are shielded from personal liability. The Articles may state a delayed effective date of organization. (Sections 21-2607 & 21-2608).

Membership requirement: Minimum number required is one. The member may be a natural person or a business entity. (Section 21-2605).

Other: The Articles of Organization should disclose the company's duration, which may be perpetual. If the company is organized to provide a professional service, the profession to be practiced must be stated.

Nevada

Address of state office for filing:
Secretary of State
New Filings Division
206 N. Carson Street
Carson City NV 89701-4299

Telephone: 775-684-5708

State web address: http://www.leg.state.nv.us/

Download state forms: http://sos.state.nv.us/business/forms

State law reference: Nevada Revised Statutes, Chapter 86.

Title of filing: Articles of Organization.

Forms available online: All packets include instructions, fee schedules, and credit card checklists. Articles of Organization Packet, Name Reservation Packet, Resident Agent Acceptance, Certificate of Change of Resident Agent or Location of Registered Office or Both, Certificate of Change of Address of Registered Agent and Registered Office, Certificate of Name Change of Resident Agent, Certificate of Resignation of Registered Agent, Initial List of Managers or Managing Members and Resident Agent Packet, Annual List of Managers or Managing Members and Resident Agent Packet, Amendment to Articles of Organization Packet, Amendment to Articles of Organization Before Issuance of Membership Interest Packet, Termination of Amendment to Articles of Organization Packet, Certificate of Correction Packet, Certificate of Resignation of Officer, Director, Manager, Member, General Partner, Trustee, or Subscriber, Customer Order Instructions (Regular or 24 Hour), Customer Order Instructions (2 Hour), Customer Order Instructions (1 Hour)

Forms provided on CD: Articles of Organization, Application for Name Reservation

Filing Fee: $75 to Secretary of State

Name requirements: The official name must contain the words "Limited Liability Company," "Limited-Liability Company," "Limited Company," "Limited," or the abbreviations "Ltd.," "LLC," "L.L.C.," "LC," or "L.C." The word "Company" may be abbreviated as "Co." (Section 86.171). A company name may be reserved for a period of 90 days for a $25 fee. (Section 86.176).

Organizer requirements: A limited liability company may be organized by one person. The organizer need not be a natural person, nor a member. (Section 86.151).

Articles of Organization requirements: Articles of Organization must contain the following: (1) name of company, (2) resident agent name and office address, and agent's mailing address if different from office address (3) name and address, either residence or business, of each of the organizers signing the Articles, (4) whether the company will be managed by members or managers, (5) name and business or residence address of each initial member, if managed by members, or name and business or residence address of each initial manager, if managed by managers, (6) if the company is to have one or more series of members and the debts or liabilities of any series are to be enforceable against the assets of that series only and not against the assets of another series or the company generally, a statement to that effect, and a statement (a) setting forth the relative rights, powers, and duties of the series, or (b) indicating that the relative rights, powers, and duties of the series will be set forth in the operating agreement or established as provided in the operating agreement, and (7) any additional matters. (Section 86.161).

Annual report requirement: Yes, to Secretary of State. The company must file annually a list of its managers or managing members and resident agent. Filing fee is $125. (Section 86.263).

Publication requirement: No.

Effective date of limited liability company organization: On the date of official approval of Articles of Organization, the company becomes a legal entity and the members are shielded from personal liability. (Section 86.201).

Membership requirements: Minimum number required is one. The member may be a natural person or a business entity. (Section 86.151(3)).

Other: By the end of the first month after filing its Articles of Organization, a company must file a list of its managers or managing members and resident agent. $125 filing fee. (Section 86.263). A registered agent is known as a "resident agent" in Nevada. The resident agent must file a written certificate of acceptance along with the Articles of Organization for the Articles to be valid. (Section 86.151). Any filing with the Secretary of State should be accompanied by the appropriate Customer Order Instructions form for regular or expedited service.

New Hampshire

Address of state office for filing:
Department of State
Corporation Division
107 N. Main St.
Concord NH 03301-4989
Telephone: (603) 271-3246
State web address: www.nh.gov
Download state forms: http://www.sos.nh.gov/corporate/Forms.html
State law reference: New Hampshire Revised Statutes Annotated, Title 28, Chapter 304-C. Professional limited liability companies are also governed by Title 28, Chapter 304-D. (Section 304-D:20).
Title of filing: Certificate of Formation.
Forms available online: Application for Reservation of Name, Certificate of Formation Packet [includes Certificate of Formation form and also Form SRA, which must be submitted together with Certificate of Formation], Certificate of Formation for Professional LLC Packet [includes Certificate of Formation for Professional LLC form and also Form SRA, which must be submitted together with Certificate of Formation], Statement of Change of Registered Office or Registered Agent or Both, Statement of Change of Registered Office by Registered Agent, Certificate of Amendment
Forms provided on CD: Application for Reservation of Name, Certificate of Formation
Filing Fee: The total filing fee is $100. This is comprised of $50 for the Certificate of Formation, plus $50 for the SRA form.
Name requirements: The official name may contain the name of a member or a manger, and must contain the words "Limited Liability Company" or the abbreviations "LLC," "L.L.C.," "L L C" or "L. L. C." (Section 304-C:3). If the company provides professional services, the name must have "Professional" or the abbreviation "P" before "Limited" or "L." (Section 304-D:6). A company name may be reserved for 120 days for a fee of $15. (Section 304-C:4).
Organizer requirements: A limited liability company may be organized by one person. The organizer need not be a natural person, nor a member. (Section 304C:2).
Certificate of Formation requirements: Certificate of Formation must contain the following: (1) name of company, (2) company purpose, (3) registered agent name and office address, (4) duration of company, if less than perpetual, (5) if management is to be vested in managers, a statement to that effect, and (6) any additional matters. (Section 304-C:12).
Annual report requirement: Yes, to Secretary of State. (Section 304-C:80). Filing fee of $100.
Publication requirement: No.
Effective date of limited liability company organization: On the date of official approval of Certificate of Formation, the company becomes a legal entity and the members are shielded from personal liability. (Section 304C:12).
Membership requirements: Minimum number required is one. The member may be a natural person or a business entity. (Section 304C:1(V), (X), (XI)).
Other: The Certificate of Formation must be signed by a manager. If there are no managers, it must be signed by a member. (Section 304-C:2(VI)). Also, an Addendum to the Certificate of Formation must be filed along with the Certificate of Formation, stating that the company complies with or is exempt from state securities laws. (Section 304-C:12). The Addendum is filed on Form SRA, which is included in each Certificate of Formation Packet.

New Jersey

Address of state office for filing:
New Jersey Division of Revenue
PO Box 308
Trenton NJ 08608-1001
Telephone: 609-292-9292
State web address: www.njleg.state.nj.us
Download state forms: http://www.state.nj.us/treasury/revenue/
State law reference: New Jersey Statutes, Title 42:2B.
Title of filing: Certificate of Formation.
Forms available online: Complete Business Registration Packet, Public Records Filing for New Business Entity, Business Entity Amendment Filing, Application for Reservation of Name, Certificate of Correction, Certificate of Resignation of Agent With Appointment of New Agent, Certificate of Resignation of Registered Agent Without Successor, Certificate of Change of Registered Name or Address or Both
Forms provided on CD: Public Records Filing for New Business Entity, Application for Reservation of Name
Filing Fee: $125
Name requirements: The official name may contain the name of a manager or member and must contain the words "Limited Liability Company" or the abbreviation "LLC." (Section 42:2B-3). A company name may be reserved for 120 days for a fee of $50.
Organizer requirements: A limited liability company may be organized by one person. The organizer need not be a natural person, nor a member. (Sections 42:2B-2, 42:2B-11).
Articles of Organization requirements: The Articles of Organization are referred to as a Certificate of Formation and must contain the following: (1) name of company, (2) registered agent name and office address, (3) duration of company, whether perpetual or limited; and (4) any additional matters. (Section 42:2B-11(a)).
Annual report requirement: Yes, to Secretary of State. (Section 42:2B-8.1). $50 filing fee.
Publication requirement: No.
Effective date of limited liability company organization: On the date of official approval of Certificate of Formation, the company becomes a legal entity and the members are shielded from personal liability. This date may be delayed to a date stated in the Certificate of Formation. (Section 42:2B-11(b)).
Membership requirements: Minimum number of members required is one. The member may be a natural person or a business entity. (Section 42:2B-2).
Other requirements: None.

New Mexico

Address of state office for filing:
Public Regulation Commission
Corporations Bureau
Chartered Documents Division
PO Box 1269
Santa Fe NM 87504-1269
Telephone: 505-827-4511
State web address: http://legis.state.nm.us/lcs/
Download state forms: http://www.nmprc.state.nm.us/corporations/corpsforms.htm
State law reference: New Mexico Statutes Annotated, Chapter 53, Article 19.
Title of filing: Articles of Organization.
Forms available online: Articles of Organization, Articles of Amendment, Statement of Change of Registered Office or Registered Agent or Both, Application for Reservation of Limited Liability Company Name
Forms provided on CD: Articles of Organization, Articles of Amendment, Application for Reservation of Limited Liability Company Name
Filing Fee: $50
Name requirements: The official name must contain the words "Limited Liability Company" or "Limited Company," or the abbreviation "LLC," "LC," "L.L.C.," or "L.C." The word "Limited" may be abbreviated to "Ltd." and the word "Company" may be abbreviated to "Co." (Section 53-19-3). A company name may be reserved for 120 days for a fee of $20. (Section 53-19-4).
Organizer requirements: A limited liability company may be organized by one person. The organizer need not be a natural person, nor a member. (Section 53-19-7).
Articles of Organization requirements: Articles of Organization must contain the following: (1) name of company, (2) registered

agent name and office address, (3) street address of company's principal place of business, (4) duration of company, if less than perpetual, (5) if company is to be managed by managers, a statement to that effect, (6) if the company may carry on its business as a single-member company, a statement to that effect, and (7) any additional matters. (Section 53-19-8).

Annual report requirement: No.

Publication requirement: No.

Effective date of limited liability company organization: On the date of official approval of Articles of Organization, the company becomes a legal entity and the members are shielded from personal liability. The effective date may be delayed to any later date stated in the Articles of Organization. (Section 53-19-10).

Membership requirements: Minimum number required is one. The member may be a natural person or a business entity. (Section 53-19-2).

Other: The Articles of Organization must be accompanied by a statement executed by the registered agent acknowledging acceptance of the appointment. (Section 53-19-9).

New York

Address of state office for filing:
New York State
Department of State
Division of Corporations
41 State Street
Albany NY 12231

Telephone: (518) 473-2492

State web address: http://assembly.state.ny.us/

Download state forms: http://www.dos.state.ny.us/corp/corpwww.html

State law reference: New York Limited Liability Company Law.

Title of filing: Articles of Organization.

Forms available online: Application for Reservation of Name, Articles of Organization, Certificate of Publication, Certificate of Amendment, Certificate of Change of Registered Agent or Office, Certificate of Change of Registered Address, Certificate of Resignation of Registered Agent, Certificate of Resignation for Receipt of Process

Forms provided on CD: Application for Reservation of Name, Articles of Organization

Filing Fee: $200

Name requirements: The official name must contain the words "Limited Liability Company" or the abbreviation "LLC" or "L.L.C." (Section 204). A company name may be reserved for a 60-day period, renewable twice, for a fee of $20. (Section 205).

Organizer requirements: A limited liability company may be organized by one person. The organizer need not be a natural person, nor a member. (Sections 102, 203).

Articles of Organization requirements: Articles of Organization must contain the following: (1) name of company, (2) county within New York where the company will be located, (3) duration of company, if less than perpetual, (4) designation of the Secretary of State as agent of the company, upon whom process against it may be served and the post office address to which the Secretary of State shall mail a copy of any process served against the company, (5) if the company will have a registered agent, the agent's name and office address, and a statement that the agent is to be the agent of the company upon whom process against it may be served, (6) if all or certain members will be liable in their capacity as members for all or certain debts, obligations, or liabilities of the company under Section 609, a statement to that effect, and (7) any additional matters. (Section 203(e)).

Annual report requirement: Yes, biennial report to Secretary of State. (Section 301(e)).

Publication requirement: Yes, company must publish a summary of its Articles of Organization in 2 newspapers of general circulation designated by the county clerk of the county in which the company's office is located. The company then must file with the Department of State a Certificate of Publication, together with the affidavits of publication from the publishers of the newspapers, within 120 days of the effective date of the Articles of Organization. (Section 206(c)). Certificate of Publication filing fee is $50.

Effective date of limited liability company organization: On the date of official approval of Articles of Organization, the company becomes a legal entity and the members are shielded from personal liability. In addition, the effective date may be delayed up to 60 days if so stated in the Articles of Organization. (Sections 203(d), 209).

Membership requirements: Minimum number required is one. The member may be a natural person or a business entity. (Section 203(c)).

Other: None.

North Carolina

Address of state office for filing:
Secretary of State
Corporations Division
PO Box 29622
Raleigh NC 27626-0622
Telephone: 919-807-2225
State web address: www.ncga.state.nc.us/
Download state forms: http://www.secretary.state.nc.us/corporations/indxfees.asp
State law reference: North Carolina General Statutes, Chapter 57C.
Title of filing: Articles of Organization.
Forms available online: Instructions for Organizing, Articles of Organization, Articles of Correction, Application to Reserve a Business Entity Name, Designation of Registered Office Address or Registered Agent or Both, Statement of Change of Registered Office or Registered Agent or Both, Statement of Resignation of Registered Agent, Articles of Restatement, Amendment of Articles of Organization
Forms provided on CD: Articles of Organization, Application to Reserve a Business Entity Name
Filing Fee: $125
Name requirements: The official name must contain the words "Limited Liability Company" or the abbreviation "LLC" or "L.L.C.," or the combination "Ltd. Liability Co.," "Limited Liability Co.," or "Ltd. Liability Company." (Section 55D-20). A company name may be reserved for 120 days for a fee of $30. (Section 55D-23).
Organizer requirements: A limited liability company may be organized by one person. The organizer need not be a natural person, nor a member. (Section 57C-2-20).
Articles of Organization requirements: Articles of Organization must contain the following: (1) name of company, (2) duration of company, if less than perpetual, (3) the name and address of each person executing the Articles and whether the person is executing the Articles in the capacity of a member or an organizer, (4) registered agent name and office address, including its county, (5) the street address, including its county, of the company's principal office, and (6) any additional matters. (Section 57C-2-21).
Annual report requirement: Yes, to Secretary of State. (Section 57C-2-23). $200 filing fee.
Publication requirement: No.
Effective date of limited liability company organization: On the date of official approval of Articles of Organization, the company becomes a legal entity and the members are shielded from personal liability. In addition, the effective date may be delayed up to 90 days if so stated in the Articles of Organization. (Section 57C-2-20).
Membership requirements: Minimum number required is one. May be a natural person or a business entity. (Section 57C-2-20(c)).
Other: All members, by virtue of their status as members, shall be managers of the company unless the Articles of Organization provide otherwise. (Section 57C-3-20(a). If the organizers want a manager-managed company, the Articles must include a statement that, except as provided in Section 57C-3-20(a), the members shall not be managers by virtue of their status as members. (Section 57C-2-21).

North Dakota

Address of state office for filing:
Business Division
Secretary of State
600 E. Boulevard Ave. Dept. 108
Bismarck ND 58505-0500
Telephone: 701-328-4284
State web address: http://www.nd.gov/
Download state forms: http://www.nd.gov/sos/businessserv/registrations/index.html
State law reference: North Dakota Century Code, Chapter 10-32.
Title of filing: Articles of Organization.
Forms available online: Articles of Organization, Reserve Name Application, Registered Agent Consent to Serve, Registered Agent or Office Statement of Change.
Forms provided on CD: Articles of Organization, Reserve Name Application
Filing Fee: $125
Name requirements: The official name must contain the words "Limited Liability Company" or the abbreviation "LLC" or "L.L.C." (Section 10-32-10). A company name may be reserved for renewable 12-month periods for a fee of $10. (Section 10-32-11).
Organizer requirements: A limited liability company may be organized by one person. The organizer must be an individual person. (Section 10-32-05).

Articles of Organization requirements: Must contain the following: (1) name of company, (2) registered agent name and office address, (3) name and address of each organizer, (4) effective date or organization, if later than the date on which the certificate of organization is issued (may be up to 90 days later), duration of company, if less than perpetual), (5) duration of company, if less than perpetual, and (6) any additional matters. (Section 10-32-07).

Annual report requirement: Yes, to Secretary of State. (Section 10-32-149). $50 filing fee.

Publication requirement: No.

Effective date of limited liability company organization: On the date of official approval of Articles of Organization, the company becomes a legal entity and the members are shielded from personal liability. (Section 10-32-09). The effective date may be delayed up to 90 day of the issuance of the Certificate of Organization, if so stated in the Articles. (Section 10-32-07)(1)(d)).

Membership requirements: Minimum number required is one. (Section 10-32-06). The member may be a natural person or a business entity. (Section 10-32-02(40)). The Articles of Organization must specifically authorize the company to have less than two members.

Other: Consent to be Registered Agent must be filed with Articles of Organization, $10 filing fee. Also, Section 10-32-07(2) contains twenty-two different provisions that will govern the company unless modified in the Articles of Organization. For example, unless stated in the Articles, the company must allow cumulative voting for governors (Section 10-32-07(2)(d)), the voting power of each membership interest is in proportion to the value reflected in the required records of the contributions of the members (Section 10-32-07(2)(m)), and a written action by the members taken without a meeting must be signed by all members (Section 10-32-07(2)(p)). For a complete list, see Section 10-32-07(2). Separately, Section 10-32-07(3) lists eighteen different provisions that will govern the company unless modified in the Articles, a member control agreement, or in the bylaws. For example, a majority of the board is a quorum for a board meeting (Section 10-32-07(3)(g)), and members have no right to interim distributions except as provided through the bylaws or an act of the board (Section 10-32-07(3)(r)).

Ohio

Address of state office for filing:
Ohio Secretary of State
Corporation Division
PO Box 670
Columbus, OH 42316

Telephone: 614-466-3910

State web address: http://www.ohio.gov/

Download state forms: http://www.sos.state.oh.us/SOSApps/SOS/FormRefbs.aspx

State law reference: Ohio Revised Code Annotated, Title 17, Chapter 1705.

Title of filing: Articles of Organization.

Forms available online: Organization or Registration of Limited Liability Company, Statutory Agent Update, Certificate of Amendment, Restatement, or Correction, Name Registration or Reservation

Forms provided on CD: Organization or Registration of Limited Liability Company, Name Registration or Reservation

Filing Fee: $125

Name requirements: The official name must contain the words "Limited Liability Company" or the word "Limited," or the abbreviation "LLC," L.L.C.," "Ltd" or "Ltd." (Section 1705.05(A)). A company name may be reserved for 180 days for a fee of $50. (Section 1705.05(E)).

Organizer requirements: A limited liability company may be organized by one person. The organizer need not be a natural person, nor a member. (Section 1705.04(A)).

Articles of Organization requirements: Articles of Organization must contain the following: (1) name of company, (2) duration of company, if less than perpetual, and (3) any additional matters. (Section 1705.04(A)).

Annual report requirement: No.

Publication requirement: No.

Effective date of limited liability company organization: On the date of official approval of Articles of Organization, the company becomes a legal entity and the members are shielded from personal liability. (Section 1705.07(a)).

Membership requirements: Minimum number required is one. The member may be a natural person or a business entity. (Section 1705.01(G), (K)).

Other: Organizers must file with the Articles of Organization an Appointment of Statutory Agent form, signed by an authorized member, manager, or other company representative, and an Acceptance of Statutory Agent form, signed by the agent accepting the appointment. (Section 1705.06(B)).

Oklahoma

Address of state office for filing:
Secretary of State
2300 N. Lincoln Blvd., Room 101
Oklahoma City OK 73105-4897
Telephone: 405-521-3912
State web address: http://www.oklahoma.gov/
Download state forms: http://www.sos.state.ok.us/business/business_filing.htm
State law reference: Oklahoma Statutes, Title 18, Sections 2000+.
Title of filing: Articles of Organization.
Forms available online: Application for Reservation of Name, Articles of Organization, Amended Articles of Organization, Change or Designation of Resident Agent or Registered Office or Principal Office, Resignation of Resident Agent, Articles of Correction
Forms provided on CD: Application for Reservation of Name, Articles of Organization
Filing Fee: $100
Name requirement: The official name must contain the words "Limited Liability Company," "Limited Company," or the abbreviations "LLC, L.L.C.," "LC," or "L.C." The words "Limited" and "Company" may be abbreviated as "Ltd." or "Co." (Section 18-2008). A company name may be reserved for a period of 60 days for $10. (Section 18-2009).
Organizer requirements: A limited liability company may be organized by one person. The organizer need not be a natural person, nor a member. (Section 18-2004, 18-2001(17)).
Articles of Organization requirements: Articles of Organization must contain the following: (1) name of company, (2) duration of company, if less than perpetual, (3) street address of the company's principal place of business, (4) resident agent name and office address, (5) if the company is to establish two or more series of members, managers, or membership interests having separate rights, powers or duties, and the debts, liabilities and obligations incurred, contracted for, or otherwise existing with respect to a particular series are to be enforceable against the assets of the series only, a notice of the limitation on liabilities of the series, and (6) any additional matters. (Section 18-2005).
Annual report requirement: No.
Publication requirement: No.
Effective date of limited liability company organization: On the date of official approval of Articles of Organization, the company becomes a legal entity and the members are shielded from personal liability. The effective date may be delayed up to nineteen days after the filing, if so provided in the Articles. (Section 18-2007).
Membership requirements: Minimum number required is one. The member may be a natural person or a business entity. (Section 18-2001(14), (17)).
Other: Registered agent is known as "resident agent" in Oklahoma.

Oregon

Address of state office for filing:
Oregon Secretary of State
Corporation Division
225 Capitol Street NE
Suite 151
Salem OR 97310-1327
Telephone: 503-986-2200
State web address: http://www.leg.state.or.us/
Download state forms: http://www.filinginoregon.com/forms/index.htm
State law reference: Oregon Revised Statutes, Chapter 63.
Title of filing: Articles of Organization.
Forms available online: Articles of Organization, Change of Registered Agent or Address, Change of Mailing Address
Forms provided on CD: Articles of Organization, Assumed Business Name, Application for Reserved Name (prepared by Nova)
Filing Fee: $50
Name requirements: The official name must contain the words "Limited Liability Company" or the abbreviation "LLC" or "L.L.C." (Section 63.094). A company name may be reserved for 120 days for $50. (Section 63.097).
Organizer requirements: A limited liability company may be organized by one person. The organizer need not be a natural

person, nor a member. (Section 63.044).

Articles of Organization requirements: Articles of Organization must contain the following: (1) name of company, (2) registered agent name and office address, (3) mailing address to which notices may be mailed until the company designates an address in its annual report, (4) if company will be managed by managers, a statement to that effect; (5) names and addresses of organizers, (6) duration of company (may be perpetual), (7) if the company will render professional services, a description of the services to be rendered, and (8) any additional matters. (Section 63.047).

Annual report requirement: Yes, registration renewal and annual report to Secretary of State. (Section 63.787). $50 filing fee.

Publication requirement: No.

Effective date of limited liability company organization: On the date of official approval of Articles of Organization, the company becomes a legal entity and the members are shielded from personal liability. In addition, the effective date may be delayed up to 90 days to a date stated in the Articles of Organization. (Section 63.011).

Membership requirements: Minimum number required is one. The member may be a natural person or a business entity. (Section 63.001(17), (21), (28)).

Other: None.

Pennsylvania

Address of state office for filing:
Department of State
Corporation Bureau
P.O. Box 8722
Harrisburg PA 17105-8722

Telephone: 717-787-1057

State web address: http://www.state.pa.us/

Download state forms: http://www.dos.state.pa.us/corps/site/default.asp

State law reference: Pennsylvania Code, Title 15, Chapter 89, Sections 8900+.

Title of filing: Certificate of Organization.

Forms available online: Certificate of Organization, Certificate of Change or Registered Office, Certificate of Amendment, Statement of Change of Registered Office by Agent, Docketing Statement

Forms provided on CD: Certificate of Organization, Registration of Fictitious Name, Application for Reservation of Name (prepared by Nova)

Filing Fee: $125

Name requirements: The official name must contain the words "Limited Liability Company," "Limited Company," or an abbreviation of either. A name may be reserved for 120 days for $70.

Organizer requirements: A limited liability company may be organized by one person. The organizer need not be a natural person, nor a member. (Section 8912).

Articles of Organization requirements: Articles of Organization are referred to as a Certificate of Organization and must contain the following: (1) name of company, (2) duration of company, if less than perpetual, (3) company purpose if the company will render professional services, (4) registered agent name and office address, (5) whether company will be managed by managers or members, and (6) any additional matters. (Section 8913).

Annual report requirement: Yes, Certificate of Annual Registration to the Department of State.

Publication requirement: No.

Effective date of limited liability company organization: On the date of official approval of Certificate of Organization, the company becomes a legal entity and the members are shielded from personal liability. In addition, the effective date may be delayed to a date stated in the Certificate of Organization. (Section 8914(b)).

Membership requirements: Minimum number required is one. The member may be a natural person or a business entity. (Section 8912).

Other: None.

Rhode Island

Address of state office for filing:
Office of the Secretary of State
Corporations Division
148 W. River Street
Providence RI 02904-2615

Telephone: 401-222-3040
State law reference: General Laws of Rhode Island, Title 7, Chapter 7-16.
State web address: http://www.state.ri.us/
Download state forms: http://www.sec.state.ri.us/corps
Title of filing: Articles of Organization.
Forms available online: Articles of Organization, Application for Reservation of Entity Name, Articles of Amendment, Certificate of Correction, Statement of Change of Resident Agent or Office
Forms provided on CD: Articles of Organization, Application for Reservation of Entity Name
Filing Fee: $150
Name requirements: The official name must contain the words "Limited Liability Company" or the abbreviation "LLC" or "L.L.C." In addition, lower case letters may be used in the abbreviations. (Section 7-16-9). A company name may be reserved for 120 days for a fee of $50. (Section 7-16-10).
Organizer requirements: A limited liability company may be organized by one person. The organizer need not be a natural person, nor a member. (Section 7-16-5, 7-16-2(20)).
Articles of Organization requirements: Articles of Organization must contain the following: (1) name of company, (2) registered agent name and office address, (3) a statement whether, under the Articles and Organization and any written operating agreement made or intended to be made, the company is intended to be (a) treated as a partnership, (b) as a corporation, or (c) disregarded as an entity separate from its member for purposes of federal income taxation, (4) the address of the principal office of the company, if it has been determined at the time of organization, (5) whether the company will be managed by managers or members, and, if the company has managers at the time of its formation, the name and address of each manager, and (6) any additional matters. (Section 7-16-6).
Annual report requirement: Yes, to Secretary of State. (Section 7-16-66). $50 filing fee.
Publication requirement: No.
Effective date of limited liability company organization: On the date of official approval of Articles of Organization, the company becomes a legal entity and the members are shielded from personal liability. (Section 7-16-5(b)).
Membership requirements: Minimum number required is one. The member may be a natural person or a business entity. (Section 7-16-2(16), (20)).
Other: The Articles may delay the effective date by up to 30 days if so stated in the Articles of Organization.

South Carolina

Address of state office for filing:
  South Carolina Secretary of State
  Corporations Department
  PO Box 11350
  Columbia SC 29211
Telephone: 803-734-2158
State web address: http://www.sc.gov
Download state forms: http://www.scsos.com/forms.htm
State law reference: South Carolina Code Annotated, Title 33, Chapter 44.
Title of filing: Articles of Organization.
Forms available online: Articles of Organization, Application to Reserve LLC Name, Amended Articles of Organization, Articles of Termination, Resignation of Registered Agent, Change of Registered Office, Agent, or Agent Address
Forms provided on CD: Articles of Organization, Application to Reserve LLC Name
Filing Fee: $110
Name requirements: The official name must contain the words "Limited Liability Company," "Limited Company," or the abbreviations "LLC," "L.L.C.," "LC," or "L.C." The words "Limited" and "Company" may be abbreviated as "Ltd." and "Co." (Section 33-44-105). A company name may be reserved for 120 days for a fee of $25. (Section 33-44-106).
Organizer requirements: A limited liability company may be organized by one person. The organizer need not be a natural person, nor a member. (Section 33-44-202(a), 33-44-101(14)).
Articles of Organization requirements: Articles of Organization must contain the following: (1) name of company, (2) registered agent name and office address, (3) name and address of each organizer, (4) duration of company, (5) whether company will be managed by managers, and if so, the name and address of each initial manager, (6) whether one or more of the members will be liable for the company's debts and obligations under Section 33-44-303(c), and (7) any additional matters. (Section 33-44-203).
Annual report requirement: No.
Publication requirement: No.
Effective date of limited liability company organization: On the date of official approval of Articles of Organization, the

company becomes a legal entity and the members are shielded from personal liability. In addition, the effective date may be delayed by up to 90 days if so stated in the Articles of Organization. (Sections 33-44-201, 33-44-202, 33-44-206). Special provisions relate to single-member companies. (Sections 12-2-25, 33-44-201).

Membership requirements: Minimum number required is one. The member may be a natural person or a business entity. (Section 33-44-202(a)).

Other: None.

South Dakota

Address of state office for filing:
South Dakota Secretary of State
State Capitol
500 E. Capitol Avenue
Pierre SD 57501
Telephone: 605-773-4845
State web address: http://www.state.sd.us/
Download state forms: http://www.sdsos.gov/busineservices/corporations.shtm
State law reference: South Dakota Compiled Laws, Title 47, Chapter 34A.
Title of filing: Articles of Organization.
Forms available online: Articles of Organization, Annual Report, Statement of Change of Registered Office or Agent or Both, Amendment to Articles of Organization, Application for Reservation of Name
Forms provided on CD: Articles of Organization, Application for Reservation of Name
Filing Fee: $125.
Name requirements: The official name must contain the words "Limited Liability Company," "Limited Company," or the abbreviation "LLC.," "L.L.C," "LC," or "L.C." The words "Limited" and "Company" may be abbreviated as "Ltd." and "Co." (Section 47-34A-105). Names are reservable for 120 days for $20 fee. (Section 47-34A-106).
Organizer requirements: A limited liability company may be organized by one person. The organizer need not be a natural person, nor a member. (Section 47-34A-101(13), 47-34A-202.1).
Articles of Organization requirements: Articles of Organization must contain the following: (1) name of company, (2) registered office address, (3) registered agent name and street address, and his or her written consent to the appointment, (4) the name and address of each organizer, (5) duration of the company, if other than perpetual, (6) whether the company is to be managed by managers, and if so, the name and address of each manager, (7) whether one or more members will be liable for the company's debts and obligations under Section 47-34A-303(c), and (8) any additional matters. (Section 47-34A-203).
Annual report requirement: Yes, to Secretary of State. (Section 47-34A-211). $50 filing fee.
Publication requirement: No.
Effective date of limited liability company organization: On the date of official approval of Articles of Organization, the company becomes a legal entity and the members are shielded from personal liability. (Section 47-34A-202.2).
Membership requirements: Minimum number required is one. The member may be a natural person or a business entity. (Section 47-34A-202.1).
Other: None.

Tennessee

Address of state office for filing:
Department of State
Corporate Filings
312 Eighth Avenue North
6th Floor, William R. Snodgrass Tower
Nashville TN 37243
Telephone: (615) 741-2286
State web address: http://www.tennessee.gov/
Download state forms: http://state.tn.us/sos/bus_svc/forms.htm
State law reference: Tennessee Code Annotated, Title 48, Chapter 249.
Title of filing: Articles of Organization.
Forms available online: Articles of Organization, Articles of Amendment to Articles of Organization, Application for Reservation of LLC Name, Change of Registered Agent or Office, Change of Registered Office by Agent, Resignation of Registered Agent, Articles of Correction

Forms provided on CD: Articles of Organization, Application for Reservation of LLC Name

Filing Fee: $50 per member with a $300 minimum fee and a $3,000 maximum fee

Name requirements: The official name must contain the words "Limited Liability Company" or the abbreviations "L.L.C." or "LLC." (Section 48-249-106). A company name may be reserved for four months for a fee of $20. (Section 48-249-107).

Organizer requirements: A limited liability company must be organized by one person or entity. (Section 48-249-201).

Articles of Organization requirements: Articles of Organization must contain the following: (1) name of company, (2) registered agent name and office address, (3) street address, county, and zip code of company's principal office, (4) statement whether company will be manager-managed, member-managed, or director-managed, (5) if company will have more than six members at date of filing, the number of members, (6) if one or more members are personally liable for all debts, obligations, and liabilities of the company, the information required under Section 48-249-114(f), (7) if the company's existence is to begin in the future (up to 90 days in the future), a statement to that effect, (8) if the company will not conduct business in Tennessee, a statement that the company is prohibited from engaging in business in Tennessee, (9) duration of company, if less than perpetual, and (10) any additional matters. (Section 48-249-202).

Annual report requirement: Yes, to Secretary of State. (Section 48-249-1017).

Publication requirement: No.

Effective date of limited liability company organization: On the date of official approval of Articles of Organization, the company becomes a legal entity and the members are shielded from personal liability. In addition, the effective date may be delayed by up to 90 days if so stated in the Articles of Organization. (Section 48-249-201).

Membership requirements: Minimum number required is one. The member may be a natural person or a business entity. (Section 48-249-501).

Other: None.

Texas

Address of state office for filing:
Secretary of State
PO Box 13697
Austin TX 78711-3697

Telephone: 512-463-5555

State web address: http://www.state.tx.us/

Download state forms: http://www.sos.state.tx.us/corp/index.shtml

State law reference: Texas Business Organization Code, Titles 1 and 3.

Title of filing: Certificate of Formation.

Forms available online: Certificate of Formation, Change of Registered Agent or Office, Resignation of Registered Agent, Certificate of Correction, Change by Registered Agent to Name or Address, Certificate of Amendment, Application for Reservation or Renewal of Reservation of Entity Name.

Forms provided on CD: Certificate of Formation, Application for Reservation or Renewal of Reservation of Entity Name.

Filing Fee: $300

Name requirements: The official name must contain the words "Limited Liability Company," "Limited Company," or the abbreviations "LLC," "L.L.C.," "LC," or "L.C." (Section 5.056). A company name may be reserved for 120 days for a fee of $40. (Section 5.101, 5.104).

Organizer requirements: A limited liability company may be organized by one person. The organizer need not be a natural person, nor a member. (Section 3.004).

Certificate of Formation requirements: Certificate of Formation must contain the following: (1) name of company, (2) duration of company, if less than perpetual, (3) company purpose, (4) registered agent name and office address, (5) name and address of each organizer, and (6) any additional matters. (Section 3.005).

Annual report requirement: Annual franchise tax reporting requirements can be found at Chapter 171 of the Texas Revised Civil Statutes.

Publication requirement: No.

Effective date of limited liability company organization: On the date of official approval of Articles of Organization, the company becomes a legal entity and the members are shielded from personal liability. Certificate may state that it takes effect up to 90 days after the date of signing. (Section 4.053).

Membership requirements: Minimum number required is one. The member may be a natural person or a business entity. (Section 101.101).

Other: If the company will be managed by managers, the Certificate must contain a statement to that effect and the names and addresses of the managers. If the company will be managed by members, the Certificate must contain a statement to that effect and the names and addresses of the members. (Section 3.010).

Utah

Address of state office for filing:
    State of Utah Department of Commerce
    Division of Corporations & Commercial Code
    PO Box 146705
    Salt Lake City UT 84114-6705
Telephone: 801-530-4849
State web address: http://www.utah.gov/
Download state forms: http://corporations.utah.gov/corpforms.html
State law reference: Utah Code Annotated, Title 48, Chapter 2c.
Title of filing: Articles of Organization.
Forms available online: Articles of Organization, Articles of Amendment
Forms provided on CD: Articles of Organization, Name Reservation
Filing Fee: $52
Name requirements: The official name must contain the words "Limited Liability Company," "Limited Company," or the abbreviations "LLC," "L.L.C.," "LC," or "L.C." (Section 48-2c-106). A company name may be reserved for renewable 120-day periods for a $22. (Section 48-2c-108).
Organizer requirements: A limited liability company may be organized by one person. The organizer need not be a natural person, nor a member. (Section 48-2c-401).
Articles of Organization requirements: Articles of Organization must contain the following: (1) name of company, (2) company purpose, (3) registered agent's name, office address, and signature, (4) a statement that the Director of the Division is appointed as the registered agent for service of process if (a) the agent resigns, (b) the agent's authority is revoked, or (c) the agent cannot be found or served with the exercise of reasonable diligence, (5) street address of the company's designated office or a statement that the company's registered office shall be its designated office, (6) name and street address of each organizer who is not a member or manager, (7) if company will be managed by managers, a statement to that effect and the names and addresses of the initial managers, (8) if company will be managed by members, a statement to that effect and the names and street addresses of the initial members, and (8) any additional matters. (Section 48-2c-403).
Annual report requirement: Yes, annual report due to Division of Corporations & Commercial Code. (Section 48-2c-203). $12 filing fee.
Publication requirement: No.
Effective date of limited liability company organization: On the date of official approval of Articles of Organization, the company becomes a legal entity and the members are shielded from personal liability. In addition, the effective date may be delayed to a date stated in the Articles of Organization. (Sections 48-2c-104, 48-2c-208).
Membership requirements: Minimum number required is one. The member may be a natural person or a business entity. (Sections 48-2c-401, 48-2c-102(14), (17)).
Other: The organizer's signature on the Articles of Organization is an affirmation that the company has one or more members, and that, if the company is managed by managers, the person or persons named as managers in the Articles have consented to serve as managers. Additionally, if the company is to be managed by members, then at the same time or prior to filing the Articles, the organizer must prepare a document, to be held with the other records of the company, stating the name and street address of each initial member of the company. (Section 48-2c-401). If the company is to be managed by managers, the Articles need not state the names and addresses of the company's members, unless the company will provide professional services. (Section 48-2c-403(2)). Finally, the Articles may state the duration of the company, which can be as long as 99 years. If the Articles state no duration, the company's duration will be 99 years from the date the Articles were filed, or 99 years from the date of the latest amendment to the Articles. (Section 48-2c-403(4), (5)).

Vermont

Address of state office for filing:
    Vermont Secretary of State
    81 River Street
    Montpelier VT 05609-1104
Telephone: (802) 828-2386
State web address: www.leg.state.vt.us/
Download state forms: http://www.sec.state.vt.us/corps/corpindex.htm
State law reference: Vermont Statutes Annotated, Title 11, Chapter 21.

Title of filing: Articles of Organization.

Forms available online: LLC Articles of Organization, Application to Reserve a Name

Forms provided on CD: LLC Articles of Organization, Application to Reserve a Name

Filing Fee: $75

Name requirements: The official name must contain the words "Limited Liability Company," "Limited Company," or the abbreviations "LLC," "L.L.C.," "LC," or "L.C." The words "Limited" and "Company" may be abbreviated as "Ltd." and "Co." (Section 3005). A company name may be reserved for 120 days for a fee of $20. (Section 3006).

Organizer requirements: A limited liability company may be organized by one person. The organizer need not be a natural person, nor a member. (Section 3022).

Articles of Organization requirements: Articles of Organization must contain the following: (1) name of company, (2) address of initial designated office, (3) registered agent name and office address, (4) name and address of each organizer, (5) duration of company, if less than perpetual, (6) if company will be managed by managers, a statement to that effect and the names and addresses of each initial manager, (7) whether the members of the company will be liable for its debts and obligations under Section 3043(b), and (8) any additional matters. (Section 3023).

Annual report requirement: Yes, to Secretary of State. (Section 3161). $20 filing fee.

Publication requirement: No.

Effective date of limited liability company organization: On the date of official approval of Articles of Organization, the company becomes a legal entity and the members are shielded from personal liability. In addition, the effective date may be delayed up to 90 days if so stated in the Articles of Organization. (Section 3022(b), 3026).

Membership requirements: Minimum number required is one. The member may be a natural person or a business entity. (Section 3022(a)).

Other: The company must file the address of its principal office with the Secretary of State within 90 days of the filing of the Articles of Organization. (Section 3023(e)). Articles must state business purpose and the month the company's fiscal year ends.

Virginia

Address of state office for filing:
Clerk of the State Corporation Commission
PO Box 1197
Richmond, VA 23218-1197

Telephone: 804-371-9733

State web address: http://www.virginia.gov/

Download state forms: http://www.scc.virginia.gov/division/clk/fee_bus.htm

State law reference: Virginia Code Annotated, Title 13.1, Chapter 12.

Title of filing: Articles of Organization.

Forms available online: Notice to Virginia LLCs, Articles of Organization, Application for Reservation or Renewal of Reservation of LLC Name, Guide for Articles of Amendment

Forms provided on CD: Articles of Organization, Application for Reservation or Renewal of Reservation of LLC Name

Filing Fee: $100

Name requirements: The official name must contain the words "Limited Liability Company," "Limited Company," or the abbreviations "LLC," "L.L.C.," "LC," or "L.C." (Section 13.1-1012). A company name may be reserved for renewable 120-day periods for a fee of $10. (Section 13.1-1013).

Organizer requirements: A limited liability company may be organized by one person. The organizer need not be a natural person, nor a member. (Sections 13.1-1010, 13.1-1002).

Articles of Organization requirements: Articles of Organization must contain the following: (1) name of company, (2) mailing address, including street address, if any, of registered office, (3) name of registered agent, (4) if registered agent is an individual, a statement that he or she is either (a) an individual who is a resident of Virginia and either a member or manager of the company, (b) a member or manager of a limited liability company that is a member or manager of the company, (c) an officer or director of a corporation that is a member or manager of the company, (d) a general partner of a general or limited partnership that is a member or manager of the company, (e) a trustee of a trust that is a member or a manager of the company, or (f) a member of the Virginia State Bar, (5) if registered agent is a domestic or foreign stock or non-stock corporation, limited liability company, or registered limited liability partnership, that it is authorized to transact business in the Commonwealth, (6) the mailing address, including the street address, if any, of the principal office of the company, which may be the same as the registered office but need not be within Virginia, and (7) any other matters. (Section 13.1-1011).

Annual report requirement: Yes, to State Corporation Commission. (Section 13.1-1062) Annual Registration Fee is $50.00.

Publication requirement: No.

Effective date of limited liability company organization: On the date of official approval of Articles of Organization, the company becomes a legal entity and the members are shielded from personal liability. In addition, the effective date may be delayed up to 15 days if so stated in the Articles of Organization. (Section 13.11004(b)).

Membership requirements: Minimum number required is one. The member may be a natural person or a business entity. (Section 13.11002).

Other: None.

Washington

Address of state office for filing:
Washington Secretary of State
Corporations Division
Box 40234
Olympia WA 98504-0234

Telephone: (360) 753-7115

State web address: http://www1.leg.wa.gov/legislature/

Download state forms: http://www.secstate.wa.gov/corps/registration_forms.aspx

State law reference: Revised Code of Washington, Title 25, Chapter 25.15.

Title of filing: Certificate of Formation.

Forms available online: Application to Form a Limited Liability Company, Articles of Amendment, Statement of Change for Registered Agent or Office, Application for Reservation of Washington Domestic Name

Forms provided on CD: Application to Form a Limited Liability Company, Application for Reservation of Washington Domestic Name

Filing Fee: $175

Name requirements: The official name must contain the words "Limited Liability Company," "Limited Liability Co.," or the abbreviations "LLC" or "L.L.C." (Section 25.15.010). A company name may be reserved for 180 days for a fee of $30. (Section 25.15.015).

Organizer requirements: A limited liability company may be organized by one person. The organizer need not be a natural person, nor a member. (Section 25.15.070).

Articles of Organization requirements: Articles of Organization are referred to as a Certificate of Formation and must contain the following: (1) name of company, (2) registered agent name and office address, (3) address of company's principal place of business, (4) duration of company, if less than perpetual, (5) if company will be managed by managers a statement to that effect, and (6) any additional matters. (Section 25.15.070(1)).

Annual report requirement: Yes, to Secretary of State. (Section 25.15.105).

Publication requirement: No.

Effective date of limited liability company organization: On the date of official approval of Certificate of Formation, the company becomes a legal entity and the members are shielded from personal liability. In addition, the effective date may be delayed up to 90 days if so stated in the Certificate of Formation. (Section 25:15.070(2)).

Membership requirements: Minimum number required is one. The member may be a natural person or a business entity. (Section 25.15.005(4), (9)).

Other: None.

West Virginia

Address of state office for filing:
West Virginia Secretary of State
Corporation Division
State Capitol Building
1900 Kanawha Blvd East
Charleston WV 25305-0770

Telephone: (304) 558-8000

State web address: http://www.legis.state.wv.us/

Download state forms: http://www.wvsos.com/business/services/formindex.htm

State law reference: West Virginia Code, Chapter 31B.

Title of filing: Articles of Organization.

Forms available online: Articles of Organization, Application for Name Reservation, Application to Appoint or Change Agent

or Office Address, Articles of Amendment
Forms provided on CD: Articles of Organization, Application for Name Reservation
Filing Fee: $100
Name requirements: The official name must contain the words "Limited Liability Company," "Limited Company," or the abbreviations "LLC," "L.L.C.," "LC," or "L.C." The words "Limited" and "Company" may be abbreviated as "Ltd." and "Co." (Section 31B-1-105). A company name may be reserved for 120 days (renewable once) for a fee of $15. (Section 31B-1-106).
Organizer requirements: A limited liability company may be organized by one person. The organizer need not be a natural person, nor a member. (Section 31B-2-202(a)).
Articles of Organization requirements: Articles of Organization must contain the following: (1) name of company, (2) address of initial designated office in West Virginia, if any, and the mailing address of the principal office, (3) registered agent name and office address, (4) name and address of each organizer and of each member having authority to execute instruments on behalf of the company; (5) duration of company, if less than perpetual, (6) if company will be managed by managers, a statement to that effect and the names and addresses of the managers, (7) whether one or more of the members of the company are to be liable for its debts and obligations under Section 31B-3-303(c), (8) the purposes for which the company is organized, and (9) any additional matters. (Section 31B-2-203(a)).
Annual report requirement: Yes, to Secretary of State. (Section 31B-2-211).
Publication requirement: No.
Effective date of limited liability company organization: On the date of official approval of Articles of Organization, the company becomes a legal entity. In addition, the effective date may be delayed up to 90 days to a date stated in the Articles of Organization. (Sections 31B-2-202(b), (c) and 31B-2-206).
Membership requirements: Minimum number required is one. The member may be a natural person or a business entity. (Section 31B-2-202(a)).
Other: Articles of Organization must be filed with an Attorney-in-fact fee, which is variable based on the month in which Articles are filed. Instruction sheet illustrating the sliding scale is attached to state Articles of Organization form.

Wisconsin

Address of state office for filing:
Wisconsin Department of Financial Institutions
Division of Corporate and Consumer Services
PO Box 7846
Madison WI 53707-7846
Telephone: (608) 261-7577
State web address: www.legis.state.wi.us/
Download state forms: http://www.wdfi.org/corporations/forms
State law reference: Wisconsin Statutes Annotated, Chapter 183.
Title of filing: Articles of Organization.
Forms available online: Articles of Organization, Name Reservation Application, Articles of Amendment, Registered Agent or Office Change, or Both, Resignation of Registered Agent, Articles of Correction
Forms provided on CD: Articles of Organization, Name Reservation Application
Filing Fee: $170 paper, $130 online
Name requirements: The official name must contain the words "Limited Liability Company," "Limited Liability Co.," or the abbreviations "LLC" or "L.L.C." (Section 183.0103). A company name may be reserved for renewable 120-day periods for a fee of $15. (Section 183.0104).
Organizer requirements: A limited liability company may be organized by one person. The organizer need not be a natural person, nor a member. (Section 183.0201).
Articles of Organization requirements: Articles of Organization must contain the following: (1) a statement that the company is organized under Chapter 183 of the Wisconsin Statutes, (2) name of company, (3) registered agent name and office address, (4) if company will be managed by managers, a statement to that effect, (5) names and addresses of organizers, and (6) any additional matters. (Section 183.0202).
Annual report requirement: Yes, to Department of Financial Institutions. (Section 183.0120) $25 filing fee.
Publication requirement: No.
Effective date of limited liability company organization: On the date of official approval of Articles of Organization, the company becomes a legal entity and the members are shielded from personal liability. In addition, the effective date may be delayed up to 90 days to a date stated in the Articles of Organization. (Sections 183.0204(1) and 183.0111).
Membership requirements: Minimum number required is one. The member may be a natural person or a business entity. (Section 183.0102(15)).
Other: None.

Wyoming

Address of state office for filing:

Wyoming Secretary of State
The Capitol Building, Room 110
200 W. 24th Street
Cheyenne WY 82002-0020

Telephone: 307-777-7311

State web address: http://legisweb.state.wy.us/

Download state forms: http://soswy.state.wy.us/corporat/corporat.htm

State law reference: Wyoming Statutes, Title 17, Chapter 15.

Title of filing: Articles of Organization.

Forms available online: Articles of Organization, Amendment to Articles of Organization, Application for Reservation of Name of LLC, Articles of Correction, Consent to Appointment by Registered Agent, Statement of Change of Registered Agent or Registered Office or Both

Forms provided on CD: Articles of Organization, Application for Reservation of Name of LLC

Filing Fee: $100

Name requirements: The official name must contain the words "Limited Liability Company," "Limited Company," or the abbreviations "LLC," "L.L.C.," "LC," or "L.C." The words "Limited" and "Company" may be abbreviated as "Ltd." and "Co." (Section 17-15-105(a)). A company name may be reserved for a fee of $30. (Section 17-15-105(d)).

Organizer requirements: A limited liability company may be organized by one person. The organizer need not be a natural person, nor a member. (Section 17-15-106).

Articles of Organization requirements: Articles of Organization must contain the following: (1) name of company, (2) duration of company, which shall be thirty years from the date of filing if no period of duration is specifically set forth, (3) company purpose, (4) registered agent name and office address, (5) total amount of cash and a description and agreed value of property other than cash contributed, (6) total additional contributions, if any, agreed to be made by all members, and when they will be made, (7) reservation of right to admit new members, (8) reservation of right of the remaining members to continue the company in the event of the termination of a member's membership, (9) if company will be managed by managers, a statement to that effect, and the names and addresses of the initial managers, (10) if company will be managed by members, the names and addresses of the members, (11) if company will elect status as a flexible limited liability company, a statement to that effect, citing Section 17-16-107, and (12) any additional matters. (Section 17-15-107(a)). A written consent to act as a registered agent must accompany the Articles of Organization. (Section 17-15-107(c)).

Annual report requirement: Yes, to Secretary of State. (Section 17-15-132). Filing fee of $25, plus annual license tax, variable based on value of company assets located in Wyoming, minimum $50. (Section 17-15-132, citing Section 17-16-1630).

Publication requirement: No.

Effective date of limited liability company organization: On the date of official approval of Articles of Organization, the company becomes a legal entity and the members are shielded from personal liability. In addition, the effective date may be delayed to a date stated in the Articles of Organization. (Section 1715109).

Membership requirements: Minimum number required is two. The members may be natural persons or business entities. (Section 17-15-106). But notwithstanding this provision, a flexible limited liability company may have one member. (Section 17-15-144(d)).

Other: License tax, variable based on value of corporate assets located in Wyoming, minimum $50.

Glossary of Business, Legal, and Accounting Terms

Account: A separate record of an asset, liability, income, or expense of a business.

Accounting method: The method of recording income and expenses for a business; can be either accrual method or cash method.

Accounting period: A specific time period covered by the financial statements of a business.

Accounting system: The specific system of record-keeping used to set up the accounting records of a business. See also *single-entry accounting* or *double-entry accounting*.

Accounts payable: Money owed by a business to another for goods or services purchased on credit. Money that the business intends to pay to another.

Accounts receivable: Money owed to the business by another for goods or services sold on credit. Money that the business expects to receive.

Accrual method: Accounting method in which all income and expenses are counted when earned or incurred regardless of when the actual cash is received or paid.

Accrued expenses: Expenses that have been incurred but have not yet been paid.

Accrued income: Income that has been earned but has not yet been received.

ACRS: Accelerated Cost Recovery System. Generally, a method of depreciation used for assets purchased between 1980 and 1987.

Agent: A person who is authorized to act on behalf of another. A corporation acts only through its agents, whether they are directors, employees, or officers.

Aging: The method used to determine how long accounts receivable have been owed to a business.

Amend: To alter or change.

Articles of Organization: The charter of the limited liability company, the public filing with a state that requests that the company be allowed to exist. Along with the Operating Agreement, the articles provide details of the organization and structure of the business. The articles must be consistent with the laws of the state of organization.

Assets: Everything a business owns, including amounts of money that are owed to the business.

Assumed name: A name, other than the limited liability company's legal name as shown on the Articles of Organization, under which a company will conduct business. Most states require registration of the fictitious name if a company desires to conduct business under an assumed name. The company's legal name is not an assumed name.

Balance sheet: The business financial statement that depicts the financial status of the business on a specific date by summarizing the assets and liabilities of the business.

Balance sheet accounts: Asset and liability accounts used to prepare business balance sheets.

Balance sheet equation: Assets = Liabilities + Equity, or Equity = Assets – Liabilities.

Business liabilities: Business debts. Also the value of the owner's equity in his or her business.

C-corporation: A business entity owned by shareholders that is not an S-corporation. Subject to double taxation, unlike S-corporations.

Calendar year: Year consisting of 12 consecutive months ending on December 31st.

Capital: Initially, the actual money or property that shareholders transfer to the limited liability company to allow it to operate. Once in operation, capital also consists of accumulated profits. The net worth of the company, the owner's equity in a business, and/or the ownership value of the business.

Capital expense: An expense for the purchase of a fixed asset; an asset with a useful life of over one year. Generally, must be depreciated rather than deducted as a business expense.

Capital surplus: Corporation owner's equity. See also *retained capital*.

Cash: All currency, coins, and checks that a business has on hand or in a bank account.

Cash method: Accounting method in which income and expenses are not counted until the actual cash is received or paid.

Certificate of Organization: Another name for Articles of Organization, used by some states. See *Articles of Organization*.

Chart of Accounts: A listing of the types and numbers of the various accounts that a business uses for its accounting records.

Check register: A running record of checks written, deposits made, and other transactions for a bank account.

Close corporation: Corporation with less than 50 shareholders that has elected to be treated as a close corporation. Not all states have close corporation statutes. (For information regarding close corporations, please consult a competent attorney.)

Closely held corporation: Not a specific state-sanctioned type of corporation, but rather a designation of any corporation in which the stock is held by a small group of people or entities and is not publicly traded.

Common stock: The standard stock of a corporation that includes the right to vote the shares and the right to proportionate dividends.

Company record book: Contains all the records of the limited liability company (except accounting records).

Consent Resolution: Any resolution signed by all of the directors or shareholders of a corporation authorizing an action, without the necessity of a meeting.

Corporate bylaws: Internal rules governing management of a corporation, containing procedures for holding meetings, appointments, elections, and other matters.

Corporation: A business entity owned by shareholders; can be a C-corporation or an S-corporation.

Cost basis: Total cost to a business of a fixed asset.

Cost of goods sold: The amount that a business has paid for the inventory that it has sold during a specific period. Calculated by adding beginning inventory and additions to inventory and then deducting the ending inventory value.

Current assets: Cash and any other assets that can be converted to cash or consumed by the business within one year.

Current debt: Debt that will normally be paid within one year.

Current liabilities: Debts of a business that must be paid within one year.

Current ratio: A method of determining the liquidity of a business. Calculated by dividing current assets by current liabilities.

Debt: The amount that a business owes to another. Also known as "liability."

Debt ratio: A method of determining the indebtedness of a business. Calculated by dividing total liabilities by total assets.

Default rules: Rules set by statute in each state that define the actual operational characteristics of limited liability companies.

Depreciation: Cost of fixed asset deductible proportionately over time.

Dissolution: Methods by which a limited liability company concludes its business and liquidates. Dissolutions may be involuntary because of bankruptcy or credit problems, or voluntary on the initiation of the members of the company.

Dividend: A distribution of money or property paid by a corporation to a shareholder based on the amount of shares held. A proportionate share of the net profits of a business that the board of directors has determined should be paid out to shareholders, rather than held as retained earnings. Dividends must be paid out of the corporation's net earnings and profits. The board of directors has the authority to declare or withhold dividends based on sound business discretion.

Domestic company: A limited liability company is a domestic company in the state in which it is organized. See also *foreign company.*

Double-entry accounting: An accounting system under which each transaction is recorded twice: as a credit and as a debit. A very difficult system of accounting to learn and understand.

Equity: Any debt that a business owes. It is owner's equity if owed to the business owners and liabilities if owed to others.

Expenses: The costs to a business of producing its income. Any money that it has paid or will pay out during a certain period

FEIN: Federal Identification Number, used for tax purposes.

FICA: Federal Insurance Contributions Act. Taxes withheld from employees and paid by employers for Social Security and Medicare.

Fictitious name: See *assumed name.*

Fiduciary duty: A duty to act with reasonable care and prudence.

FIFO: First-in, first-out method of accounting for inventory. The inventory value is based on the cost of the latest items purchased.

Financial statements: Reports that summarize the finances of a business; generally a profit and loss statement and a balance sheet.

Fiscal year: A 12-month accounting period used by a business.

Fixed assets: Assets of a business that will not be sold or consumed within one year. Generally, fixed assets (other than land) must be depreciated.

Foreign company: A limited liability company is referred to as a foreign company in all states other than the one in which it is actually organized. In order to conduct active business affairs in a different state, a foreign company must be registered with the other state for the authority to transact business and it must pay an annual fee for this privilege.

FUTA: Federal Unemployment Tax Act. Federal business unemployment taxes.

Gross pay: The total amount of an employee's compensation before the deduction of any taxes or benefits.

Gross profit: Gross sales minus the cost of goods sold.

Gross sales: The total amount received for goods and services during an accounting period.

Gross wages: The total amount of an employee's compensation before the deduction of any taxes or benefits.

Income: Any money that a business has received or will receive during a certain period.

Income statement: Financial statement that shows the income and expenses for a business. Also referred to as an "operating statement" or "profit and loss statement."

Indemnify: To reimburse or compensate. Members and managers of limited liability companies are often reimbursed or indemnified for all the expenses they may have incurred in organizing a company.

Initial capital: The money or property that an owner or owners contribute to starting a business.

Intangible personal property: Generally, property not attached to land that you cannot hold or touch (for example: copyrights, business goodwill, etc.).

Inventory: Goods that are held by a business for sale to customers.

Invoice: A bill for the sale of goods or services that is sent to the buyer.

Ledgers: The accounting books for a business. Generally, refers to the entire set of accounts for a business.

Liabilities: The debts of a business.

LIFO: Last-in, first-out method of valuing inventory. Total value is based on the cost of the earliest items purchased.

Liquidity: The ability of a company to convert its assets to cash and meet its obligations with that cash.

Long-term assets: The assets of a business that will be held for over one year. Those assets of a business that are subject to depreciation (except for land).

Long-term debts: Debts that will not be paid off in one year.

Long-term liabilities: The debts of a business that will not be due for over one year.

Long-term loans payable: Money due on a loan more than one year in the future.

Long-term notes payable: Money due more than one year in the future.

MACRS: Modified accelerated cost recovery system. A method of depreciation for use with assets purchased after January 1, 1987.

Managers: In a limited liability company, those persons selected by the members of the company to handle the management functions of the company. Managers of limited liability companies may or may not be members/owners of the company. Managers are roughly analogous to the officers of a corporation.

Members: In a limited liability company, those persons who have ownership interests (equivalent to shareholders in a corporation). Most states allow single-member limited liability companies.

Minutes: A written record of the activities of a meeting.

Natural person: An actual human being, not a business entity.

Net income: The amount of money that a business has after deducting the cost of goods sold and the cost of all expenses. Also referred to as "net profit."

Net loss: The amount by which a business has expenses and costs of goods sold greater than income.

Net pay: The amount of compensation that an employee actually will be paid after the deductions for taxes and benefits.

Net profit: The amount by which a business has income greater than expenses and cost of goods sold. Also referred to as "net income."

Net sales: The value of sales after deducting the cost of goods sold from gross sales.

Net wages: The amount of compensation that an employee will actually be paid after the deductions for taxes and benefits.

Net worth: The value of the owner's share in a business. The value of a business determined by deducting the debts of a business from the assets of a business. Also referred to as "owner's equity."

Nontaxable income: Income that is not subject to any state or local sales tax.

Not-for-profit corporation: A corporation formed under state law that exists for a socially worthwhile purpose. Profits are not distributed but retained and used for corporate purposes. May be tax-exempt. Also referred to as "nonprofit."

Officers: Manage the daily operations of a corporation. Generally consists of a president, vice president, secretary, and treasurer. Appointed by the board of directors.

Operating Agreement: The internal rules that govern the management of the limited liability company. The agreement contains the procedures for holding meetings, appointments, elections and other management matters. If this agreement conflicts with the Articles of Organization, the provision in the articles will be controlling.

Operating margin: Net sales divided by gross sales. The actual profit on goods sold, before deductions for expenses.

Operating statement: Financial statement that shows the income and expenses for a business. Also referred to as "income statement" or "profit and loss statement."

Owner's equity: The value of an owner's share in a business. Also referred to as "capital."

Paid-in capital: Total amount of money or property transferred to the limited liability company upon its beginning business.

Partnership: An unincorporated business entity that is owed by two or more persons.

Payee: Person or business to whom a payment is made.

Payor: Person or business that makes a payment.

Per capita: One vote per member.

Perpetual duration: Existence of a limited liability company forever.

Personal property: All business property other than land and the buildings that are attached to the land.

Petty cash: Cash that a business has on hand for payment of minor expenses when use of a business check is not convenient. Not to be used for handling sales revenue.

Petty cash fund: A cash fund. Considered part of cash on hand.

Petty cash register: The sheet for recording petty cash transactions.

Physical inventory: The actual process of counting and valuing the inventory on hand at the end of an accounting period.

Plant assets: Long-term assets of a business. Those business assets that are subject to depreciation (other than land).

Pre-paid expenses: Expenses that are paid for before they are used (for example: insurance, rent, etc.).

Profit and loss statement: Financial statement that shows the income and expenses for a business. Also referred to as an "income statement" or "operating statement."

Proxy: A written member authorization to vote shares on behalf of another.

Qualify: Having a Certificate of Authority to Transact Business from another state in order to actively conduct business in that state.

Quorum: The percentage of ownership shares in the limited liability company that must be represented at a members meeting in order to officially transact any company business.

Real property: Land and any buildings or improvements that are attached to the land.

Reconciliation: The process of bringing a bank statement into agreement with the business check register.

Registered agent: The person designated in the Articles of Organization who will be available to receive service of process (summons, subpoena, etc.) on behalf of the limited liability company. A limited liability company must always have a registered agent.

Registered office: The actual physical location of the registered agent. Need not be the actual principal place of business of the limited liability company.

Resolution: A formal decision that has been adopted by either the shareholders or the board of directors of a corporation.

Retained capital: Limited liability company member/owner's equity. See also *capital surplus*.

Retained earnings: In a limited liability company, the portion of the annual profits of a business that are kept and reinvested in the company, rather than paid to the members/owners.

Revenue: Income that a business brings in from the sale of goods or services or from investments.

S-corporation: A type of business corporation in which all of the expenses and profits are passed through to its shareholders to be accounted for at tax time individually in the manner of partnerships. A specific IRS designation that allows a corporation to be taxed similarly to a partnership, yet retain limited liability for its shareholders.

Sales: Money brought into a business from the sale of goods or services.

Sales income: Revenue derived from selling a product of some type

Salvage value: The value of an asset after it has been fully depreciated.

Service of process: To accept subpoenas or summonses for a company.

Shareholders: Owners of issued stock of a corporation and, therefore, owners of an interest in the corporation. They elect the board of directors and vote on major corporate issues.

Short-term loans payable: Money due on a loan within one year.

Short-term notes payable: Money due within one year.

Single-entry accounting: A business recordkeeping system that generally tracks only income and expense accounts. Used generally by small businesses, it is much easier to use and understand than double-entry accounting.

Sole proprietorship: An unincorporated business entity in which one person owns the entire company.

Straight-line depreciation: Spreads the deductible amount equally over the recovery period.

can hold and touch (for example machinery, furniture, equipment).

Taxes payable: Total of all taxes due but not yet paid.

Termination: End of legal existence of company.

Trial balance: In double-entry accounting, a listing of all the balances in the general ledger in order to show that debits and credits balance.

Wages: Hourly compensation paid to employees, as opposed to salary.

Wages payable: Total of all wages and salaries due to employees but not yet paid out.

Working capital: The money available for immediate business operations. Current assets minus current liabilities.

Index

Nova Publishing Company
Small Business and Consumer Legal Books and Software

Law Made Simple Series

Advance Health Care Directives	ISBN 13: 978-1-892949-23-3	Book w/CD	$24.95
Estate Planning Simplified	ISBN 1-892949-10-5	Book w/CD	$34.95
Living Trusts Simplified	ISBN 0-935755-51-9	Book w/CD	$28.95
Living Wills Simplified	ISBN 0-935755-50-0	Book w/CD	$28.95
Personal Bankruptcy Simplified (4th Edition)	ISBN 1-892949-34-2	Book w/CD	$29.95
Personal Legal Forms Simplified (3rd Edition)	ISBN 0-935755-97-7	Book w/CD	$28.95
Powers of Attorney Simplified	ISBN 13: 978-1-892949-40-0	Book w/CD	$24.95

Small Business Made Simple Series

Corporation: Small Business Start-up Kit (2nd Edition)	ISBN 1-892949-06-7	Book w/CD	$29.95
Employer Legal Forms	ISBN 13: 978-1-892949-26-4	Book w/CD	$24.95
Landlord Legal Forms	ISBN 13: 978-1-892949-24-0	Book w/CD	$24.95
Limited Liability Company: Start-up Kit (2nd Ed.)	ISBN 13: 978-1-892949-37-0	Book w/CD	$29.95
Partnership: Start-up Kit (2nd Edition)	ISBN 1-892949-07-5	Book w/CD	$29.95
Real Estate Forms Simplified	ISBN 0-935755-09-1	Book w/CD	$29.95
S-Corporation: Small Business Start-up Kit (2nd Edition)	ISBN 1-892949-05-9	Book w/CD	$29.95
Small Business Accounting Simplified (4th Edition)	ISBN 1-892949-17-2	Book only	$24.95
Small Business Bookkeeping System Simplified	ISBN 0-935755-74-8	Book only	$14.95
Small Business Legal Forms Simplified (4th Edition)	ISBN 0-935755-98-5	Book w/CD	$29.95
Small Business Payroll System Simplified	ISBN 0-935755-55-1	Book only	$14.95
Sole Proprietorship: Start-up Kit (2nd Edition)	ISBN 1-892949-08-3	Book w/CD	$29.95

Legal Self-Help Series

Divorce Yourself: The National Divorce Kit (6th Edition)	ISBN 1-892949-12-1	Book w/CD	$39.95
Incorporate Now!: The National Corporation Kit (4th Ed.)	ISBN 1-892949-00-8	Book w/CD	$29.95
Prepare Your Own Will: The National Will Kit (6th Edition)	ISBN 1-892949-15-6	Book w/CD	$29.95

National Legal Kits

Simplified Divorce Kit (2nd Edition)	ISBN 1-892949-20-2	Book only	$19.95
Simplified Family Legal Forms Kit (2nd Edition)	ISBN 13: 978-1-892949-41-7	Book w/CD	$19.95
Simplified Incorporation Kit	ISBN 13: 978-1-892949-33-2	Book w/CD	$19.95
Simplified Limited Liability Company Kit	ISBN 1-892949-32-6	Book w/CD	$19.95
Simplified Living Will Kit	ISBN 1-892949-22-9	Book only	$15.95
Simplified S-Corporation Kit	ISBN 1-892949-31-8	Book w/CD	$19.95
Simplified Will Kit (3rd Edition)	ISBN 1-892949-21-0	Book w/CD	$19.95

Ordering Information

Distributed by:
National Book Network
4501 Forbes Blvd. Suite 200
Lanham MD 20706

Shipping: $4.50 for first & $.75 for additionall
Phone orders with Visa/MC: (800) 462-6420
Fax orders with Visa/MC: (800) 338-4550
Internet: www.novapublishing.com
Free shipping on all internet orders